THE INFLUENCE OF ENGLISH ON MARATHI

A Sociolinguistic and Stylistic Study

THE INFLUENCE OF ENGLISH ON MARATHI

A Sociolinguistic and Stylistic Study

BHALCHANDRA NEMADE

Published by
Harsha Bhatkal
for Popular Prakashan Pvt. Ltd.
301, Mahalaxmi Chambers
22, Bhulabhai Desai Road
Mumbai - 400 026
www.popularprakashan.com

First published in 1990 by
Prabhakar Bide, Rajhauns Vitaran
Panaji, Goa

Republished 2014

(4365)
ISBN 978-81-7991-806-7

Cover design: Mahendra Ghanekar

Printed in India by
Saurabh Printers Pvt. Ltd.,
A-16, Sector-IV, Noida 201301

CONTENTS

PREFACE

I have had the opportunity of developing my own views on influence study into this project while teaching Marathi in England and English in Maharashtra in the non-interfering and healthy academic life at the School of Oriental and African Studies, University of London during 1971-72 and then at the Marathwada University, Aurangabad during 1975-80. I recall with gratitude the quiet generosity of the two institutions. In the course of this long preoccupation with the two languages I have contracted intellectual debts that I shall never be able to fully acknowledge.

As a writer I am given to liking the idea of the whole language — semiotic and aesthetic, past and present, standard and non-standard with the entire range of its verieties, so that in many places the linguist has had to make room for the critic. I have also experienced that the model of linguistic influence is equally effective in the study of literary influence by drawing an analogy between the behaviour of a linguistic subsystem and that of a literary subsystem under influence.

I would like to record my sense of gratitude to my scholar friends with whom I discussed a number of practical problems and with whose help I could solve them. I like to express here my indebtedness especially to Ashok R. Kelkar, R. B. Patankar, G. S. Amur, Ian Raeside, Chandrakant Patil, R. M. Pai, Y. M. Pathan, S. G. Malshe, Ravindra Kimbahune, Afzal Khan, Manavendra Kachole and Pradeep Deshpande.

I wish to express my appreciation of the staffs of the following libraries for their assistance : the India Office Library, the Library of the School of Oriental and African Studies, the London University Library and the British Museum, London; the Marathwada University Library, Aurangabad; the Deccan College Library and the Jayakar Granthalaya, Pune; and the Mumbai Grantha Sangrahalay, Bombay.

I thank the authorities of the Goa University for providing U.G.C. assistance for the publication of this book. And I thank Shri Prabhakar Bhide of Rajhauns Vitaran, Panaji, who has taken a very enthusiastic interest in publishing this book.

A Note : I have not used diacritical marks in the transliteration of Marathi and Indian words (which are naturally many) in order to facilitate easy reading.

All translation of quotations from the original Marathi cited in this work is mine.

Bhalchandra V. Nemade

THE INFLUENCE OF ENGLISH ON MARATHI

A SOCIOLINGUISTIC AND STYLISTIC STUDY

CHAPTER ONE

INTRODUCTION

1.1 THE SCOPE OF THE STUDY

The present work is a linguistic study of the influence of the English language on Marathi prose style during its different phases in the nineteenth century. In this study the term *prose style* implies a broad spectrum of period style covering within it several substyles of prose genres, individual authors and individual works. It is mainly confined to written literary prose as against non-literary prose, though in the formative phase of any national style this distinction is often blurred. *National prose* connotes the prose characteristic of the whole language community.

Specific terms denoting specific styles are used when diverse varieties of prose style such as *individual* or *genre* style, *written* or *oral* style are under discussion. The term *genre* signifies form of writing, rather than form of literature.

The terms *contact* and *confrontation* are indicative of a wide range of political, socio-cultural and literary-aesthetic overtones, though in the present study the terms are used primarliy for linguistic phenomena, suggesting two successive stages of the initial impact of a foreign language before the actual process of linguistic borrowing begins.

The term *influence* implies linguistic borrowing systematized in the receiving language.

Non-linguistic description of style is avoided for the sake of clarity in argument. The term *language* is used in both literary and non-literary forms and the various binary concepts of language such as *langue* and *parole;* individual and social variables are taken as influencing factors whenever the influence of the English language as a whole is under discussion.

The focus of the study is on stylistic influences of English, although the broad cultural setting in which the language contact took place has been taken into account as an integrating factor in the formation of period style. The contact marked a break in the oral and manuscript cultures of the Indian society by initiating the formation of modern print culture of a literate society which stores up its social memory in prose. Since the formation of Marathi prose style during the nineteenth century is the natural result of such a contact, reference is made to the formative processes alone, and other factors which would have contributed to the evolution of Marathi prose style are either hypothesized or indicated in the Notes. Also, since several linguistic and non-linguistic phenomena are at work in the formation of a national style, only those that directly or indirectly relate to stylistic influences are attended to. The broad principle that seemingly arbitrary influence of one culture on the other follows definite laws on the level of language is the basic hypothesis of the study.

1.1.1 THE CONTACT OF ENGLISH

Marathi, after its formation as a New Indo-Aryan language between the fifth and the eighth centuries, developed a considerably rich, though broken, tradition of prose writing from the eleventh century.[1] Scholars have pointed out that the distinct characteristics of Marathi are attributable to the peculiar geographical environment of the Marathi-speaking people.[2]

English education was the most powerful instrument of social change in nineteenth-century British India. It resulted in the development of the people on entirely new lines, affecting their political, social, religious and economic outlook. This phase marks the belated transformation of the Indian society, from the medieval to the modern. Meyer Schapiro's dictum that "every style is peculiar to a period of culture" and that it is "a pervasive rigorous unity" not only in prose or in literature but in the entire epoch of a given culture is true of Marathi[3] (see Chapter 5.2).

The influence of the English language on Marathi has been circumstantially acccepted by scholars in various fields.[4] This influence is invariably linked with a renaissance in arts and life by Indian critics and social scientists. Foreigners visiting different parts of India during the last century and a half have recognised it as a dominant feature of Indian social life.[5] This is a unique phenomenon in terms of its magnitude and size and is thus capable of multiple interpretations, from the historical-political-sociological to the literary-aesthetic.[6] As a classic example of culture contact it gave rise simultaneously and at different phases to various nativistic movements, opposed to one another in nature and kind, such as neo-Hinduism and anti-Brahmanism, Brahmanization and Westernization, glorification of the West and revulsion against the West, anglomania and anglophobia, revivalism and modernization (see 3.2.3 and

                    The Influence of English on Marathi

4.2.4.). The studies of concrete problems arising out of this contact present a rich field for future research. The areas of confrontation are indeed numerous (see 4.2.1), though the present study confines itself to the confrontation of two linguistic systems.

1.1.2 THE THREE PHASES

The downfall of the Peshwa rule in 1818 marked the emergence of the British as the sole political power in India. It also made the British the cultural guardians of the backward and stratified Hindu society.[7] The sense of wonder nurtured by visitors from Marco Polo to Vasco da Gama, with this colonial undertaking dissolved itself into a realistic encounter between two distinct cultural traditions in human history. The culmination of this encounter became more material and real after the 1857 mutiny when the concept of *Pax Britannica* assumed precedence over all other relationships. This concept assumed the form of 'the white man's burden' in the twentieth century.

The contact of the English language with Marathi had preceded the political contact when the Missionaries started their proselytization activities at the beginning of the nineteenth century.[8] The contact had been a durable and prolonged type, giving rise to several socio-linguistic phenomena peculiar to Indian situation (see Chapter 4). The role of the English language in the cultural renaissance in India during the nineteenth century has been unanimously acceptd by social scientists, linguists and critics.[9] The most popular description of this contact in Marathi is "English incarnation of Marathi prose".[10] Several contemporary British educationists and officials compared the role of English in India to that of Greek and Latin in Europe during the late Middle Ages.[11] The impact of Western thought through the English language was all-pervasive. It gradually encroached upon the oral culture and encouraged written culture as the sole literary style of expression in all walks of life. Even a slight shade of the English language in the writing increased the acceptability and prestige of an argument in Marathi. As the total cultural contact ushered in a new age in Maharashtra and India, the need for a new mode of communication, namely prose, was felt as essential towards new uses of the language (see 1.1.4). The direct or indirect effects of colonization on the linguistic situation in India are of far greater significance than the meagre studies of these problems done so far would reflect.

Learning, throughout the nineetenth century, became synoymous with the ability to read and write the English language, a social substitute for the ancient system of learning the Sanskrit language (see 3.3 and 4.2.5). English education was institutionalized and this involved learning the

English language together with English literature. There was little freedom to choose the aspects of learning other than those institutionalized and this perpetuated definite linguistic influences. All educational institutions were started with a view to transforming the Hindu view of life, dominated by the *karma* theory, to the modern European outlook of science and rationalism. Since learning in the nineetenth century was monopolized by the upper caste Brahmans, both modernization and revivalism bore the stamp of Brahmanization (see 3.2.3, 3.4 and 3.5). The socio-linguistic implication of Brahmanization was that it helped speedy standardization of Marathi prose, because the written standards, formulated mainly by Brahman writers, were imitated wholly by other writers and there was least interference from other sociolects (see 4.4).

The influence of English on Marathi prose can be divided broadly into three phases, 1 : 1818 to 1847, 2 : 1847 to 1874, and 3 : 1874 to about 1890. By the last decade of the nineetenth century a standard prose style was clearly evolved, as it is evident in the works of English educated prose writers such as Vishnushastri Chiplunkar, Gopal Ganesh Agarkar, Bal Gangadhar Tilak and Hari Narayan Apte. This division into phases is intended more to mark the different stages of the influence of English than for suggesting that any startling change was to be expected merely because one phase ended in 1847 and another began in the same year. Although these stages of influence are by no means clearcut, each of them can be correlated with the prose works written during the successive phases of increasing bilingualism. Of the many indices of the influence the most important has been the steady growth of English education, and consequently, of borrowing from the English language. At the deeper level, a new view of life and change in the sensibility of society was steadily taking place, replacing the old traditions which had been well-suited only for the needs of the medieval society. By the end of the century, the old tradition of oral literature was almost forgotten by the intelligentsia and it had to be revived by nativistic movement as part of the revival of pride in Indian culture (see 3.2.3 and 4.2.4). As the language was being increasingly anglicized, isolated cries for purity were voiced regularly though these were not backed up by tangible cultural or social behaviour. However, even the extremist type of nationalism did not totally denounce the continuous role of English as a civilizing force, and puristic movements did not succeed beyond substituting translation loans for the earlier direct loans from English. English influence had, by that time, already become firmly established in several subsystems of language structure. As the influence matured by 1885 several substyles of literary genres (also borrowed from English) and of individual works and authors became specialized under the influence of

English. The process of standardization began earlier than that of stylistic norm formation, as language standardization is the prerequisite of the formation of stylistic norms.

The influence of English was thus absolute and all-round and penetrated deeply into the structure of the language, giving little scope to revival of old forms of expression in the oral tradition of Marathi. Various literary forms of the oral tradition still continued to be active in the illiterate rural masses, while the new English forms like the novel, tragedy, comedy and essay were being established along with the new prose style. At the end of the century, there was a clear division between two types of language use : the elitist and the proletarian, the distinguishing factor being bilingualism (see 4.3.2). The transition from the oral to the written and from manuscript to print culture was the first requisite of the new prose style, which was laboriously accomplished by the first generation of the prose writers in the First phase (1818-1847). Specialization of the features of the written language took place along with the emergence of a new standard in the Second phase (1847-1874), and as the standard was consolidated in the Third phase (1874-1890), the transition form Sanskrit bilingualism to English bilingualism of Marathi writers was complete.

1.1.3 THE ORAL AND THE WITTEN CULTURES

In the Indian literary tradition a clear division can be said to have existed between the written and the oral cultures. Writing was by no means unfamiliar to the people, but the oral culture was consciously encouraged for various socio-political reasons, the chief being the fact that reading and writing was the privilege of the upper castes and that oral expression was the only available medium to the masses.[12] Among the Hindus, writing had a lower ritual status than oral delivery and there were separate 'writer castes' like the Kayasthas. The learned Brahman could boast of his ability to recall orally from memory (*upasthiti*). Marathi has had both written and oral cultures equally active throughout its history, from its formation as a New Indo-Aryan language, which it inherited from the known history of the Indo-Iranian linguistic culture via Sanskrit and Apabhransha.[13] In Maharashtra the written culture is more or less prosaic, discontinuous, elitist, courtly, fluctuating in respect of its uses and users, and deeply influenced by an alien or artifical *supraglossia* such as Sanskrit, Prakrit, Persian and, in modern times, English (see 1.1.4 and 4.2.5).[14] On the other hand, the oral culture is more or less poetic, continuous, proletarian, rural and comparatively standardized in its uses.

The entire linguistic repertoire of the Marathi society historically shows several oral, written and intermediate styles of expression, both in verse and prose before it came in contact with English. The rich variety of Marathi prose, both written and oral, was however broken, discontinuous and was only occasionally belletrist in spirit (see Chapter 2). The various autonomous cycles of prose independent of one another and running parallel developed different standards of prose writing until the early nineteenth century.[15] Most of the prose writing was temporal in motivation and was not intended to be 'literary' or 'artistic'. Some of the great prose works in these cycles became classics only by accident. This was a natural consequence of the low prestige prose received in the Indian medieval literary culture. Moreover, the voluminous verse tradition possessed several substyles of utilitarian and discursive types which bordered on prose styles. Most of these, biographies, philosophical commentaries on Sanskrit texts and monastic and historical documents, could be called rhymed prose. However, it is true that the verse forms were the most favoured expression of the Marathi people associated as these were with eminent saint-poets like Namadev, Dnyanadev, Janabai, Eknath, Tukaram, Ramadas, Shridhar, Mahipati, Moropant and with the Shahirs. With the single exception of the Mahanubhava cycle of prose, which produced classics in prose in the thirteenth and early fourteenth centuries, the great talent was rarely attracted to prose writing. Even this cult soon went underground owing to persecution by Muslims as well as orthodox Hindus. Thus, until the nineteenth century, dominance of verse literature remained unchallenged.

1.1.4 THE NEW PROSE

Since Language and culture are capable of a high degree of reciprocal reinforcement, the movement of the new prose in Maharashtra can be studied both as a literary product and as an instrument of new sensibility created by the contact situation in the nineteenth century. New situations create need for new channels of social communication. Culture contact also produces semantic situations which can be transformed by the literary artists into linguistic features. The English contact opened up a new psycho-social reality. The Hindu view of life (inadequately expressed in the term 'Hindu religion' in English), with its otherworldly philosophy, underwent a severe reformation giving rise to several protestant movements in Maharashtra. The political defeat of the Brahman rulers of Maratha confedaracy of Pune was a unique symbolization of a white race deposing the holy twice-born rulers under whose patronage the Hindu view of life flourished as it did nowhere else in India after the Vijaynagar kingdom in the fifteenth century. The establishment of the British rule, therefore, meant the end of an epoch, the beginning of something entirely new in the history of India. The cultural superiority of the white race was admitted even by Brahaman leaders like Lokahitavadi (Gopal

Hari Deshmukh : 1823-1892) and Mahadev Govind Ranade (1842-1901).
The public opinion on the whole turned in favour of British values such
as democracy, justice and civil liberties never enjoyed by the masses in
the known history of India.

A general feeling that a new age was beginning to dawn upon the ex-
ploited *varna* ridden society was the first discernible sign of the contact
situation and it was vigorously propagated by the first generation of
writers whose natural choice of expression was prose. Since prose is
particularly conducive to judicial argument, the psycho-social reality
even justified the colonial rule and the consequent economic exploitation
of society. The Anglo-Indian intellectuals have initiated a process of
respecting each other's culture, which mitigated the expected reaction of
violence, contrary to Frantz Fanon's observation that "in a colonial
situation, culture, which is doubly deprived of the support of the nation
and of the state, falls away and dies."[16] The interest in Indian culture,
both by Western Orientalists and Indian revivalists increased national
consciousness as well as nationalism. A new philosophy of rational
interpretation of East-West contact and comparative culture commenced,
the most powerful expression of which is Gandhism in the twentieth
century.[17] The new philosophy, as L. S. S. O'Mally observes, roused
India from the 'intellectual coma' and turned it to western literature,
science and philosophy for cultural inspiration, "just as western Europe
woke from the lethargy of the middle ages and turned to the literature
of Greece and Rome for models of thought and style."[18]

Thus the movement of new prose in Marathi can be interpreted as one
of the cultural elements that constitute 'deep structures' beneath the
synthecizing organic unity of a national culture and a national literature.
It provided the philosophical basis of a literary period, which, according
to René Wellek and Austin Warren, is "a true selection defined by a
system of norms embedded in the historical process and irremovable
from it."[19] A socio-linguistic analysis of this period would reveal how
conscious linguistic phenomena are connected to their unconscious infra-
structure.[20] Otto Jespersen states, "if we find a particular period especially fertile in linguistic change, it is quite natural that we should turn
our attention to the social state of the community at that time in order,
if possible, to discover some specially favouring circumstances."[21]

The new attitudes developed in the nineetenth century Maharashtra
had their roots in the educational policies of the East India Company (see
Chapter 3.3). The new elite who were benefitted by English education
assumed leadership of the masses. It is important to note that the new
prose writers were also the leaders of the cultural movements of the
period.

Among the new attitudes developed by English education the most crucial was rationalism (see 4.2.3). The dominant Hindu ideas about man's relation to universe were either supernatural or mythical, in turn giving rise to the attitudes of awe and indifference towards the universe. The more radical thought of Kanada, Charwaka, the Buddha, and Shankara and others had become part of history. The new inductive thinking inculcated philosophical spirit of enquiry. The universe as a hostile phenomenon to be conquered by the spirit of man revolutionized the entire thinking of the Hindus; and new concepts of individualism, women's rights, humanism and new social administration replaced the 'absurd' Dharmashastras and outdated Arthashastras which had outlived their usefulness. The ideas propagated in England by Hume and Locke, Darwin and Thomas Huxley, J. S. Mill and Herbert Spencer, Bentham and Adams had established at least a superficial authority over the Maharashtrian elite who vigorously preached these ideas in their prose. A new view of social relationship often superficially accepted by the Brahman writers exercised a double authority over the Hindu social ethos— one of being western and the other of being Brahmanical[22] (see Chapter 3). The new prose thus favoured new canons of judgement, judicial enquiry, order and balance : the great virtues consciously developed by the post-Restoration English prose writers.

Ready models for several substyles of prose were provided by English courses in schools and University examinations. In the first half of the century, imitation rather than borrowing of stylistic features from English dominated the literary scene in Marathi. Literary trends, movements and schools modelled on English literary tradition rose by the middle of the century. Introduction of printing and the consequent growth of periodicals and printed books greatly increased the volume of published prose. These media favoured a particular substyle which dominated the prose written during the entire period, especially in the second and the third phases. It was prose of controversy, of purely logical dependence on the English argument of similar controversy, of satire and persuasion and of rhetorical presentation of argument. It introduced a critical dimension to writing and reinterpretation of man's attitude to man and to self, making obsolete symbolist or lyrical verse narrative in Marathi. English literary culture itself became a model of new writing. The influence of English was felt in technical as well as thematic aspects of writing. As anglicized features did not fit into the old traditional verse genres, the seven-century-old verse tradition dried up as soon as the new prose register began to expand in various genres of Marathi.

Since traditional prose was not readily available for reading and most of it was not even known, the vacuum of entertainment, instruction and information was to be filled by the new prose whose inspiration was wholly derived from an alien literary culture. The teaching of English was not a carefully planned curriculum, but rather an administratively useful programme of examinations in certain popular texts (see Chapter 3). When the Government undertook translation projects with a view to promoting vernacular language as a medium of instuction, the English-educated writers extensively borrowed English terminology, and along with a view to promoting vernacular languages as a medium of instruction, the English-educated writers extensively borrowed English terminology, and along with it, lexical, morphological and syntactic elements into Marathi. The puritanical discipline of pontificating British officers like Major Candy who supervised Marathi works, whether translated or original, allowed little variation in grammatical structures. Most British officers, building up their own careers and too busy with numerous military campaigns and operations such as those against Thugs and Pindharis, were understandably not in touch with new developments in Europe. These nostalgic expatriates recommended the books they had read and loved most. The more important English books were not always available in India and the same classical texts were prescribed over and over through several decades.[23] The British Civil Servants under the East India Company popularized the eighteenth century post-Augustan and pre-Romantic literary taste of their prime days, representing Richardson, Johnson, Gibbon, Burke, Campbell, Cowper and Scott.[24] These became the models for the newly educated Indian elite. The later generation of civil servants under the Crown popularized Palgrave's *The Golden Treasury* and writers like G. W. M. Reynolds, Meadows Taylor, Bulwer Lytton, Macaulay and Dickens. What was popular in England was thus authoritatively imposed as great literature on the Indian mind, without much concern for relevance to the native culture.[25]

Anthropologists and, more specifically, linguists are of the opinion that language contact is a necessary component of acculturation studies.[26] In the multilingual situation of the subcontinent, however, there has been a permanent feature of bilingualism that requires a special treatment and also a special term, denoting a kind of geopolitical need of the numerous ethno-linguistic groups. For centuries, the vehicle of this need was Sanskrit to be replaced by Prakrit languages between 300 B.C. and A.D. 100; this was followed by the revival of Sanskrit in the second century. Later Sanskrit was replaced by Persian after the twelfth century.[27] English has been firmly established in this place since the nineteenth century. We may use the term *supraglossia* to describe this sociolinguistic phenomenon peculiar to the Indian linguistic situation (see Chapter 4.2.5). English has accelerated not only the traditional role of a *supraglossia* within India, but also linked Indian literary culture to the Atlantic culture and through it to the wider world literary culture. Apart from the direct influences on individual styles and genre styles it has also offered inter-state and international communication to the Marathi writers. Thus a totally new world of ideas entered into the Marathi psyche. Under the influence of this *supraglossia* of unprecedented status Marathi was standardized at a speedy rate. The literary-aesthetic, graphic and structural features of its prose style developed steady norms within a century. The widening dialectal differences were reduced considerably in the written style under the influence of English. The caste-and-profession-specific variants were absorbed in the period style so as to make the nineteenth-century prose a standard 'national' prose.

1.2 THE PROBLEM

The influence of one language over the other and the change caused by the borrowed features through bilingualism is a fairly accepted phenomenon in acculturation studies, studies of languages in contact and anthropological models of social evolution. However, these processes of linguistic acculturation in stylistic studies have always remained unexplored both by literary scholars and linguists. Most pioneers in modern linguistic theory have expressed their awareness of this problem. For example, Edward Sapir in his article "Language" (*Culture, Language and Personality*, 1962) refers to the same phenomenon of stylistic influence when he states :

> "A type of influence which is neither exactly one of vocabulary nor of linguistic form, in the ordinary sense of the word, and to which the insufficient attention has so far been called, is that of meaning pattern."[28]

The influence of one literary culture on the other is an area on the borderland of linguistics and stylistics, or more particularly comparative literature, comparative linguistics and comparative stylistics. As J. R. Firth observes, "At the present time, descriptive linguistics is suffering from a pre-occupation with phonemics and other forms of segmental phonology, and in the next decade it is probable that linguistic theory and practice will turn to synthesis."[29] The 'synthesis', however, could be better done in the context of literature, which, according to Ashok R. Kelkar, is an inter-section between Aesthetics and language, or more specifically, between art and letters.[30] In the context of the culture contact, such influences can be best studied in a close-up of stylistic study, as André Martinet states : "the changing needs of a community influence he more intimate fibre of its language, namely its syntax"; and "the way

  The Influence of English on Marathi

increasing social complexity determines the expansion of the functional complexities of the corresponding linguistic medium."[31]

The influence of English on Marathi prose style is a problem important in two ways : 1. as a case study and 2. as an enquiry into the mechanism of stylistic influence.

1.2.1 A CASE STUDY

As a case study, the problem has many dimensions. First, there is a need for the study of historical situations in which the language contact took place (Chapter 3), and an investigation of the making of a national prose under the influence of a well-developed foreign tradition. Second, the native prose style prior to the contact of English has to be reconstructed with available primary sources belonging to the eighteenth century. Third, the work of examining the type of culture contact which gave rise to the various acculturation processes contingent upon language contact has to be undertaken, a fact to be determined on the basis of the contemporary primary and secondary sources in English and Marathi; as also the areas of confrontation related to the language contact and consequently to the stylistic norms formation. Modern Marathi prose in its evolution towards modern syntax affords a fine illustration of language contact arising out of culture contact, and free acceptance by the people of the linguistic standards which the alien government had consciously introduced through the education system. It is difficult to distinguish the standards which were imposed by the government upon the subject people from those freely accepted by the people, till social historians show the way. Stylistic influences can be seen as a broad index of culture contact and as an expansion of the functional complexity of the linguistic medium corresponding to the increasing social complexity.[32] This involves socio-linguistic study of the background of the period under consideration on the linguistic plane. The resistance of a language against reorganization required by new social and communicative needs is clearly evident in the variants eliminated at successive stages of development. Several borrowed features, mostly interpreted as culture tags, may meet with zero resistance throughout the period. Since in Marathi the new age marks a sudden transition from the oral to the written, from the verse to the prose style of expression, there was little clash between linguistic features of the same contextualization in prose. Overborrowing with complete disregard to the capacity of the system was evident in the first phase of contact. Readjustment of existing features along with the borrowed ones and their contextualization began during the second phase along with elimination of unwanted variants. The continuous contact still brought in new features, so that by the end of the century, norms had to be formed to organize or discard multi-   farious variants (aesthetic-literary, graphic, and structural) in the stylistic system.

The most important feature of this study is the simultaneous occurrence of several linguistic processes and phenomena at one and the same time (see Chapters 4 and 9). It is not always possible to carry out analysis of all the linguistic processes from inside, as self-contained contexts, exclusively internal to linguistic systems, are insufficient to account for several aspects of stylistic influence. It is for this difficulty that an extrinsic approach is adopted with constant recourse to historical and social background.

1.2.2 AN ENQUIRY INTO THE MECHANISM OF STYLISTIC INFLUENCE

As an enquiry into the mechanism of stylistic influence the problem would first demand analysis of the processes of linguistic influence leading to standardization of written prose, and consequently, the stylistic norm formation. Secondly, it would seek to establish its own procedures and goals with necessary modifications of the already available comparative descriptive methods in linguistics, without claiming necessarily either the unique or the universal implications of itself in any formalistic sense. Provided with available researches in anthropological studies, linguistics and stylistics, this study would attempt a comparative descriptive model for functional analysis of the linguistic influence for the purpose of investigating stylistic norm formation under the influence of a foreign language. Select representative texts chosen from the period before the influence and during the period of influence serve as concrete data for comparison of the standards. Observations in this regard have been based on the careful reading of numerous texts in Marathi before and after the influence. Similarly, the different substyles in English prose from the sixteenth century to the nineteenth are utilized for the investigation of borrowing from English into Marathi.

Within the broad extra-linguistic framework of linguistic acculturation the linguistic study of the mechanism of stylistic influence itself can be directed to the well defined areas of confrontation. Of these areas (see Chapter 4.2) the confrontation of two linguistic systems has to be explored in greater detail. The mechanism of linguistic influence leading to the formation of stylistic norm (4.3) begins with the initial contact of the languages by means of bilingualism (4.3.2) which opens several channels to facilitate borrowing (4.3.3). This gradually effects change in the receiving language (4.3.5) and interference in the linguistic systems (4.3.4). Standardization then follows (4.4). Other areas of confrontation, especially in literary-aesthetic systems, are   complementary to

The Influence of English on Marathi

stylistic influence, though their investigation is difficult in the area of *langue* which is abstract, while the area of *parole* has to be more thoroughly investigated. In a study related to the period style, such as the present one, the collective use of literary-aesthetic sytems is to be kept in the background. As for sociolinguistic processes there is a general agreement on the essential nature of some of these processes which become active during the period of contact.[33] The situation in India, which is multilingual, however demands radical modification in the established view of sociolinguistic processes generated by the contact of an alien language. For example, socio-linguistic needs require English to act as *supraglossia* (4.2.5) replacing Sanskrit, while linguistic nativism makes Marathi increasingly dependent upon Sanskrit, the disappearing *supraglossia*.

In the absence of a well-developed model for the analysis of stylisitic influence a purely functional model has been constructed (Chapter 5), which uses a reconstructed base line (Chapter 2) to detect the borrowings during the period of contact. The borrowed linguistic features used as free variants are clearly evident in the first two phases (1818—1847 and 1847—1874), when they were tried and accepted or eliminated in the successive stages of the formation of the period style. The levels of investigation have been, in the present study confined to sentence levels, which is more than adequate for the present stage of research in this field, though a deeper and more microscopic investigation will further strengthen the conclusions drawn purely on the basis of comparative descriptive analysis of the sentence and near-sentence levels of two written languages in contact.

1.2.3 THE LIMITS OF THE STUDY

The present study does not presume to be even an outline of the linguistic influence of English on the nineteenth century Marathi prose in general. It limits its scope to the genesis of a period style under a foreign influence over the span of about seventy years, only selected problems of language contact are discussed. It makes no attempt to furnish a complete picture of the nineteenth century Marathi prose styles in all their individual and genre varieties. Since the focus is on period style, less attention is paid to the style of individual authors and of individual works as well as to genre styles, though these substyles are utilized in pointing out the concrete impact of English features.

The limits of the methods used are the limits of the linguistic-stylistic methodology in general. These deficiencies are admitted by all the leading European and Indian authorities in the areas of language contact, namely, acculturation, bilingualism and borrowing, language standardization and literary style.

While detecting the effect of a foreign element, dating of innovation or its adjustment in the system has been approximately fixed in three phases (30 years, 27 years and 16 years respectively), on the basis of their first appearance in published documents during the prolonged contact situation. Thus any change could be located in a span of thrity years. This is ascertained in several passages of the period. The lack of uptodate primary and secondary sources which could indicate the earliest attested sources makes it difficult to fix a borrowed feature more precisely. The test adopted is the discovery of the continuous occurrence of a particular feature in literary works. The eliminated features do not appear noticeably frequently in the following phase. Statistical tests, in future research, would be able to give a more accurate picture of the gradual disappearance of a borrowed feature, though such studies will have to be always microscopic and limited in respect of textual volume. In a bilingual situation of the type that existed in the nineteenth century, several stylistic features might have had their beginning in the spoken language, a study of which would present numerous other problems as well. The chronology of such features will always remain uncertain within a considerably long period of time.

Short-lived variants have been ignored and attention is paid to the major variants in period style. The possibility of internal development in some cases cannot be denied. Fossils revived owing to the contact, directly or indirectly, to fill the empty cells of the growing structures constitute another important class of variants.

Sample texts accounting for the changes which seem to have taken place are selected with the view to indicating the broad spectrum of representative substyles in a particular phase. Repetition is avoided in successive phases of the same substyle. Since a handful of people learnt English and still less wrote in Marathi, there is scarcity of primary sources representing different castes, classes, dialects, sexes and different age groups.

Borders between individual styles and genre styles were diffuse even until the middle of the last phase and distinctions between the styles were blurred. In such cases differences rather than similarities decide the characteistic foreign element.

The English models that influenced Marathi writers were limited and they are traceable in the references that appear in the primary sources. However, some room must be left for unknown (because unrecorded) models of English works in the period.

Non-linguistic description of style is avoided, though some important graphological features like punctuation are given more prominence,

                                    The Influence of English on Marathi

since the graphic level is closely involved in the structural aspects of prose style (see 5.5.2). Preoccupation with the sentence-level linguistics has obviously thrust to the background microlinguistic aspects of influence (see 1.3.2 and 5.5), but a marginal use of phonological-morophological and lexical-grammatical features is made whenever analytical exigencies demand them.

1.3 SOURCES AND METHODS

Neither linguists nor anthropologists have so far produced systematic work on comparative stylistics of linguistic equivalents. In the absence of ready models of study pertaining to stylistic influence of one language on the other, the present study of the influence of English on Marathi has to be based on the researches done in a number of related areas, namely, Anthropology, History, Linguistics, Stylistics, English studies, Marathi studies and a few allied disciplines like structuralism, literary theory and criticism, aesthetics and comparative literature. The problems raised by incomplete or neglected coverage of questions in the field of modern stylistics and the unequal treatment of these very questions in linguistics have been explicitly recognised by all the experts in these sciences and disciplines (see 1.2,3 : Limits). Attempts, in this study, are made at all possible stages to supplement these inadequacies by a careful (and cautious) use of available inter-disciplinary studies, more particularly in the field of acculturation studies and applied linguistics.

1.3.1 SOURCES

Numerous works in English and Marathi have contributed directly or indirectly to the theoretical base of this study though the initial thinking was formulated by the exercises in translation of the texts both from and into English, as well as Marathi. The books and articles which have indirect bearing on the formation of this problem are many.

Most of these sources deal with some theoretical discussions on the problem of acculturation, but none either in English or in Marathi with the specific problems of stylistic influence. The most valuable study on language contact is Uriel Weinreich's *Language in Contact* (1953). The structural appraoch developed by Russian Formalism and the Prague School is of great help in preparing the levels for the analysis of stylistic influence. Most works on bilingualism and multingualism casually discuss the issues in the study of syntactic changes as a result of linguistic influence. Sociolinguistic studies offer useful methodology in the treatment of language variation. Most linguists are permissive as to the final results of bilingualism and borrowing, namely, change and standardization. These have to be correlated with anthropological research in linguistic acculturation as a counterpart of cultural change.[35] Marathi studies lack preciseness in respect of linguistic borrowing and most of them have a philological odour. Some English studies are useful as models in stylistic analysis, but rarely so in the study of the influence of a foreign language on English, and even these do not go beyond lexical borrowing. Identifying language with dictionary was a common lapse in British linguistics until Firth and Halliday.

Stylistics and stylistic studies provide important guidelines, especially for the preliminary level analyses of lexical-syntactic features, though using the same models for comparative stylistics present a serious difficulty of stretching the level too deep into the sentence structure which often runs tangential to the lexical-syntactic level. Stray observations in Marathi criticism about the influences of English authors on Marathi individual and genre styles are, despite being unsystematic, quite useful in the absence of a complete picture of generic influences of English on Marathi. The lexical level dominates all such studies in Marathi.

1.3.2 THE PROBLEM OF METHODS

A brief account of the major problems, both in methods and approach recorded by experts in different areas related to stylistics will help to know where and how the enquiry into stylistic influence should begin its own premises. This will also help in deciding the approach to the subject of the present study.

Experts like Harry Hoijer affirm that little work is done on the processes of linguistic change and on the possibilities of relating these to the processes of change in the non-linguistic aspects of culture. Hoijer suggests that causes of language change must be sought in these cultural contexts, for it is here that the complex fabric of language is made to fit the numberless meaningful situations provided by the daily experiences of the members of a society.[37] A similar view is voiced by Ralph Beals, who says :

> " Studies [on linguistic acculturation] thus far published are relatively preliminary and have included few theoretical statements. Generally, stress has been laid upon the interrelationship between sociocultural and linguistic factors in change. Despite some suggestions that linguistic studies could provide indices for acculturation, the field is little developed and ... it appears to offer unexplored potentialities".[38]

This opinion from anthropologists is confirmed by linguists like André Martinet : "linguistic research has so far favoured the study of divergence at the expense of convergence." According to him, the study of linguistic convergence " becomes particularly rewarding when it results from the contact of two clearly distinct structures."[39]

Since change in style is closely related to linguistic change when language changes to adjust itself to the new conditions, modernization in both language and style is the natural consequence of acculturation. Charles Ferguson reiterates this fact by interpreting modernization of a language as a " process of its becoming the equal of other developing languages as a medium of communication, a process of joining the world community of increasing interstatable languages recognized as appropriate vehicles of modern forms of discourse." He veiws the process of modernization at two levels : First—lexical, or expansion of the lexicon of the language by new words and expressions. Second, stylistic—the development of new styles and forms of discourse". Further, he admits that the second level has less often been studied than the first. He is of the opinion that the poetic structures like metre, rhyme, assonance, allusion, stanza forms etc. are, being highly distinctive, more difficult to transfer to other languages than prose structures like paragraphing, ordered sequences, transitions etc.[40]

Lubomir Dolezel thinks that two essential properties of text structure defy any linguistic theory : 1. The organization of textual units in a temporal sequence, the sequential 'growth' of text representing time dimension of the text structure; and 2. the context dimension of text.[41]

The complex subject matter covered by the *language of literature* has to be concentrated upon if some progress is to be made in the field of stylistics. Tzvetan Todorov maintains that "literature has language both as point of departure and its destination."[42] In the contact situation, especially at the initial stage, the pole of departure naturally predominates the pole of destination, and affects the harmony of linguistic variants in style. Linguists who are concerned with this aspect have been explicitly critical of the established canons of descriptive micro-linguistics. The need for developing macro-linguistic sentence-level description of language is strongly felt in the recent years.

Archibald A. Hill, for instance, most emphatically ascribes this lack of methodology to micro-linguistics, and states :

"Microlinguistics does not cover the whole of language activity, and since it covers neither the correspondence between symbol and the object designated nor the artistic structures of literature, it does not cover these parts of language activity which have the most importance for us as members of society."[43]

Aphonse G. Juilland goes so far to say that " from the differential point of view, phonology and morphology naturally would give nothing", and that in the micro-approach " the most significant material is in danger of becoming irrelevant from the definitional point of view, because, being found elsewhere, it has lost its differentiating value."[44]

The need for isolating such differentiating features of language, which we will call *stylistic features* (see 5.1.2) from the non-differentiating features of language, is essential in any study of style.

To relate *contact stylistic features* to language change is another important problem that concerns modern linguistics. It is traditionally dealt with in studies on comparative methodology and historical procedures. André Martinent points out that " on the plane of general linguistics it [historical linguistics] amounts to determining how and why languages change through time ... This problem was a favourite with some language theorists, but mainly as far as sound changes were in question." He further admits that it is easy to notice the vocabulary changes, but it is all the more difficult to imagine " how the changing needs of a community influence the more intimate fabric of its language, namely its syntax."[45]

Similarly, Wallace Chafe rejects the possibility of reconstructing stylistic features. Internal reconstruction of stylistic features like phonetic features is not possible, as stylistic features have two components : contexts and phonemes. The obscuring of language history by the various types of language change is cumulative , and may vary greatly in effect both from language to language and within different environments in the same language ; so that it is impossible to set well defined historical limits to the applicability of internal reconstruction. Internal reconstruction is a procedure for inferring part of the history of a language from material available for synchronic description of the language, and from that alone. Chafe, however, admits that in other situations such as partial availability of records, " it can be useful supplement to and confirmation of the comparative and other historical procedures."[46]

Naomi S. Baron gives some concrete guidelines to overcome procedural difficulties. In her opinion, historical linguistic records are extremely crude approximations of normal spoken style, leaving room for only conjectures regarding spoken bilingual behaviour. However, within the proposed framework the data of texts may be used to help evaluate some diachronic hypothesis on the bases of synchronic and diachronic descriptions. The feature at two points of time offer a hypothesis that the change is due to the existence of some intervening agent, force or state of affairs. This is identified as the cause. She recommends sociolinguistic methods for the study of social, economic and cultural factors that introduce the use of new linguistic expressions and also advocates the inte-

                                    The Influence of English on Marathi

gration of synchrony and diachrony. However, she admits that although there would seem to be several ways of studying such phenomena, "there is almost no discussion of this topic in literature to date."[47]

In Einar Haugen's opinion, the use of the comparative method for the study of influences on the morphemic and higher levels would be very complex, involving the organization of the morphemic into words and constructions and the syntactic sequences. He too states that "much less has been done in this field than in the phonological."[48]

James M. Anderson classifies various types of structural change in contact situations as substratum, superstratum and adstratum, and emphasizes motivation factors behind all these types of linguistic influence. He refers to the researches by C. D. Durlington and L. F. Brosnahan, and indicates that phonetic peculiarities of a language may be a genetic trait. Thus phonetic elements in influence studies require minimum attention. In his opinion, " treatments of syntactic change generally have not shown much insight into the nature of the processes at work on the syntactic level of language."[49]

Harold Weinreich, who pleads for increasing need of macrolinguistic methodology in text-linguistics or linguistic stylistics, expresses his dissatisfaction with the undue stress laid by traditional linguistics on phonology, morphology, semantics and words at the expense of syntax, clauses and sentences. this distribution of language units cultivates the wrong notion of " a science built out of small units which pass gradually into larger units, finding its limit at the level of sentences—the Hercules Columns of linguistics. "He argues that " linguistics is necessarily textual. Syntax should be conceived of as textual or macro-syntax."[50]

A number of other linguists have passingly voiced similar opinions on the ineffectiveness of narrow approaches and on the micro-linguistic procedures in stylistics analysis.[51]

All experts on style are unhappy about the "multiple implications with which the basic vocabulary of stylistic criticism reverberates."[52] Language being a heuristic discipline , the subject matter of the language of literature, which possesses a large connotative spectrum of stylistic meaning, escapes from one level of analysis to another. This behaviour of the language of literature is put to scrutiny in studies of contact comparative linguistics or more particularly in theory of translation, because in these situations the two structures along with their elements and subsystems are face to face with each other. The application of linguistic methods of stylistics facts gives us an objective knowledge of their bipolarity, language as a semiotic code and language as an aesthetic code.[53]

The enquiry into the methods of the influence of one language on the stylistic systems of another language presents one crucial problem which has been clearly stated by Michael Riffaterre in his two articles "Criteria for Style Analysis," *Word*,   15 (1959), 154-174; and "Stylistic Context" *Word*, 16 (1959), 207-218). Riffaterre sees the dangers of applying linguistics methods to literary facts without a specific viewpoint, and deals with the difficulty in distinguishing stylistic facts from purely linguistic facts. He points out that " outside of the Structuralist schools linguists side with the stylisticians and do not satisfactorily clarify the position of stylistics inside or outside of linguistics."[54]

Another important procedure for the study of individual text is suggested by Efim Etkind, who defines a stylistic feature in relation to its peculiar function : its differentiating value.[55]

The views of Riffaterre and Etkind need to be suitably modified in the context of contact comparative methodology (see chapter 5). Finally Roman Jakobson's observation provides a valuable point of view for the study of borrowing in style. He says :

> " Any stage discriminates between more conservative and more innovatory forms. Any contemporary stage is experienced in its temporal dynamics, and on the other hand, the historical approach, both in poetics and linguistics is concerned not only with changes but also with continuous, enduring, static factors. A thoroughly comprehensive historical poetics or history of language is a superstructure to be built on a series of successive synchronic descriptions."[56]

1.3.3 METHODS : THE APPROACH

(A)   The sources of the problem reveal that inadequacies in the relationship between different theories leave large areas to be bridged by entirely new methods of enquiry, the development of which is itself a problem of considerable magnitude in a relatively new science like stylistics. Whatever the method used, therefore, it cannot be refined except through an increasingly exact knowledge of its own subject matter. A too narrowly empirical method develops its own disintergration, as it has happened in Practical criticism and New criticism. A too broad method, on the other hand, does not go beyond a simple approach or procedure. The subject matter of stylistic influence contains numerous sets of contexts, from historical-cultural to literary-aesthetic.[57]

The present study is, therefore, conducted with the help of a broad-based methodology from extra-linguistic contexts to micro-linguistic features relevant to the particular type of contact between English and

Marathi (see 4.1). The major thrust of stylistic analysis, however, is on macro-linguistic features, which begin with the syntactic subsystems and end with the paragraph. An attempt is made to juxtapose alternate theories which combine language use and objective techniques of description of language change due to foreign influence, which modern linguistics makes available. The methodology inevitably tends to become comparative descriptive.[58] Style is taken as a section of language, more particulary of the written language.[59] The written language is always seen with reference to the socio-cultural setting of the language contact.[60] Sometimes in particular cases style boundaries do not coincide with the socio-cultural phenomena, which is expected in view of the multi-dimensional role style plays in linguistic text.[61] The influence of one language on the other has to be seen as rearrangment of the existing or conservative stylistic features with the innovatory borrowings, not only an itenerary of borrowings but their adjustment with the *superstructure* of the previous stage. Stylistically irrelevant and stylistically redundant features have to be ignored so that the homogeneity of stylistically relevant features can be established. Such an approach which sanctions reduction and simplification of data is an approach which every science adopts.

Though the studies of linguistic acculturation reflect the fact that such studies are described in a vast, scattered literary divergent, yet all are essentially complementary to one another. Purely linguistic studies of acculturation, once coordinated with stylistic studies of individual authors, individual works and genres, a distinct phenomenon of period style emerges as a common denominator. The knowledge of period style is often *a priori*, particularly for the native speaker who can react to it intuitively. The native speaker's intuition is by no means a hindrance, provided the extra-linguistic experience or reality inherent in such intuitive approach is checked by rational principles of enquiry and rigid laws of investigation. Objectivity for its own sake is by no means a sufficient end of any science.

A contrastive perspective is maintained throughout the treatment of cultural theories, language contact, linguistic theories and literary texts, because it is impossible to carry out the analysis of influence merely from the inside. Linguistic and non-linguistic (the social, political, cultural) factors are seen as complementary in the making of a period style. However, stylistic interpretation of texts in Chapters 6, 7 and 8 is done by purely linguistic methods.

The influence of English is verified by both external and internal evidence. Though languages are in a constant process of change, the style of a text catches the still equilibrium at a particular point of time. An approach which combines both the synchronic description of text, and the diachronic view of prose written at different points of time is developed. At the same time, the literary aesthetic component of text has not been cast aside entirely.

(B)   The study is conducted on four levels :

1. Historical linguistic, to establish the norms of Marathi prose prior to the contact of English. A descriptive analysis of the different styles is reconstructed at different stages of the development of Marathi prose.[62]

2. Socio-linguistic or, more particulary, contact comparative linguistic, to investigate the processes of standardization in written language under the influence of a foreign language.[63]

3. Comparative descriptive linguistic, to prepare a model for functional analysis of the linguistic influences established *a priori* by linguistic description for the purpose of investigating stylistic norm formation at different stages of the contact.[64]

4 Linguistic stylistic, to analyse the prose texts written in the three phases of the contact so as to establish the influence of English in the formation of a standard period style.[65]

It should be mentioned here that the serial order of these four levels of investigation is by no means rigidly maintained in the actual treatment of stylistic contexts and of stylistic data ; any of the four levels may precede others or operate simultaneously in the discussion of various points. However, there is a greater degree of exchange at levels 3 and 4. This precludes attempts at mathematical formation, and checks parasitic tendencies which develop in undue adherence to one method alone.

Stylistics has established some crucial characteristics of style as a linguistic variation. A synthesis of these characteristics yields fruitful results in the analysis of period style (see Chapter 5) and prevents a disintegration of the method. Two of these characteristics, namely, style as a choice of alternate forms and style as deviation from norm are complementary to each other in investigating influence in a period style. Contact helps in broadening the course of selection in freely borrowing from a well-developed language like English. The direction of selectivity is always decided by foreign models for the lack of any available prose tradition. Variants thus borrowed facilitate selection within the language as the range of alternate choices widens.

According to M. A. K. Halliday, deviation is the result of choice.[66] However, when norms do not exist in a language, as was the situation in Marathi before the contact with English, deviation from the norms naturally does not take place (see 5.3). Ready norms from a source language may enter a receiving language like Marathi, still the variants need a fairly long time to develop into stylistic devices in the system. This was the situation in Marathi in the first and second phases of the influence. It is only when the norms and the variants both find their correspondences and family relations within the system that tangible stylistic relationship begins to develop. steady variant formation precedes the norm formation and then deviation, which is a conscious stylistic process, comes into existence.

Of the other theories of style, translation theories are most useful in influence studies as, among other things, they emphasize the high degree of reciprocal reinforcement between language and culture which is also a dominant element in the acculturation situation. The transfer and re-structuring of textual elements in translation reveals *language universals* shared by the two languages under consideration.

Transformational-generative grammar has not been employed mainly because it offers no awareness of the problem of language contact and as a tool it is too crude to be applied to period style. It constantly points to the area of *language universals,* and in contact studies the *borrowed universals* would be difficult to distinguish from *original universals* in the bilingual behaviour. Morever, there are serious doubts regarding its applicability to a verb-final language like Marathi.[67] Again, all the three levels of the structure in the grammar, namely, 1. base component including semantic component, 2. transformational component and 3. phonological component, impose a microscopic restraint on the study which works against the methodology adopted in the present study.[68]

Quantitative linguistics offers better techniques of generalization, but the frequency of norms and variants in the study of period style would be a stupendous task and is beyond any single individual's ability. Moreever, outside the purely structural level of occurrence, statistical methods would contribute little to the totality of the statement regarding style.[69]

Contextual analysis is equally unwieldy, as contextual taxonomies in a contact situation are likely to be numberless and the results will be most often irrelevant to the problem. Some linguists regard contextuali-zation as a pseudo-procedure.[70]

Thus the limitations of several methods in stylistics present problems which can be solved only by utilizing the present provisional theroretical bases in stylistics as cautiously as possible in concrete comparisons of English and Marathi features. At each stage of the transfer of features from the source language to the recipient language, i.e., from their se-lection to their accomodation in the new system of prose style, different complementary methods can be applied so that some advance is made in the present condition in comparative stylistics.

CHAPTER TWO

PRE-NINETEENTH-CENTURY MARATHI PROSE STYLE

2.1 HISTORICAL VIEW OF STYLE

While tracing the history of style in any language it is worth noting that progress in literary style cannot be viewed as linear. Croce suggests a view which can be adopted in the historical study of style. He states : "At the most . . . it may be asserted that the history of literary productions shows progressive cycles . . . Progress begins with the beginning of a new cycle."[1] The theory may be used, with a slight modification, in the study of stylistic influence. Linguistic acculturation as a part of culture contact associates itself with a number of psycho-linguistic and socio-linguistic processess which we may call *confrontations* (see 4.2). When the contact is overwhelmingly one-way the structure of the receiving language could be shattered and could give way to a process of pidginization but for the native conservatism of linguistic behaviour[2] (see Chapter 6). To test this hypothesis, a baseline consisting of the state of the language in the period antecedent to the particular contact needs to be reconstructed with the help of available primary sources belonging to the period.

The influence of English on Marathi in the nineteenth century begins a new cylce in Marathi prose in Croce's sense. The concept of language as a semiotic system as well as a literary medium takes care of linguistic behaviour of style to its full extent, although it gives rise to another concept of style, namely, style in history as an *archaic* phenomenon. However, any analysis of contemporary style presumes its historical dimension. *Archaism* is not an evaluating denominator, but a historical descriptive tenn. Hence the problem is not of magnitude. Theoretically all written literature of the past is created long before it is read and

therefore bears a kind of archaism. With the contact of a foreign system
this continuity of style is disturbed. The only compensating factor in such
a situation is linguistic influence which begins with bilingualism (see
4.3.1).

2.2 MARATHI PROSE BEFORE THE CONTACT WITH ENGLISH

A broad historical perspective of Marathi prose up to 1818 reveals four
autonomous cycles developing independently and simultaneously. There
does not seem to be even a broken tradition comprising all the different
cycles from thirteenth century to the period under consideration. Unlike
Marathi verse, which has an unbroken tradition all through the centuries,
Marathi prose with its scattered works can be organized in four distinct
cycles. The psychological basis inherent in any national tradition was
totally missing in Marathi prose tradition until linguistic   nationalism
provided such a base under the influence of English (see 3.2.3, 3.3.5 and
4.2.4). The reasons for its discontinuity can be summed up as follows :
1. Lack of adequate primary sources. A large number of texts have
become extinct, and some of the extant ones were not even known before
the twentieth century. Even today faithfully printed primary sources are
rare. 2. Lack of language standardization owing to Brahmanical adherence to Sanskrit lore and Vedic tradition which despised Marathi. 3.
Various socio-political causes such as lack of peace and stability in the
region, alien rulers being often hostile or indifferent to local culture. 4.
Dominance of oral culture which favoured lyrical rather than rational
aesthetic systems. It is true that several major poetic works in the oral
tradition were very close to discursive narrative prose. Many of these
works, utilitarian in character, used simple metres which were very close
to colloquial speech, thus obviating the need for prose writing. Yet the
rational basis was completely missing. Marathi prose writers in the
nineteenth century were not aware of the fact that a considerably rich
prose existed prior to their contact with the English prose tradition.[3] The
British educationists who were responsible for language planning were
ignorant of even the masterpieces of Marathi prose.[4] It is in the twentieth
century that hundreds of manuscripts have been discovered, only a few
of which are available in print even today.[5] Marathi is unique in having
a prose tradition among all the Indo-Aryan group of languages. Though
discontinuous and only partly belletrist, this tradition had developed several substyles of considerable variety.

2.3.1 THE FOLK STYLE

Oral prose forms, some of which are only recently graphized and printed,
reveal numerous substyles dating back to Middle Indo-Aryan and Old
Indo-Aryan literary traditions.[6] The oral literary style seems to be domi-

nant in society throughout the centuries and its influence on other cycles is considerably deep. This is a subject of independent research. The works in Mahanubhava and Bakhar cycles contain numerous fables, allegories, humorous tales, tales of son-in-law, vow tales and tales of supernatural beings. Having their origin in the various ethnic groups they abound in linguistic features coming from different language families such as Dravidian, Austro-Asiaitic, Tibeto-Burman and different Aryan dialects. The sentence-level analysis of this cycle would reveal a rhythmic quality which is mostly lost in the written prose of later centuries (see Annexure A1). This prose reveals a fine sense of genre. Simple recurring patterns of short sentences closer to colloquial rhythm, emphasis on semantic rather than grammatical units, freedom of word order entirely subsidiary to the prosodic qualities and repeated use of a limited number of sentence-linkers—are the distinguishing features of the prose in this cycle. A very important characteristic of this prose which is missing in other cycles is the partial-sentence construction. The folk cycle which is not fully explored as yet offers several varieties of individual and genre styles all over the Marathi speaking area. (For its South Indian Dramatic prose style see Annexure A2.)

2.3.2 THE PUNDIT STYLE

A few works belonging to this cycle, scattered over broken periods of time, suggest an unbroken tradition.[7] From Shripati Bhatt's *Jyotisharatnamala* (circa A.D. 1039) to the late nineteenth century this cycle has produced utilitarian works and discources and critical commentaries. This cycle gradually merged with the Bakhar cycle during the seventeenth and eighteenth centuries. These works reveal a kind of quasi-style made to a suit a wide variety of subjects like medicine, simple arithmetic, astrology and textual exegesis. It has been observed that this cycle has developed its own standard norms common to all regions and communities.[8]

This prose reveals a rigorous internal discipline of arguments with specialized artificial syntax tending to rhetorical norms. The prosodic values tend to depart from colloquial rhythm. The script does not exhibit rigorous graphic norms. Punctuation is frugal and often inadequate. There is no sense of paragraphing, though haphazard sections roughly guide the reading of text. Structurally, however, it is rich in numerous sentence-linkers and with a wide range of clausal patterns. The sentences are of varying length from to short to too long. On the lexical level it is dominated by Sanskrit elements. On the morphologiical, grammatical and phonological levels it exhibits dialectal varieties within a common syntactic standard. (See Annexures B1, B2, and F1.)

   The Influence of English on Marathi

2.3.3 MAHANUBHAVA STYLE

The richest of these cycles is the Mahanubhava prose. I. M. P. Raeside lists over 300 works, mostly unpublished, lying scattered in monasteries and private possessions of the devotees of the Mahanubhava sect.[9] A monastic cult, founded by Chakradhara (d. 1276), who preached radical principles of monotheism and equality, it offered equal status to women and shudras and revolted openly against Brahmanism. Chakradhara and his followers strictly prohibited the use of Sanskrit in the rich lore of the sect and established, for the first time in the history of Marathi, a broad-based colloquial prose style. The Mahanubhava prose works can be classified under four major heads : 1. Biographies of Mahanubhava leaders. 2. Philosophical works 3. Textual criticism and 4. Works of practical nature such as worship, prayers, rituals etc. The stylistic range of Mahanubhava prose is wide, inclusive of variants from local dialects, folk style and Sanskrit propositional style. This prose prospered during the latter half of the thirteenth and early fourteenth centuries. The Mahanubhava writers anticipated great upsurge of written culture, but unfortunately became ineffective politically as well as socially in the following centuries as a result of Brahman opposition and Muslim antipathy. In order to preserve their identity the Mahanubhava writers adopted several esoteric scripts which led to the stagnation of their prose literature, so that by the eighteenth century the sect along with its literature became almost obsolete. However, some devotees have continued to write textual commentaries and pseudo-style prose until today.

The Mahanubhava style reflects a standard shared by a host of writers from different regions and of different castes[10] Much of this prose was even committed to memory and was recited orally like verse.[11] Some of the most distinguishing featurs of this style can be enumerated as follows : 1. It is mainly propositional style based on Sanskrit Sutra style which is highly cryptic. Being nominal it emphasizes concepts and their interrelationships, thus avoiding Transformational possibilites. 2. The overall austere sense of genre is missing. The same style is monotonously used for biographies, memoirs, tales, character sketches, descriptive prose and textual criticism. 3. Individual style is evident only in a limited context. 4. At all major levels (prosodic, graphic and structural) the Sanskrit elements are reduced to the minimum. 5. Sentences are invariably short, which increases their capacity for parallelism and rhythmic matching. Colloquialism in the early texts greatly encouraged polarization of Marathi prose. 6. The scripts, with independent codes of diacritical signs and short forms particular to each of the several schools of the sect, defy any kind of standardization from punctuation to sentence boundaries. Paragraphs are absent. Structurally Mahanubhava style presents a varied and rich prose, making numerous experiments at intersentential and intrasentential levels. However, the contracted sentences and too loose a word order were prohibitive of stylistic norm formation at the syntactic level (see Annexures C1 to C4 and F2).

The style continued to be used in its historical form until the beginning of the nineteenth century and did not develop any outside contact [12] (see Annexure C 5).

2.3.4 THE BAKHAR STYLE

A *bakhar* is a historical chronicle, one of the many products of the Persian contact with Marathi during the fourteenth to seventeenth centuries. The Bakhar cycle is actually a complex of several cycles. It is most important from the point of view of the present study because the stylistic system of the bakhars written in the eighteenth century, with appropriate adjustment serves as a baseline to study the change that occurred after the nineteenth-century shift in the written standard. The first in this wide cycle, *Mahikavatichi Bakhar,* written from the latter half of the fifteenth century intermittently to the late eighteenth century, is written partly in verse and partly in prose. The last bakhar, *Indore Sansthanchi Bakhar,* was written in 1896, long after the new prose style under the influence of English had been firmly established. This shows that the bakhar style had been the most representative prose standard of the old tradition. R.V. Herwadkar in his study lists 140 works extant.[13] The cycle contains an admixture of several styles current in the past tradition. The large bulk of all these chronicles can be classified into several sub-genres, namely, biographical, autobiographical, sectarian, mythological, educational accounts; historical accounts of battles; family histories, news reports topical in nature, travelogues and geographical accounts.

The bakhars have been generally written by professional writers of Kayastha Prabhu and Deshastha Brahman castes employed by Princes and feudal lords.[14] This explains the courtly mode of writing, conspicuous use of Persian vocabulary and syntax and the strong sense of medieval tradition. The Marathi bakhars have been written in different regions of India, from Punjab to Tanjore, yet they exhibit some common standard of well-established prose. After the ascendency of the Maratha power from the end of the seventeenth century, the Persian features were reduced to the level of variants along with newly introduced Sanskrit variants. Local varieties of spoken dialects were also adjusted.

It is true that most bakhars are written in a quasi-style and that even the great classics in this cycle are literature only by accident. However, the bakhar style is a conscious attempt to develop a nativistic style out of the shattering Persian influence, that had penetrated deep into the structural level of Marathi prose. Sentence linkers, clausal structures, words and syntactic patterns, idioms and genre features are borrowed as wholes in bakhar prose. The long periodic sentence with its dominant main clause and balanced clausal structure was the organic growth of sentence linking devices of old Marathi. Several other additional features were developed under Persian influence[15] (see Annexures E1 and E2). The bakhar style was inclusive as regards stylistic devices and excepting the esoteric Mahanubhava cycle, it has borrowed stylistic devices from all other varieties of prose style, oral as well as written, available in the eighteenth century (see Annexures D1 to D3 and F3).

2.4.1 MARATHI PROSE IN 1818 : THE BASE FOR COMPARISON

Most scholars are of the opinion that old Marathi prose was unknown to the writers of the nineteenth century.[16] They argue that there was no standard Marathi prose before 1818, that the early nineteenth century writers had naturally no backgound of any significant prose norms existent in the history of Marathi, and that even if there were any, they were in manuscript form beyond the reach of the new literati.

To a large extent this observation is true. No writer until the middle of the nineteenth century has referred to any of the old classics. The Mahanubhava works remained undeciphered until the beginning of the twentieth century. The works in the Pundit cycle were in the possession of traditional professionals and village priests. The oral tales were not regarded as literary works as this awareness came to the educated people much later in the twentieth century. The bakhars were read only in limited circles of courtly families. In short, the stylistic awareness of the English-educated writers was exclusively controlled by English models (see Chapter 3).

However, the primary sources of the nineteenth century reveal several interesting facts related to the literary activities of the period. The popular literary traditions of prose were kept alive in old religious prose, mythologicial tales, Puranas and classical Sanskrit prose.[17] Several religious works in Sanskrit contained prose commentaries. Some of these were printed as soon as printing facilities were available.[18] These native influences, along with the widiely popular verse tradition, continued to be alive in society, though they had little prestige as compared with English influences. M. M. Kunte mentions a disitinct *Shastri* style of literary taste in the preface to his epic *Raja Shivaji* (1871). He says : "The inhabitants of Maharashtra, including Brahmans, Shudras and others, may be divided into 3 classes in reference to their taste. 1. The Shastris and whom they really guide. The class is large. 2. The educated, that is, those who know English. 3. The unducated, especially those who are indifferent to the Shastris or the educated, and who follow what their instinct prompts, and delight in what their nature likes."[19]

The overdone rhetoric in classical Sanskrit writers like Dandin, Kalidasa and Bhavabhuti, with their extravagant figures of speech and too obvious *Kavyagunas*, artificial sentence structures and correspondences were the models before this 'large class of Shastris'. The leading prose writers of the nineteenth century came from this very class. It is no wonder that these writers found close affinity with the rhetorical tradition in the eighteenth-century writers like Johnson, Burke and Gibbon. Even the anglicized writers could not escape the influence of the 'Shastri style'. For example Baba Padamanji, the first Indian novelist, says in his autobiography how folk tales, religious literature and other traditional works were popular even among the Shudras.[20]

The old Marathi prose works thus constitute the undercurrents in the nineteenth century literary culture. The drawbacks of these works were generally the drawbacks of the old tradition—limited variety of language use, lack of standardization and absence of rationality. The professional writers at the courts vanished with the old times. The area of the influence of the new learning increased and suppressed the old learning, which was, however, kept alive by a few traditional readers.

In the history of style there is always a possibility of archaism replacing the current features as soon as a stylistic system fails to supply differentiating features (see 2.1) needed by individuals, genres and by the whole period. The undercurrents stored by *langue* are always available whenever the need arises. Literary historians of English prose who see continuity of English prose from Anglo-Saxon to the Elizabethan period have confirmed this opinion.[21] Ian A. Gordon maintains that "the presence or absense of texts proves nothing against the weightier evidence, the actual survival of a rich and expressive language, with a sentence structure that was modified and expanded but always without alteration of its essentials."[22] In Marathi the actual survival of several sub-styles was at stake as long as the influence of English continued. During the last phase of the nineteenth century the oratorical variety of the Shastri style reappeared with great vigour. The other varieities such as the lyrical, the discursive and the priestly however did not appear until the beginning of the twentieth century.

As a result of the total absense of grammatical studies, Marathi was never subjected to prescriptivism and the language grew on its own or under the changing language policies of the British Government till the

                                        The Influence of English on Marathi

mid-nineteenth century (see Chapter 3.3). Though Sanskrit grammar was religiously studied, the descriptive methodology was never applied to the Marathi language; and English grammar provided an unscientific basis for the description of Marathi.[23] S. M. Katre observes that the process of decay which began in the Middle Indo-Aryan (MIA) period had continued in its uninterrupted line and that "the process had continued in the NIA [New Indo-Aryan] stage, and worked an absolutely new change from the synthetic to the analytic stage."[24] Neither English nor Sanskrit grammar was capable of studying this 'process of simplification' and a new grammar was needed. The numerous Marathi grammars during the second phase prescribed wrong rules and created anomalies in the understanding or written language by the English-educated prose writers. On the other hand, the Persian and English borrowings created confusion in the writing system especially on the graphic level and hampered the progress of natural style. A contemporary writer, M. M. Kunte laments the 'indiscriminate' introduction of Sanskrit words and says that "Marathi words are not writiten as they are pronounced . . . So long as this difference between Marathi written and Marathi spoken, is not removed, or at least recognized . . . the cause of metrical Marathi composition should suffer."[25]

Thus it can be safely said that despite the unconnectedness of the prose cycles and the apparent brokenness of the prose tradition, there existed certain norms which survived the onslaught of English prose. It is essential to reconstruct this framework which would serve as the basis of comparison between the then existing old tradition of bakhar-pundit-popular-religious written prose and the norms that came into existence in the early nineteenth century. This comparison would be restricted to a few but definite stock of categories so that the dynamic processes of language change can be analysed with some accuracy (see Chapter 4). A more detailed framework comprising all the norms of prose writing in the eighteenth century can be developed at a future stage of research (see Chapter 9).

2.4.2 LANGUAGE AND STYLISTIC VARIETIES

That the norms of eighteenth-century Marathi prose styles were generally formed by the speech of upper classes in the Desh part of Maharashtra is confirmed by the early nineteenth-century lexicographers, grammarians and educationists.[26] In the event of any controversy regarding the medium of instruction, choice of lexemes, standard and vulgar features and translation borrowing the balance went in favour of the Desh variety, more specifically the dialect spoken in the Pune area of the Bombay Presidency. This area, apart from being centrally located, had the advantage of being the political, cultural and literary centre in the eighteenth century. Great poets from Namadev (thirteenth century) to Moropant (eighteenth century) had used the dialect variety of this region in their verses. Marathi verse tradition had developed its own standard. As for prose, only a few genres seem to have developed independnent genre styles. Descriptive historical accounts, biography and letters claim some kind of standardization, but even here the component of rationality and the overall sense of literary form was entirely missing. In the treatment of time and chronological details, this prose could not develop any techniques. Utilization of the verbal space does not show any aesthetic basis. Literary conventions are absent. As a result, no deviation from the norm was possible. Individual styles, however, are exceptionally well-developed. For example, the four accounts of the debacle of Panipat (1761) show four distinct styles.[27]

2.4.3 GRAPHIC NORMS

(A) SCRIPT

The writing system was notoriously defective (For the three major scripts see Annexures F1, F2 and F3). The Modi script had virtually replaced the Balbodh or Devanagari on the sole strength of its easy calligraphy (see Annexure F3). However, the principles of this script were equally irrational. The characters and especially clusters of characters do not show uniformity. Length of vowels being non-phonemic in Marathi the two *i*'s and two *u*'s were always interchangeable. The placing of the nasal point was not uniform. Moreover, it was also given an additional function of indicating grammatical properties. The reading became confusing when irregularities occurred at the hands of careless copyists. Since interpolations by the copyists are many, omissions and additions in most manuscripts give rise to a number of textual problems. It is important to note that this is a serious handicap for undertaking microlinguistic studies in comparative stylistics, though its effect on the present study which concerns itself with sentential and near-sentential categories in the main is minimal.

Strange forms of *Sandhi* are frequent. The dental and the palatal affricates are indicated by a single series of letters. The oblique forms of dental affricates are palatalized in Marathi, but the scripts has no provision to make this change and the phonetic values are mixed up. Graphization of words was even more defective, as Sanskrit orthography was adopted in toto. Since the relationship between prose and writing system is very important from the point of view of language standardiztion, this hampered the very function of prose style. The manuscript culture of Marathi prose was thus ineffectual until the advent of printing (cf. 5.5.2 and Chapter 6).

(B) PUNCTUATION

Punctuation was too inadequate to reduce the confusion in reading. Traditionally, a vertical bar was the only punctuation mark to indicate sentence boundary, and usually two such bars to indicate section boundary. Statement, question, exclamation, clause, phrase, group of words—all these were distinguished by this single bar. In several manuscripts even the bar does not exist and words and sentences as well as sections are allowed to run into one another till the end of the page which was the natural boundary. Thus, lack of punctuation and of aesthetic use of space affected the written style at all its levels. The sense of graphology was almost totally missing. (cf. 5.5.2 and Chapter 6).

2.4.4 STRUCTURAL LEVEL

(A) INTERSENTENTIAL LINKING

As paragraphs did not exist, the links between groups of sentences are totally absent. The links between·sentences were comparatively more developed though they were never precisely formed. Sentence linkers assume a full stop between the two sentences. Often certain connectors, especially conjunctions, are substituted for real sentence linkers. The number of such connectors was very high as they were borrowed extensively from Sanskrit, Persian and native verse tradition.[28]

(B) SENTENTIAL NORMS

The prosodic qualities of oral style are seen disappearing in the eighteenth century prose and the rhythm of purely written style, dominated by Persian sentence structure, was developing as a norm. Variation was allowed to a large extent and clarity was not sacrificed at the cost of rhythm. The eighteenth century sentence style is essentially a short sentence style, the long sentences being joined smoothly by numerous connectors such as conjuctions, verb forms and adverb clauses.[29] A full stop before the sentence connector is common, showing attempts by the writers to develop the badly needed sentence linkers. On the whole the sentence structure was being developed to meet the needs of standardization.

(C) SYNTACTIC NORMS

The eighteenth century Marathi retains a considerable freedom from the stringent rules of syntax inherited from old Marathi. As in Old Indo-Aryan, Sanskrit, Middle Indo-Aryan, Prakrit and New Indo-Aryan, the word order is loose. The eighteeenth century Marathi retains this trait and develops new patterns of word order, though minimally.[30] R. B. Joshi attributes the freedom of word order in Marathi prose to the rich verse tradition which does not recognise too many of word order, and

observes context of meaning as the only principle.[31] In such a work order
where only the verb has a fixed position, other elements being broadly
positioned, confusion occurs in the semantic links.[32] The subject and the
verb are separated to the degree of polarization and the verb can give a
sudden turn to the whole meaning is suspended up to the end. Such a
word order is not particularly helpful for accurate reasoning since it
encourages ambiguity, rhetorical acrobatics and obscurity—lyrical elements which go against rational thinking and consequently good prose
writing.

(D) LEXICAL-GRAMMATICAL NORMS

Not even a brief account of this vast area can be attempted in this
section, as microlinguistic studies alone can give a proper picture. However, a few observations especially related to the function of verb, are
possible.

Borrowing at all levels appears to be a trend encouraged by the eighteenth century Marathi writers. Sanskrit lexical borrowings are numerous.[33] Sanskrit words are seen adjusted as variants of the norms of
Marathi style.[34] Words and grammatical features are extensively borrowed form other Indian languages. Persian borrowings have already
become part of the stylistic system of Marathi. Along with the Persian
borrowings Arabic and Urdu features are commonly found, especially in
the registers of administration and jurisprudence, military sciences and
courtly formalities.

An important development is seen in the use of the verb. Old Marathi
had a tendency of making the verb redundant. This tendency has been
curtailed and the presence of the verb has been made essential in the
eighteenth century prose. The usefulness of a verb as an indicator of
important semantic processes was recognized for the first time in Marathi. The verb was gradually becoming a strong element. The growth of
the new compound verb can be related to this fact. As John Beames
observes : "The modern [Marathi] verb, while throwing aside all the
intricacieis of the synthetical system of tenses, still manages to lose
nothing of its power of expressing minute shades of the meaning. On the
contrary, by its almost unlimited power of forming compound tenses, it
obtains a fullness and delicacy of expression which even the synthetic
verb cannot rival."[35]

As for grammatical properties of nouns and verbs this style does not
show a conscious tendency toward standardization and the behaviour of
genders, numbers, cases, voices, tenses and inflections has been carried
forward in the same way as in old Marathi with appropriate adjustment
of borrowed Persian lexical-grammatical categories. However, the more

minute features and finer characteristics at this level can be determined only through detailed stylo-linguistic studies with micro-linguistic methods.

2.5 CONCLUSION

With this idea of a base-line for comparison, the areas of Marathi prose styles which proved to be susceptible to the influence of English in the early inneteenth century can now be hypothesized. It should be kept in mind that such a skeleton model is not in any way intended to be a complete philological description of Marathi prose in the eighteenth century. As a purely a functional model for comparison, it is restricited to a few subsystems most relevant to the study of stylistic influence. The written prose of different historical cycles shows the following limitations as a system :

1.   The whole manuscript culture as against the oral culture was courtly and dependent upon the medieval feudal system. The collapse of the feudal system would naturally create a need for reorganization in the literary tradition as a whole.

2. Marathi had been in contact with other Eastern languages having religious culture as their background. With the contact of a western language like English the contexts of confrontation would be totally different. Similarly the literary-aesthetic systems would also be rdically changed. Individual styles had little freedom of expression in the feudal system. Radical social change would encourage individual styles.

3. The graphic system of eighteenth-century Marathi, especially its compositional and punctuation subsystems, was to a large extent irrational, fragile and detrimental to standardization. Confrontion with a more standardized graphic system would result in radical changes.

4.   Structural subsystems of the eighteenth-century Marathi prose, especially the intersentential cohesion and sentence structure, show signs of internal development. These would be further expanded with the passage of time. Logical relationship of structures is the most immediate need of the eighteenth-century prose.

Since Marathi sentence at this stage is essentially short and plain branching, downgrading, relativization and coordination being almost absent for lack of clausal linkage, the rhythmic patterns and length of the sentence would undergo unexpected changes with its expansion. Again the eighteenth-century prose shows little sense of actor-action construction. The excessive freedom that the word order in the eighteenth-century prose permits has severely reduced the possibility of standardization in syntactic rules. Though this word order is stylistic and capable of infinite patterns, it encourages haphazard sentence structures which are impervious to rational discourse and micro-cohesion of thought units in the text. The looseness of the word order also restricts the syntactic rules needed to be framed. Lexical cohesion is the only possible means of sentence linking at this stage. All these features would be modified under the influence of new modes of order and cohesive devices other than lexical.

The vocabulary is limited to the sphere of feudal life, though it bears great capacity of word formation processes such as compounding, reduplication and formation of verbal nouns. New lexical stocks containing other elements depending upon the need of the prose would enter the lexical subsystem. Inflectional categories, especially genders, and verb forms, and morphological processes are too strong to undergo basic changes. Verbal forms are sufficiently flexible to absorb new modifications.

When the written style of English with a strong unbroken prose tradition of at least three centuries comes into contact with Marathi in the early nineetenth century, a wide range of stylistic influences is expected in its writing system. Every influence is indicative of two characteristics of language as a system : 1. The strength of the tradition, 2. The limit of the orginality of the language.[36] It will be seen at the end of this study that after about a hundred years of contact not all the areas we have hypothesized here have been necessarily influenced. The reasons for this unequal impact in the acculturation is a problem that needs separate investigation.

ANNEXURES

The passages in Annexures A to E are taken from modern printed editions of old texts originally written in different old scripts particular to the cycles described in the preceding pages. The texts, transcribed or transliterated in standard Devanagari script and punctuation, are reproduced with a view to facilitating their comparison with those printed in the nineteenth century reproduced in Chapters 6, 7 and 8. They are selected from different periods and cycles so as to give sufficient idea of the variety of structural subsystems of the old Marathi prose.

The passages in Annexure F are, however, reproduced from the original manuscripts in order to give the idea of the graphic subsystems of old Marathi texts.For the full bibliographicial details and other information regarding the sources of the texts in these annexures, see **Notes and References** : Chapter 2 and **Bibliography.**

A1

आटपाट नगर होतं. तिथं एक गरीब ब्राह्मण रहात असें. तो दरिद्रानं फार पिडला होता. त्याची बायको शेजारणीच्या घरीं एके दिवशीं बसायला गेली. आपल्या गरिबीचं गान्हाणं गाइलं. शेजारणीनं तिला शुक्रवारचं व्रत सांगितलं. ती म्हणाली बाई बाई शुक्रवारचं व्रत कर. हे शुक्रवार तू श्रावणापासून धर. सारा दिवस उपास धरावा, संध्याकाळीं सवाष्णीला बोलवावं, तिचे पाय धुवावें, तिला हळदकुंकू द्यावं, तिची ओटी भरावी, साखर घालून दूध प्यायला द्यावं. भाजलेल्या हरबऱ्यांची खिरापत द्यावी, नंतर त्याचं उद्यापन करावं, असं सांगितलं. ही घरीं आली, देवाची प्रार्थना केली व शुक्रवाराचं व्रत करूं लागली.

A2

सूत्रधार : (नालगु भाष लटिके वानिनि अडिगेदी), तूं कोण रे ?

कंचुकीराय विनोदी   : तूं कोण रे ?

सूत्रधार : आह्मीं भागवंत.

कं. :   भाग्यवंत जाले तरी, मंदिल कोठें ? चादर कोठें ? झगा कोठें ?

सूत्र. :   अरे, भाग्यवंत नव्हे रे. आह्मी दशावतार .

कं. :   अरे, दश जाले तरी कोठें रे ?

सूत्र. :   हेंगे तरु बुरु नटु मुटु हेंगे श्रुदंग.

कं. :   तरु बुरु नटु मुटु मीरु देंगु.

सूत्र. :   अरे, आह्मांस पुसतोस कां ? तू कोण ? तुझें नांव काय ? सांग.

कं. :   माझें नांव कंचुकीराय विनोदी.

सूत्र :   काशास आलास रे ?

कं. :   मी, श्रीमन्नारायण जगदाधार सभेस येताती, सभा सिद्ध
           करायाकारणें आलों.

B1

अथ नेत्र उपचार ॥ मकियाचे मूळ तांबियावर उगाळून डोळा घालिजे चिपडे जाति ॥ सोनवळिचा रस नेत्रि घालिजे रक्त फाके ॥ जटांमासि निंबाची पाने वाटुन रस डोळा घालिजे रक्त फाके ॥ आघाडियाचें मूळ, गाईचें तूप, दहि याचे पाणि सेंधव, गोरोचन, हे तांबियावर उगाळून नेत्रि घालिजे झडल्यापात ज्याये ॥ तीळ, सतांजन, मदे उगाळून डोळा घालिजे त्रिमिर जाय ॥ तिळाचें फुलें ८० पिंपाळिचे तांदूळ ६० एकत्र करुन नेत्रि धुईजे वरि जोपकिजे त्रिमिर जाय ॥ हेंच औषथ दहियेचे पाणिये घालिजे रातांध जाय ॥ पाणी ये रक्त फाके कांजिये पडळ जाये ॥ कमळ सेंधव रातांजन त्रिफळा वस्त्रगळींत करून नेत्री घालिजे त्रिमिर जाय ॥ बेलाच्या मुळाचा रस, घोडियाचे मुत्र डोळा घालिजे फुल जाय ॥

B2

न क्लेशपंचकमिदं भजते कृतकोशपंचविवेक : ।
अत एव पंच कोशान् कुशलधियः सन्ततं विचिन्वन्ति ॥७॥

॥ टीक ॥ पंचकोशविवेक ज्या पुरुषानें केला आहे त्यास पंचक्लेश होत नाहींत ॥ यास्तव कुशल बुद्धिवंत निरंतर पंचकोशविवेक करित आहेत ॥ ते पंचक्लेश कोणते ॥ अविद्या ॥ अस्मिता ॥ राग ॥ द्रेष ॥ अभिनिवेश ॥ पंचक्लेशा : ॥ याचा अर्थ कथितों ॥ अविद्या म्हणजे मूलविद्या आत्मविषइं अज्ञान ॥ अस्मिता म्हणजे देहादि अनात्मा याचे ठायीं आत्मबुद्धि 'अहं देहीत्यादी' ॥ देहानुकूल शब्दाविषयीं प्रीति तो राग ॥ देहास प्रतिकूल शब्दादि विषयिं अप्रीति तो द्रेष । रागद्रेषाचे ठाइं दुराग्रह तो अभिनिवेश ॥ दुराग्रह म्हणजे अनुकूलच संपादावें प्रतिकूल सर्वथा नसावें । हे पंचक्लेश माहा दुर्धर ॥७॥

आतां पंचकोशाचिं नामें तत्पूर्वक विवेक सांगतों ॥

C1

गावीं एकी व्रक्षाखालि आसन : तव पारधी वाटे ससा सोडीला : तया पाठी सुणी सोडीली : काकूळती येउनि ससा जानूतळि रीगाला : सूणी उभी राहींली : मागील कडौनि पारधी आले : तेहीं वीनवीलें : 'ससा सोडीजो जी' : सर्वज्ञें ह्मणीतलें : 'हा एथ सरण आला' : पुडती तीहीं ह्मणीतलें : 'जी जी : हा होडेचा ससा जी : या कारण सूरीया काढणीया होती : जी जी : हा सोडावा जी' : एकी वासना : 'काल लागैल जी : ससा सोडीजो जी' : सर्वज्ञें ह्मणीतलें : हां गा : एथ सरण आलेया काइ मरण असे' : 'जी जी : तरि हा : गोसावी राखीला' ॥ रामेश्वरबास ॥ निरूपण केलें : हां गा : ए रानीं असति : पाणी पीति : यातें तुम्ही कां मारा : तीहीं ह्मणीतलें : जी जी : आजि लागौनि न मारूं : मग : तें निघालें : मग सर्वज्ञें ह्मणीतलें : 'माहात्मे हो : आतां जाए' ऐसें : भणौनि : जानु उचलिली : मग ससा निगाला ॥

C2

गांवा हस्ति आलाः तेथ जात्यंध हस्ती पाहों गेले : एकें पावो देखीला : एकें सोंड देखीली : एकें कानु देखीला : एकें पाठि देखीली : एकें पोट देखीलें : एकें पूंस देखीलें । मग एकमेका संवादति : आरे तुवां हस्ती देखीला : पावो देखीला तो म्हणे हस्ती खांबासारीखा : सोंड देखीली तो म्हणे हस्ती मूसव्ळासारीखा : कानु देखीला तो म्हणे हस्ती सुपासारीखा : पाठि देखीली तो म्हणे हस्ति भींतीसारीखाः पोट देखीलें तो म्हणे हस्ती कोथव्ळेयासारीखा । पुंस देखीलें तो म्हणे हस्ती खरांटेयासारीखा : ऐसें एकमेकां उरोधीति । तयांमध्ये डोळसु असे तो म्हणे हा हस्तीचा एकु एकु अवएवु होए : परि हस्ति नव्हे : ऐसा अवएवीं युक्त तो हस्ति ॥४३॥

C3

तंवः अरुणोदयो : होए आधीली दिसी भटोबासी सीलीका दोनि आणुनी ठेवलीया असति : आंबीयाचीया : बाबुळेचीया : कदाचीत बोरीचीया : तो दोन्ही गोसावीया : श्रीकरी ओव्ळगवीति : गोसावीयाची : एकि जानु वरि ठेवीति : एकी दंतधावन करीति : दंतधावन करूं सरे : ते परी त्यजीति : दुसरी घेति : ते : डावीये श्रीकरीचेया आंगुठेयाचेनि नखें : चीरूनि दोनी फोडि करीति : एकि आंगुळीयां मध्यें धरीति : एकी धनुषाकार वळीति : त्या जीव्ह्यामळ आकर्षीति : जीव्ह्यामळ आकर्षूं सरे : आणि परीतेजीति : दुसरी घेति : तेही : धनुषाकार वळीति : त्या जीव्ह्यामळ आकर्षीति : जीव्ह्यामळ आकर्षूं सरे : आणि परीत्यजीति :

C4

तथा संबंधी-संबंधु-प्रदानिं माझा केसव शुकयोग्गिंद्र म्हणणें : ॥

मग एक दी केसोबासांचि संबंधियें आइकोनि नेयावया आलीं : भाउ गोपाळदेव : आणि सासुरे यैसें प्रतिकूळत्वें नेवों आलें : केसोबासातें नेलें : भिक्षा सांडवूं आदरिली : तवं ते काही केलेयांही न संडीतिचि : मग विद्रांसिंहीं हात झाडीले : तेहीं म्हणितलें : हे आम्हां जिनवति ना : आतां यांची ब्राम्हणि यांतें जिणेल : तरि : जिकतीं : आतां ये दोंधें येका घरांत कोंडावि : मग कोंडीली : तेथ तियें बाजेवरि निजति तरि ते खालि निजति : (तियें खालि निजति) तरि आपण बाजेवरि निजति : यापरी रात्रि जाये : दिवसा गंगेकडे जाति : तेथ दृष्टीचीं राखणें घालीति : केसाबास गंगे विजन करीति : तेथ 'रत्नमाळा' स्तोत्रें करीति : मग गांवांतु आणिति : यापरी सातपांच दिवस जाले : मग ब्राम्हणी म्हणितलें : आतां यांसि जावों द्या : आतां हे योगीये जाले : यांचे मज पाप लागत असे : मग अवधा केसोबासां अनुज्ञा दीधलिः निगाले : भटोबासांसी भेटि जालीं : मागील सांघितले : तें आइकोनि-परीसौनि भटोबासीं म्हणितलें : माझा केशव शुकयोग्गिंद्र किं गा : म्हणौनि थोरचि प्रसंसीले : ॥१३॥

C5

रत्नपुर नावं नगर : तेथें देवदत्तु नांव ब्राह्मणु आसे : तयाची स्त्री व्यभीचारिणी : परपुरुशरत : ते सीनाळी : प्रत्यहिं ते सीनाळासी पक्वांनें रांधी : भर्तारासी ठाउकें पडों नेदी : सीनाळाचें घरीं जाऊनी तयासंगातें सुरतसंभोग करि : ऐसें तीचे लोक अपवाद बोलती : तेनें ब्राह्मणें परशधरें आईकीलें : मग म्हणे : "हें सत्य कीं मीथ्या : केवी ठाउकें पडे ?" तवं एके दिवसी तेणें ब्राह्मणें पक्वांनें रांधितां देखीली : तेणें पुसीलें : "आजी पक्वांनें काशालागी करतो (ते) सी :" तवं ते म्हणें : "तुम्हांसी दुखत होतें : तै म्यां देवतेसी बोनें नवसीलें होतें : आतां नैवेदु दाखवावेया देउळा जाईन :" तवं तो म्हणें : "बरवें केलें :"

D1

तेधवा थारेसि भोज या जवळ गेला ॥ राया केशवदेवाची पदें वाखाणिली ॥ पितामोहो यैसि गद्यपद्य म्हणता जाला ॥ तेधवा राजा भोज कोपला ॥ कालिचें पोर ऐसा अभिमान धरिला ॥ दळवै बोलाविला ॥ आज्ञा दिधली जर सेना सिद्ध करावी ॥ हल्ला ठाणे कोकणि म्हणोन ॥ दळ सिद्ध जालें ॥ मुहिम केली ॥ थेट कळव्यास आले ॥ परदळ देखतां हाहाकार जाला ॥ येक केशवदेवा प्रति सांगो आलें ॥ जर कटक भोजरायाचे आलें ॥ देसायाला हुंकारा केला ॥ देसाय देसाय देस मिळाला ॥ सिंध्याचा जमाव थोर जाला ॥ नगान्या घाव घातला ॥ करणे बांके सिंगे डफ काहाळा विराणी वाजली ॥ पाईकापाईक जालि ॥ कळव्या युद्ध थोर जालें ॥

D2

७७ तों इकडे जनकोजी सिंदे निशाणापासीं झोंबत होते. त्यांचे उजवे दंडास येकायेकीं गोली लागोन दंड मोडला , हाड बाहेर आलें. जनकोजी सिंदे यांस कलम येऊन घोड्चाखवालीं आले. तो जवळ खिजमतगार उभा होता. तो धांवत दताजी सिंदे यांजकडे आला आणि घाबरेपणें वर्तमान सांगितलें कीं, "बाबासाहेब गोळी लागोन पडले." आसें वर्तमान ऐकतांच दत्ताजी सिंदे यांणीं जवळ लोक उभे होते त्यांस बोलिले कीं; " बाबा आम्हांस सोडून गेले. आतां आम्हांस देशीं तोंड दाखवावयाचे कारण नाहीं. रणांत मृत्यु आला तर उत्तम आहे; नाहीं तर विष खाऊन प्राण द्यावा." आसें बोलोन दताजी सिंदे यांजपुढें दाहा हजार कुतुबशाहा व दुराणीचे लोक उभे होते, त्यांजवर अठरा असामींनीं घोडीं घातलीं.

D3

श्री

त्यात बुदले भरून छ ३ सफरीं कुल अवघी सिद्धता करून लोकांस सुरुंग उडतांच हल्ला करण्याविशीं ताकीद केली. छ ४ रोजी सुरुंगास बत्या दिल्या. राजश्री राणबाकडील पांच सुरुंग उडावे. त्यांत चार उडाले. एक उडावयाचा होता तोंच लोकांनी तांतड करून हल्ला केली. तो पांचवा सुरुंग उडाला. तेणेंकरून लोक बहुतकरून दगडांनी हडपले. तैसे हल्लेस हशमाचे लोक चढले होते तेही उडाले; व फिरंगी यानें हुक्के व गरनाळा, दारूचीं मडकीं बरखंदाजी, रंजिगिरी येणेंप्रमाणें अतिशय मार दिला. यामुळें ते दिवशीं लोक कचमोहरे जाले. मग कारेगार जालें नाहीं. दुसरे दिवशीं दोन सुरुंग उडतां राहिले होते, त्यांचा शोध करून, बत्या ठीक करून, सान्या लोकांची निवड करून, हल्लेविशीं ताकीद केली; आणि सुरुंगास बत्ती दिली. त्यानें निम्मे बुरुज उडाला. लोकांनी जीवित्वाकडे दृष्टी न देतां चालोन गेले.

E1

अर्जदास्त अर्जदार ॥ बंदगी बंदे नवाज ॥ आलेकुम्सलाम ॥ साहेबांचे शेवेशीं ॥ बंदे शरीराकार ॥ जिवाजी शेखदार ॥ बुधाजी कारकून ॥ परगणे शरीराबाद ॥ किल्ले कायापुरी ॥ सरकार साहेबांची आज्ञा घेऊन स्वार झालों ॥ तो परगणे मजकुरचे जमेदार ॥ दंभाजी शेट व लोभाजी महाजन व मनीराम देशमूख व ममताई देशपांडीण व क्रोधाजी नाइकवाडी ॥ ऐसे हरामजादे फार आहेत ॥ ते सरकार कामाचा कयासा चालूं देत नाहींत ॥ दंभाजी शेठ्या कचेरीस येऊन जोम धरून बसतो ॥ मनीराम देशमूख आपलें काम परभारें करून घेतो ॥ ममताई देशपांडीण इणें तमाम परगणा जेरदस्त केला ॥ क्रोधाजी नाइकवाडी यानें तमाम तफरका केला ॥

E2

"मशहुरुल हजरत राजश्री जिवाजी विनायक सुबेदार व कारकुन सुबे मामले प्रभावळी, प्रती राजश्री शिवाजीराजे दंडवत. दौलतखान व दरियासारंग यासी ऐवज व गल्ला राजश्री मोरोपंत पेशवे यांणीं वराता सुबे मजकुरावरी दिधल्या. त्यास तुम्हीं कांहीं पाठविले नाहीं म्हणोन कळों आलें. त्यावरून अजब वाटलें कीं, ऐसे नादान थोडे असतील ! तुम्हास समजलें असेल कीं याला ऐवज, कोठेंतरी ऐवज खजाना रसद पाठविलिया मजरा होईल म्हणत असाल. तरी पद्मदुर्ग वसवून राजपुरीच्या उरावरी दुसरी राजपुरी केली आहे. त्याची मदत व्हावी, पाणी फाटी आदिकरून सामान पावावें, या कामास आरमार बेगिनें पावावें, तें नाहीं. पद्मदुर्ग हबशी फौजा चौफेर जेर करीत असतील. आणि तुम्ही ऐवज न पाववून, आरमार खोळंबून पाडाल ! एवढी हरामखोरी तुम्ही कराल; आणि रसद पाठवून मजरा करूं म्हणाला त्यावरी साहेब रिझतील कीं काय?

F1

F3

CHAPTER THREE

THE SOCIAL, POLITICAL AND LINGUISTIC BACKGROUND OF NINETEENTH-CENTURY MAHARASHTRA

3.1 PRELIMINARIES

One of the most important characteristics of language is its binary relationship with culture : Language is both a result of culture and the condition of culture. When culture contact takes place, the receiving language maintains its first, causal relationship with culture vigorously, while the second, namely, its being the condition of culture is disturbed to the degree of the force of the alien contact. In the long-term colonial type of culture contact the language of the dominant group becomes an instrument of ethnic superiority. The dominant group use their language as the instrument of spreading their values; and the dominated, being left with no other alternative, accept the value systems of the dominant as their own. The medium of this transfer is the bilingual behaviour of the dominated group. A closer study of the political and social background in respect of the socio-linguistic phenomena is essential in order to "abstract the structure which underlies the many manifestations," a view confirmed by anthropologists and linguists concerned with the study of acculturation.[1]

Excellent source material on the history of nineteenth century India is available in personal memoirs, contemporary historical documents and studies made by social scientists, British as well as Indian. (see Bibliography). The political and social developments in nineteenth-century Maharashtra pertaining to the formation of a national prose are briefly reviewed in this chapter. The chapter is intended to serve as a reference guide to the following chapter and also as a general background to Chapters 6,7 and 8. It attempts to analyse the special characteristics of the English contact leading to acculturation as distinct from other types of acculturation presented by the studies published so far (see Bibliography).

3.2 POLITICAL SETTING

3.2.1 THE FIRST PHASE (1818-1847)

The Maratha power was dominant in Western India in the second half of the seventeenth century and grew into the most dominant political power in India by the end of the eighteenth century. During this period, the Europeans (mainly British, Portuguese and French) had confined their activities to modest trade and to proselytization on the west coast. The East India Company was established in A.D. 1600. Interpreters and informers on the British as well as the Maratha side had established some linguistic contacts from Shivaji's days (mid-seventeenth century), but sources reveal that these contacts were limited to a few individuals.[2] The Battle of Plassey (A.D. 1757) raised the political status of English traders, missionaries and diplomats in India. The Third Anglo-Maratha War (1917-18) extinguished the Maratha power, which was their most powerful rival at the beginning of the nineteenth century, and established the British as the sole political power in India. In 1819 the Bombay Presidency was formed with Bombay, which had been in British prossession since 1668, as its headquarters. The cultural life of Bombay, therefore, was more anglicised than that of any other city in Maharashtra throughout the nineteenth century.[3]

The social change in nineteenth-century England together with industrial-capitalist-democratic-colonization developments had ensured the emergence of Britain as the most powerful nation state of a new type in the world.[4] With the contact of such a nation the ancient socio-political structure of India was bound to collapse. Total absence of nationalism, backward political and social economy, caste compartmentalization and numerous factions of language, religion, profession and region combined to favour the strong impact of well-organized British industrial power.

India had been for the European since Marco Polo's accounts in the thirteenth century, a place of romance, exotic beings, haunting customs, landscapes and pomp.[5] This image of India began to disappear with the nineteenth-century British occupation. The first scientific knowledge of India began with William Jones's account, *Objects of Enquiry during my Residence in Asia* and with the studies of the first western scholars of Sanskrit like Charles Wilkins.[6] These studies initiated modern comparative disciplines including linguistics in Europe. The average Englishman coming to India was thus regarded as the scholar, the scientist, the missionary, the trader or the soldier.

                                   The Influence of English on Marathi

When the British captured and retired the last Peshwa in 1818 and later, in 1839, deposed the Chhatrapati of Satara, there was little unrest among the masses. Though the upper class proteges of the feudal lords and Princes were greatly displeased, and later, supported the desperate battle fought all over west-central India in 1857, there was little sympathy for them among the masses. The common man in the early nineteenth century, having known little of what can be called freedom, accepted the new rule rather as an act of deliverance. Even the sense of the lack of freedom developed among the elite in the late nineteenth century, mainly as a result of English education. The rule of law and order, of justice and peace replaced the terrible anarchy of caste fanaticism and lawlessness of the late Peshwa period, and on the whole people were happy with the new rulers.[7] The trend to praise and welcome British rule reached its climax in the mid-nineteenth century. In the last quarter of the century nativistic movements, mainly led by political extremists and English-educated Brahmans, gained strength among the masses. However, even the leaders of these movements are found accepting British rule as a blessing in disguise. Some non-Brahman minorities even preferred British rule to self-government.[8]

In 1820 Mountstuart Elphinstone became Governor of the newly formed Bombay Presidency which was the most difficult province for the British to administer on account of its peculiar historical background of Brahman dominance and the martial traditions of its people. However, the administrative policy Elphinstone adopted was that of respect for the local culture.[9] Despite pressures from British administrators and native reformers he continued to appease the orthodox section of society. With an undaunted zeal he encouraged a number of government and private institutions to educate the natives and became a most respected British administrator of his time in India. An introspective and sensitive whig, he was influenced by the French revolution and shared the thoughts of the early Romantics.[10] Like other founders of British power in India, such as Warren Hastings (Governor-General of India from 1774 to 1785), Elphinstone was convinced that the British Power must be an Indian power, and encouraged Oriental learning in India in the spirit of Indian tradition.[11] However, the younger generation of officers employed by East India Company did not share this spirit. The 'British India' trend prospered at the beginning of the nineteenth century with Sir Thomas Munro in Madras, Elphinstone in Bombay, Sir John Malcolm in Central India, Charles Metcalfe in Delhi and Wellesley in Bengal. With the background of the Romantic Movement, French revolution and the martial epoch through which Britain passed in the Napoleonic wars, Industrial Revolution, American war of Independence and Parliamentary reforms the British administrators had developed a kind of liberal attitude toward Indian society within the imperial and colonial framework. They were generally in favour of preserving Indian institutions with suitable anglicization of the administrative system. They were very proud of the historical role the British were to carry out in modernizing India. Many of them introduced radical reforms with full awareness of the risk of losing their power in India in the long run. For example, Sir Erskine Perry says : "Whether we desire it or not our educational efforts undoubtedly tend to make the Hindus able to govern themselves, I think the object is noble and to propose ourselves anything more restricted would be a dereliction of our duty."[12]   Similarly, Mountstuart Elphinstone's remark that the Marathi books he was encouraging were "a high road back to England" is well known.[13]   This tradition continued throughout the nineteenth century. "We are here to educate the natives", was the motto of the early British administrators in India, though for all of them, India was a career. Even Macaulay says : "To have ruled them as to have made them desirous and capable of all the privileges of citizens would be a title of glory of our own".[14] In his famous Charter speech of 1833, he states that Indians "having become instructed in European knowledge, . . . may, in some future age demand European institutions . . . Whenever it comes it will be the proudest day in English history." The British seemed to prefer, in Macaulay's words, "the imperishable empire of English arts and English morals, English literature and English laws" in Independent India to slavery and superstition of British India of that period.[15]

Though this silver lining of British colonialism proved to be favourable to acculturation, the motives behind British policy of India on the whole do not show any consistency in instituting real reforms in India. Nor did they always encourage progressive forces. For example, a later Utilitarian, John Lawrence, Governor General of India in 1864, emphatically says : "We are here by our own moral superiority, by the force of circumstances and by the will of Providence. They alone constitute our charter of Government and in doing the best we can for the people we are bound by our conscience and not by theirs."[16] So the Utilitarian belief in 'the greatest happiness of the greatest number' met with the paradox between the principle of liberty and the principle of authority, and a reference to moral right became necessary to legitimize exploitation of India. It was out of a feeling of guilt that the British rulers introduced and sometimes even forced radical reforms on the Hindus. After Frantz Fanon's model of colonialism the British rule in the nineteenth century could be treated as a period of accumulation of capital in the long term capitalism of British economy. Some of the most honest British administrators like Martin Montgomery have confessed how the

                                     The Influence of English on Marathi

British were plundering the people shorn of their political and military powers.[17]

The native intellectuals also show conflicting responses to the good and evil caused by British rule in India, and these are equally human and mature. They reveal a conscious acceptance of the superiority of the western civilization though they still preserved national pride and religious sentiments in a concealed form. The British respected these sentiments by recognizing the merits of the native culture. The Indians, in turn, wanted more and more of material culture to be imported to India. The Benthamites of the first half of the nineteenth century upheld the leadership of the world that England undertook, and forced utilitarian reforms on the Hindus. This spirit is best revealed in the Indian career of William Bentick, Governor-General of India from 1828 to 1835. Jeremy Bentham wrote to Bentinck on 18th November 1829, that it appeared to him "as if the golden age of British India were lying before me," and desired that he should encourage the diffusion of education and useful knowledge in India. Bentinck promptly promised compliance.[18]

The utilitarians' 'golden age' was already evident in the multifarious activities encouraged by the British rulers in India and in Bombay Presidiency. The pioneers in almost every branch of learning were the British, such as Drummond and Carey, Major Candy and Captain George Ritso Jervis, Molesworth and Monier Monier-Williams, Horace Wilson and H.T. Colebrook, William james and Charles Wilkins. It remains to be investigated whether most of the British who loved Indian culture were of non-English background, and whether their Scottish, Welsh or Irish sentiments were reflected unconsciously in their attitude toward India where colonization was just beginning. This can be an interesting problem for research for cultural anthropologists.

3.2.2 THE SECOND PHASE (1847-1874)

The phase is marked by increasing racial cleavage between the Indians and the British. Several princely states, many of them under Maratha Princes, were annexed to British India by Dalhousie, Governor-General of India between 1848 and 1856. Unification of Greater India took place for the first time in known history. Dalhousie introduced several dazzling reforms which linked distant parts of the Indian subcontinent to the main ports, and India to the western world. This in effect increased further exploitation of India, though it also meant greater communication between India and the West. The Indian image of British underwent a radical change. The trading motives had gradually developed into Imperial designs. As the industrial centres grew in size and number, agriculture suffered. The feudal professions vanished completely, creating imbalance in rural economy; and when colonization was complete, several nativistic movements, from the Bombay Association (1852) to Tilak's Ganpati festival (1893) rose (see 3.2.3). The racial cleavage was most terribly demonstrated by the Mutiny of 1857, when the British demonstrated a most barbaric spirit in their destructive acts like burning down an invaluable library of rare manuscripts at Jhansi, and when the politically divided Hindus and Muslims made common cause against the white race.[19] Savage massacre of Englishmen, their wives and children in several places in North India and the eqully savage measures to root out the rebels revealed the deep racial rift between the Indians and the British. The East India Company was forced to liquidate itself; and with the establishment of *Pax Britannica* and the Proclamation by the Queen in 1858 that the British Government would not interfere with the religion of the natives, the relationship between Hindus and the British became truly political.

3.2.3 THE THIRD PHASE (1874-1901)

This is a period of spread of education and rise of great nativistic movements, of alternate British policies depending upon the Conservative and the Liberal governments in Britain. The belated transformation of the Indian society from Medieval to Modern age began during this phase. The Indian National Congress was born and soon the development of a rift between the moderates and the extremists within it followed. A number of terrorist organizations were active in Maharashtra. Phule's mass movement and Tilak's neo-Hinduism symbolized the two directions in which social change was taking place. Constitutional struggle for fundamental rights posed a threat to the British rule at the end of the century. Lord Curzon, the Viceroy of India from 1901 to 1905 and Tilak, the leader of the violent nationalist agitation polarize the almost century-old relationship between the British and the Hindus. The rise of Japan made Indians more confident. Both cultures claimed superiority at this stage and the neo-Hinduists even started saying that England had much to learn from India. Pan-Indian nationalism, one of the most notable consequences of Indo-British for freedom no longer remained a political movement but a cultural necessity as well

Standardization of public administration, growth of towns and communications directly strengthened the formation of educational centres in Bombay and Pune. On the other hand, the impoverishment of the rural population increased due to the depletion of agriculture, recurring famines and epidemics. A general feeling that change was necessary dominated the intellectal world. In other words, there was a spirit of unrest

                                    The Influence of English on Marathi

with a demand for both social and political reforms from the educated sections of society.

Some of the nativistic movements had their roots in the Second phase, though they raised their heads during this phase. The wide spectrum of nativistic movements suggests organized efforts to assert the native culture at various levels, confirming that change was essential. Each movement seems to adopt its own specific devices. These have important bearing on the prose literature of this phase. The movements can be grouped as under :

I   NON-LITERARY NATIVISTIC MOVEMENTS :

1. Perverted—religious—quasi-nativistic : the Thugs, and Shaktas
2. Irrational—non-constitutional : The Bhil rebellions
3. Well-organized political : The 1857 mutiny
4. Temporary : The Deccan Riots of 1873
5. Terrorist-underground : Vasudeo Balwant Phadke's riot

II   SEMI-LITERARY NATIVISTIC MOVEMENTS

ORAL AND WRITTEN :

1. Rural mass : The starting of Satyashodhak Samaj
2. Urban mass : The Bombay Association, the National Congress
3. Revivalistic : Sanskritism, Reprint of old Marathi poets, Renewed interest in Maratha history; Starting of the Swadeshi movement, Neo-Hinduism such as activitieis of Prarthana Samaj, Brahmo Samaj and Arya Samaj
4. Progressive : Paramahansa Sabha, Widow Remarriage Association, various Christian Associations, Educational Institutions, Dhnyan Prasarak Sabha, Manav Dharma Sabha, Kallyannonayak Mandali, Dhnyan Prakash Sabha, Public speeches etc.

III LITERARY NATIVISTIC MOVEMENTS :

1. Periodicals, printing, theatre and such other channels
2. Literate or written bilingualism
3. Professional writing : The essay, the novel, drama and other prose genres.

The above classification indicates the multiple means of expression the society was trying. For example, Dnyan Prasarak Sabha (Students' Literary and Scientific Society) regularly organized paper readings on literary and scientific subjects wherein use of English in papers and discussions was strictly prohibited.[20] Some of these movements were initiated and encouraged by the liberal British intellectuals.[21] It is important to note that bilingualism of the literate type (see 4.3.2) and nativistic movements have directly contributed to the development of Marathi prose under the influence of English.

3.3 THE ENGLISH EDUCATION AND LANGUAGE POLICIES

3.3.1 THE BACKGROUND OF BRITISH EDUCATION

Modern education in Maharashtra began as an act of charity with the initiative of European and American Missionaries. After 1823 the East India Company framed its educational policy. There was hardly any 'system' of education before the British introduced their system in India.[22] Even in England there was nothing like a national system of education, as education was mostly left to private agencies. About half the population of England and Wales could not read, and about three fourths could not write.[23] The Elementary Education Act was passed in 1870. Thus it is clear that the haughty colonial administrators from Britain tried inexperienced methods on the vast subcontinent in their utilitarian zeal. Sir Thomas Munro claimed in 1822 that the state of education in India, though low compared with England, was higher than in most European countries.[24] The primary sources of the nineteenth century Britain like Charles Dickens's novels, especially *David Copperfield* (1850), Thomas Hughes's *Tom Brown's School Days* (1856) and Matthew Arnold's scornful views on British education reveal that the British system was far from being satisfactory. However, the Victorian complacency made the Anglo-Indian administrators believe that their educational methods were the best in the world. Only the rich 'barbarians' in Matthew Arnold's term had access to expensive public schools, and the middle class started receiving the benefits of cheap grammar schools only in the last quarter of the century after the passing of Elementary Education Act in 1870.

It may also be assumed that most British officers who passed the Indian Civil Service examination did not possess a sound knowledge of their own language and literature. According to a report entitled *The Teaching of English in England*, being the report of the Departmental Committee appointed by the President of the Board of Education "to enquire into the position of English in the Educational system of England," higher education in the nineteenth century was strongly classical, Latin and Greek were the more important subjects, and English was until the middle of the nineteenth century a 'soft option' in British Universities. Latin Grammar dominated until the end of the eighteenth century, and "English Grammar did not become a widely recognized school subject before the nineteenth century." The Report further shows that English language studies were never encouraged in British universities.[25] Several other scholars such as J. A. K. Thomson, Ian A. Gordon and

                    The Influence of English on Marathi

George Campbell speak of the unmethodical teaching of the English language.[26]

But at the same time it is also true that eighteenth-century England greatly desired standardization in their own language. George H. McKnight speaks of the 'great attention' to the study of grammar of English in England in the first half of the nineteenth century.[27] Purism was a dominant trend among the nineteenth century British grammarians. The *zeitgeist* is well reflected in the policies of British educationists coming over to India in the first half of the nineetenth century. Molesworth, George Jervis, E. I. Howard, Major Candy and several others who are responsible for language planning in Maharashtra were great purists as regards the writing of Marathi. Their insistence on standardization and perseverence in persuading the native writers to use 'idiomatic Marathi' are of catalytic significance in the process of stylistic norm formation in the nineteenth-century prose.[28]

3.3.2 THE FOUNDERS

After the initial misgivings among the natives that English education was an enticement leading to their conversion to Christianity (see 3.5), English education established itself and soon caught the people's fancy. Its public base and humanistic motives, combined with the more alluring economic advantages and prestige, attracted such huge numbers that demand for more schools increased everywhere.[29] The Public Instruction Department could not meet the demands, nor could they plan education properly for the vast area. Therefore short-cuts were preferred to long-term policies. The gap between the early Romantic dreamers of ideals and the later careerists who had to execute their predecessors' policies widened. The early founders of the Raj were inspired by the ideal of change which they had received from the imperialistic zeal of Europeans undertaking the total leadership of the orient. The role of English was compared to that of Greek and Latin of the Renaissance.[30] Nearly all the early nineteenth-century Marathi prose writers have recorded their gratitude to the fact that Marathi prose grew solely with the British patronage, and that writing in Marathi gained status only because of British encouragement.[31] By the mid-Victorian era, moral responsibility was further added to the old burden.[32] The later British educationists planned and envisaged full growth of Marathi on the same pattern as English developed on the classicial Greek and Latin, without, of course, granting the same status to Marathi. Macaulay's Minute of 1836 clearly states this anomaly in British policy. Wood's dispatch in 1854 reiterates the same confusion. For the British rulers educating the Indians was inseparable from teaching them the English language.

3.3.3 THE FIRST PHASE : THE CONTROVERSIES

The colonial phenomenon of "the European elite undertaking to manu-
facture a native elite" noticed by Jean-Paul Sartre began in India with a
nativistic undercurrent encouraged by the usurpers themselves.[33] The
Charter of 1813 granted by the British Parliament to the East India
Company specified that "one lakh rupees per year be spent for the dissemination of knowledge to the Natives" for the revival and improvement of literature and encouragement of the learned natives of India and
for the introduction and improvement of a knowledge of sciences." This
was partly the effect of Lord Minto's Minute in 1811 for revival of
letters in India, which did not in effect materialize until 1823.[34] This
policy was adopted to check the missionary influence which was growing
and was dangerous for the East India Company's existence in India (cf.
3.5). The missionaries had always preferred to use the vernaculars as
medium of communication and instruction in all their activities.

A dominant minority of enlightened Hindus like Raja Ram Mohan
Ray, however favoured western knowledge and 'English' learning as they
had seen the dangers of oriental superstition and prejudice that had devas-
tated India. The British administrators who favoured English as a medium of instruction joined hands with the enlightened Hindus. Thus the
problem of whether modernization of India can be effected by English or
vernaculars was got mixed up with the problem of whether European
sciences or Sanskrit and Arabic learning should be the content of instruction.

In the beginning the Vernacularists had the upper hand in policy
making. As the knowledge of Marathi was essential for Civil Servants,
Marathi was taught in several institutions such as Haileybury College
near London, Fort William College, Calcutta and Fort St. George College, Madras. Several British officers wrote good Marathi prose, and the
discipline of written prose was first taught to the native writers by missionaries and British officers.[35] In the controversy regarding the medium
of instruction, the Anglicists were outdone by the Vernacularists who
argued vigorously in favour of Marathi as the sole medium of instruction
in schools.[36] The early British founders of the educational system in
Maharashtra had to fight against both native and British rivals as well as
all kinds of material difficulties. They ordered from England printing
machinery and specially cast Nagari types for the printing of Marathi
books. They carefully planned the numerous series of translations, science books, reference books, reading courses and grammars.They also
encouraged a number of agencies that introduced the new learning in
Marathi. All this diffusion of European knowledge they did without

                          The Influence of English on Marathi

supercession of the vernacular, and revolutionized the popular education. No ruler in the history of Maharashtra, with the exception of the Yadavas in the thirteenth century, had offered so much loving patronage to Marathi as a national language.[37] During the Peshwa period, the Daxina fund, a yearly gift amounting to five to eighteen lakhs of rupees, was being distributed to thousands of Brahmans all over India. This fund was gradually converted into useful expenditure on the printing of Marathi books on a variety of new subjects, translation projects and fellowships to deserving candidates of all castes.

The First Reforms Act of 1832 had its echoes in Indian adminstration too. With the Whigs dominating British Government, their counterparts in India ushered in a number of radical reforms in the educational system, introducing gradually western science and English literature to the newly educated Brahman students, who constituted more than 94 per cent of students in Bombay Presidiency.[38]

The renewal of the East India Company's charter in 1833 and Macaulay's famous Minute of 1836 can be viewed together as the Utilitarian objective of making the best of everything. No Indian "shall by reason only of his religion, place of birth, descent, colour or any of them be disabled from holding any place, office or employment under the Company," states the charter.[39] It in effect meant allowing cheaper recruitment of Indians with a view to keeping down the cost of administration in India and more profits. The natural corollary of this was training English-educated Hindus in large numbers. The Whig wave in Britain after 1830 established more firmly the notion of 'useful learning'.[40] The Romantic debates initiated by the earlier rulers about spreading new cultural values while still preserving the great Oriental heritage vanished. A new policy specifically directed toward establishing the importance of English language and English learning was initiated by Bentinck. According to George Jervis, it "neglected the benefits of 300 years of experience in Europe" where Latin had created barriers between the learned class and the masses, and these barriers were destroyed only when modern European languages came in common use.[41] The Filtration theory, introduced by Macaulay, thus crushed the Romantic idealism of the Elphinstone school and the textual Orientalism of the early founders of the Raj. In the Indian social context, the Filtration theory in effect only helped Brahmans to gain all the benefits of the new learning, including economic gains, prestige and enlightenment[42] (cf. 3.4). According to G. R. Potter, the result of Macaulay's Minute was disastrous :

> "The higher education of the Indian people ceased to be traditional and Oriental and was made merely English, not even European . . . It proved to be an irrevocable decision of tremen-

dous import. The path to success lay through the mechanical repetition of text books written in English and the English language was thus imposed upon the Continent".[43]

In 1844 Governor General Hardinge made English education compulsory for public services and in 1848 Lord Dalhousie introduced several P.W.D. works that required thousands of English educated employees at lower levels of administration.

The first genertion of the Shastris who received their education in both traditional Sanskrit subjects and new English sciences in Bombay and Pune schools started writing literary Marathi prose at the end of the first phase. The early prose writers like S. K. Chhatre, B. G. Jambhekar, H. K. Pathare, Bhau Mahajan, Jagannathshastri Kramvant and Balshastri Ghagave were rightly called "English Shastris" on account of their bicultural English-Sanskrit background (see Chapter 6).

3.3.4 THE SECOND PHASE : ANGLICIZATION

The Bombay Government postponed the implementation of Macaulay's Minute and did not give up the policy of Vernacularism despite warnings from Calcutta.[44] Still under the influence of the Bombay school of Vernacularists, the British officials took genuine interest in spreading vernacular education in distant places. opening primary schools and printing old Marathi classicis like Tukaram's *Abhangs, Navaneet,* and useful books like diictionaries and grammars in Marathi.

Charles Wood's educational dispatch of 1854, founded on the Filtration theory of Macaulay, was intended to put an end to the prolonged controversy regarding the content and medium of instruction. It explicitly stressed that the objective of the educational system should be "to spread western knowledge and science," and to create an English-educated middle class who would be 'interpreters between us and the millions whom we govern.' The dispatch introduced a new system of schools, colleges and the university at the top. The new system emphasized the diffusion of western, and not Indian, knowledge. The University of Bombay was established in 1857. Though Wood's dispatch emphasized the importance of the study of vernaculars, the vernaculars were never encouraged in the new system. On the other hand proficiency in the English language became the precondition of success in education and consequently of future career of young men, who slaved to gain efficiency in English. The mother tongue could be ignored after the primary stage of education (cf. 4.3.2). The British objectives of making the upper class Indians "English in tastes, in opinions, in morals and in intellect" meant in effect that they need not be aware of the cultural tenets of their own country (see 4.2.2 and 4.3.2). This wave of unbal-

                                                                    The Influence of English on Marathi

anced bilingualism and biculturalism in favour of English language and culture resulted in increasing anglicization of Marathi (see Chapters 6 and 7). The nativists as well as balanced thinkers like M. G. Ranade, however, severely reacted to the gross negligence of the vernacular at the hands of these English-educated bilinguals[45] (cf. 4.2.4).

With the second generation of English-educated Hindus the process of anglicization in Marathi prose became noticeable. It is most clearly expressed in the prose written in this phase. Lokahitavadi, Moroba Kanhoba, Dadoba Pandurang, G. N. Madgaonkar, V. J. Kirtane, N. J. Kirtane, Baba Padamanji, R. B. Gunjikar, Vishnubuva Brahmachari, L. M. Halbe, Krishnashastri Chiplunkar and about a hundred other significant prose writers had started writing in different kinds of genres, mostly under the influence of English literary models (see Annexure). Thus the wisdom of the policy-makers became evident when western values were seen steadily modernizing the intellectual life of Maharashtra, without evoking strong reactions (cf. 4.2.3). The ideas of Adam Smith, Burke, Bentham, J. S. Mill, Herbert Spencer and Charles Darwin were spreading among the upper classes, giving birth to a kind of Hindu protestantism. The new sceptical questioning Hindu mind was most forcefully expressed in the rational arguments about the Hindu view of life and the role of the English in India. The spirit of acculturation began to appear first in the prose essay (see Chapter 7).

3.3.5 THE THIRD PHASE : NATIVISTIC REACTIONS

After the 1857 Mutiny the Indian Government lost whatever autonomy it had under the East India Company. The new Government was directly controlled by the frequently changing Liberal and Conservative parties. At no stage until the end of the century any real educational reforms were introduced. The educational system continued to be excessively literary. Industrial, economic or vocational education was ruled out in colonial planning. However, the system of grants-in-aid introduced as a result of Wood's dispatch greatly proliferated the network of private institutions of higher education mainly in urban centres. As high school teachers who taught in English were well paid, the low paying primary schools did not attract the new graduates who mainly belonged to Brahman castes.[46] On the other hand this English-educated bilingual class was concentrated in metropolitan centres and district places. Consequently, the entire literary activity was confined to Bombay and by the end of the century to Pune.

The new education reached only the male population of a few urban communities. The women, the rural masses, and the lower classes had little participation in the literary world. [47] The Hunter Commission appointed in 1882 again favoured the use of English as a medium of instruction in Secondary schools.[48] The Government had already seen the political danger of educating Indians because English education had, by this time, given birth to a number of nativistic movements which began challenging British suzerainty over India.

The English language syllabuses were full of outdated literary works.[49] Most contemporary writers are found quoting only older English writers and the poems selected by F.T. Palgrave for his *The Golden Treasury of Songs and Lyrics,* published in 1864. The British 'official' literary attitudes permeated the Marathi literary taste.[50] Therefore, Sir Richard Temple finds the failure of the educational system of this period "in the undue and disproportionate attention devoted to literature and philosophy."[51] This observation is supported by the excessively literary attitudes to English culture taken by several writers of this phase. They reveal, perhaps, that the English contact had reached the limits of borrowing. Jotirao Phule and Vishnushastri Chiplunkar mark the new phase with their incisive humour and strong nativistic spirit. Tilak and Agarkar, Pandita Ramabai, Kashitai Kanitkar and Tarabai Shinde, Ranade, Telang and Bhandarkar, Kirloskar, Kirtane and Deval, H. N. Apte and Keshavsut are a few names who represent individual styles expressed in distinctly new genres, though under the common influence of English.

3.4 SOCIAL CHANGE

The nineteenth-century acculturation initiated a diffused social movement under the pressure of western culture. The modern sociology of Hindu society distinguishes between Brahmanization and Westernization, but nineteenth-century studies do not propose these two as separate sociological processes.[52] As a result of the Filtration theory, western values permeated the lower class only through the Brahman bilinguals. As a result, westernization and Brahmanization were mixed up.[53] On the other hand, Jotirao Phule's writing and activities seem to initiate an anti-Brahmanical movement similar to the Dravida Munnetra Kalhagam movement. It has also been observed that the British contact left the caste system stronger than it was before the contact.[54] An aggressive Brahmanism was initiated by the prose writing of Vishnushastri Chiplunkar and Tilak.

These trends serve as important guidelines to the study of the growth of a period style. The Brahman dominance has indirectly helped language standardization. Similarly the urban setting of Bombay and Pune provided one-community register to Marathi prose. Speedy elimination of unwanted linguistic features was not hampered at any stage. The other communities accepted the standards as they accepted the new cultural values from the Brahmans.

Connected to the twin process of Brahmanization and Westernization is the processes of Modernization. Since the channels of the new educational system were controlled by Brahmans living in urban centres, the most radical ideas came from the Brahman leaders. With the single exception of Jotirao Phule, nearly all modern values were introduced by Brahman leaders. The new novel, the new drama, the short story, literary criticism and the new poetry, incorporating the modern values, revolutionized the literary tradition. It need not be emphasised here that prose is one of the most distinct characteristics of a modern society.[55]

One of the most important features of modernization that emerged at the end of the century was the rise of the new middle class in urban centres. The urban middle class was largely of Brahman composition. Industrialization, confined only to the city of Bombay, did not make any impact on the literature of the period. On the other hand, the colonial links of Bombay with England gave the city an alien status, a fact which is amply utilized in Marathi fiction of the following period.

In the cities the joint family gradually came to mean an anachronism. Similarly, several Hindu institutions, festivals, rituals and customs ceased to afford aesthetic appreciation under the growing impact of English social values. There is no literary work in the century which attempted to portray the beauty of the crumbling social order; on the other hand, it is difficult to find a writer, barring Godsebhataji, who is not affected by English values. A modern individual is an economically free individual, but the colonial system enforced and maintained by the British in India would not be naturally interested in strengthening the indigenous economic system on modern lines. The lag between the backward economic system on the one hand and the other advanced socio-political and literary-aesthetic systems on the other created serious anomalies in the Indian society[56] (cf 4.1.2.). Few prose writers of Maharashtra in the nineteenth century could overcome this anomaly. All prose genres, therefore, offered, as it were, freedom in the cage (see 4.2.2 and Chapter 8).

The villages and the rural population were the worst hit in the nineteenth century renaissance of scholarly ideas and values. All benefits went exclusively to the urban classes. Modern transport only increased their economic exploitation manifoldly. Old methods of farming, the recurring famines and total depletion of agriculture affected the age-old democratic institutions like the *balutedari* system.[57] No intellectual activity was seen taking place in the village, with the single exception of

Satyashodhak Samaj. The traditional oral culture continued to survive in a stagnated form.

3.5 THE MISSIONARIES AND NEO-HINDUISM

One of the most significant results of the English contact is the rise of neo-Hinduism toward the end of the century. The Hindus accepted the material benefits of the western Christian tradition, but the spiritual values of this tradition were always despised. It is a matter of independent discussion as to why the English rulers, knowing fully well the religio-nationlist temperament of the Brahmans, still allowed and encouraged the orthodox elements in Hinduism. The ethnocentricism of the Brahmans was fully known to the British administrators. For example, Sir Richard Temple records in his book, *Men and Events of My Time in India* (1882)

> "The Mahratta Brahmans . . . some of the very ablest among the eleves of the modern education keep their minds riveted upon national models, and would strenuously repudiate the notion of their inner thoughts being transferred by what they have been learning . . . They will learn much from us, and may even acquire new faculties, for all that, as a race, they will retain their individuality."[58]

The missionaries, who had recognized the strength of Brahmans, were very honest about their motives. So they began their indefatigable assaults on the more vulnerable sides of Hinduism such as the uncritical Hindu habit, coarse idolatry, the Hindu law which sanctioned many barbarisms like the Sati and Thugee, prostitution and infanticide, obscenities, and ignorance among the low castes. Many prose writers of the Second phase, like Baba Padamanji and Lokahitavadi—shared their views, though the missionaries always mistook practical Hindu religion for the theory of Hinduism, and so could not make much progress in their endeavours. The English-educated Brahmans of the later years, however, found that the core of Hinduism was not so debased as practical Hinduism reflected it to be. They soon familarized themselves with the history of Christainity and, with unbridled arguments, refuted the Missionaries' charges on Hindu view of life.[59] The missionaries thus provided a stimulus to the prose writers and indirectly contributed to the growth of prose literature.

The missionaries also circulated radical literature such as Thomas Paine's *Age of Reason* (1795 and 1807) which could not have possibly entered the Universities.[60] They aimed at the masses and adopted the more colloquial style of spoken Marathi, which is at the source of the totally pidginized substyle of missionary prose in Marathi (see Chapter 6). The religious controversies between the missionaries and the English-

The Influence of English on Marathi

educated Brahmans occupy a large area in the prose of the period. It is an area which deserves independent treatment.

Besides this role, the American and Scottish missions also played another, more positive role in strengthening the literary culture of the period. They had pioneered in several branches of learning, they were the first in opening schools for the low classes and for girls. The first printed Marathi books for example are from Serampore mission.[61] The missionaries themselves wrote textbooks on the sciences, history and grammar, printed philosophical and ethical treatises, compiled dictionaries, and thus provided a rational base to Marathi prose style in its formative period.

The Hindus, who had lost mental stability and spiritual confidence during the first stage of the contact with western civilization, discovered that Hinduism, the most powerful element of their culture, had enough sources of inspiration for the nation as a whole. So they organized themselves, and together with numerous reformist movements, regained their strength. The foundation of Brahmo Samaj in 1845, Prarthana Samaj in 1867 and Arya Samaj in 1875 in Bombay and in various other parts of the country and of the Theosophical Society in America in 1875 marked the upsurge of neo-Hinduism. A rational interpretation of Hinduism followed. Neo-Hinduism prevented the alienation of those westernized Hindus who faced the dilemma of living in a religious society with intellectual commitment to western ideals. This revival had played a significant role in the development of the prose literature of the last phase. This trend encouraged Sanskritism in prose. It encouraged the growth of journalism and various public forums.[62] The new prose writers often employed aggressive rhetoric and satire to criticise the dominant culture. They claimed superiority for their culture, in order to combat the sense of inferiority among the dominated Hindus. The spiritual thought of the West offered nothing new to the Hindus, whose scriptures, they believed, contained multiple values. This created a poisonous complex in the minds of most of the other writers of this phase. Bigotism on the one hand and indirect acknowledgement of inferiority on the other reveal their split personalities. The rhetorical prose they wrote bears the marks of this split. In the prose of some writers like B. G. Tilak, neo-Hinduism was inseparable from nationalism (cf. 4.2.4).

CHAPTER FOUR

LINGUISTIC ACCULTURATION :
A SOCIO-LINGUISTIC APPROACH TO THE INFLUENCE OF
ENGLISH ON MARATHI

4.1 PRELIMINARIES

Contact comparative linguistics presumes reconstruction of the specific
processes active at the deeper level of society during the historical period
of contact. Since language contact neither occurs in a vacuum nor can be
studied in a vacuum, the linguistic acculturation in a particular space
time dimension must necessarily reveal specific phenomena at work.
The specificity is in fact one of the components of period style (see
Chapter 5.2).

The period from the advent of British rule in 1818 to the rise of
nationalism toward the end of the nineteenth century covered in Chapter
3 presents the backdrop to the linguistic situation in Maharashtra. The
new prose has come about by synthesis out of English influence and nativistic tendencies (4.2.4). A period style in prose arose again syntheti-
cally out of the confrontation of the two literary-aesthetic systems (4.2.2
and 4.2.3). The aesthetic component of style is also the result of the
personal evolution of writers themselves. When a literary tradition of a
society possesses literary conventions which are inadequate and insufficient, the tradition requires a stimulus, an impulse indicating some new
path.[1] At the end of the nineteenth century, such a situation existed in
Marathi (cf. Chapter 2). The present Chapter attempts to specify the
socio-linguistic processes that led to standardization of Marathi as a
result of linguistic acculturation. These processes will be documented by
a stylistic analysis of the texts written in different phases of the contact
with English at a later stage. The acculturation situation can be studied

by the use of documentary material, which has a double advantage in stylistic studies.[2] It provides data both for the study of acculturation and for diachronic stylistic study.

4.1.1 THE TYPE OF THE CONTACT

As stated in 3.2.1 the first contact of the West in India made itself felt through the activities of the Christian missionaries and the educational policies of the early British rulers. Both at first emphasized the usefulness of the vernacular as a medium of instruction. The early nineteenth-century westerners were possessed by the idea of renovating the Indian civilization by introducing western ideas of empirical science and rationality, ethical values and literature of ideas. Acculturation, therefore, began mainly with textual contacts. The European policy makers were on the whole ignorant of the deep structure of the then static Hindu tradition.[3] Even the Indians were generally unaware of their own heritage (see 4.2.4). The policy makers who introduced new learning and channels of reaching it to the Hindus therefore began with a misconstrued notion about them. However, the rapid progress made by the Hindus in various branches of learning and their enthusiasm in the acquisition of new learning surprised the later Europeans.[4] Forcing greater quantum of English language and literature into the educational curricula, however selfish and colonial it may seem on the part of the rulers, only increased the passion of the Hindus for acquiring more materialistic benefits from the western learning. It is difficult to say, on the basis of contemporary primary and secondary sources, whether the Hindus forced the British rulers to give them more of western knowledge or the alien Government imposed to acquire western standards on the dominated people.

Another important characteristic of the contact is the comparatively smooth conduct of the acculturation processes. It evoked little conflict, as mature responses from both sides developed a unanimous consensus as regards the need for the Hindus to change and modernize. Several factors including the growing impact of the Aryan myth of common racial origin of English and Indian peoples contributed fundamentally to the respect for each other's culture. Enlightened self-interest and political wisdom prevented the rulers from creating a situation of violence. Mountstuart Elphinstone wrote in one of his letters :

> "It is for our interest to have an early separation from the civilized people, rather than a violent rupture with a barbarous nation, in which it is probable that all our settlers and even our commerce would perish, along with all the institutions we had introduced into the country."[5]

                    The Influence of English on Marathi

This feeling was warmly reciprocated by the natives themselves who encouraged the ventures of moral education and spread of knowledge undertaken by the British rulers.[6] The Aryan myth of common origin, orientalism of the Sanskritists and British liberalism on the one hand and rational introspective Hindu intellectuals on the other are largely responsible for the non-violent conduct of the contact. Indian acculturation of the nineteenth century is thus a unique phenomenon in world history. It defies all the models of colonization in the Americas, Africa and East Asia. There is no evidence to suggest that Indians suffered from the complex of racial inferiority or from what Frantz Fanon calls, "the complex of not being white".[7] .

Another reason for the smooth conduct of the contact is in the fact that the two cultures maintained separate geographical identities. The English never intended to make India their home. For them England was the *vilayat*, a wistful Anglo-Indian term meaning 'home'. India remained in their view a farmyard, need of the growing industrialization at home. Within the colonial framework their attitude toward the impoverished peoples of India was charitable. Indians on the other hand lauded the various reforms introduced by the British and recognized the political superiority of the ruling race. In the controversy regarding the medium of instruction, there were Indians who favoured English, as there were the British who sincerely fought for Marathi (see 3.3.3). In the first half of the nineteenth century, the British had done so much for Marathi that no later writer including Tilak could ignore their good intentions. The British encouraged the writers to write in Marathi, printed the old classics like Tukaram's *Abhangs* and *Navaneet* for the benefit of the natives, and even wrote the first history of the Marathas. Some of them openly spread the concept of Aryan brotherhood. They introduced the system of public education and threw open the gates to jealously guarded Brahman learning. Many British officials did not think of just building career and devoted their energies to compiling Marathi dictionaries, making translations, writing useful books out of sheer love of the native culture.[8]

The Anglo-Indians of the period also exhibit a peculair reaction toward India, which can be summed up as a love-hate relationship. The Anglo-Indian writers up to Rudyard Kipling reflect this particular pattern.[9] The more appropriate description of British Indian through British eyes is however supplied by an Indian Babu, namely, that India is the "Continent of Circe".[10] A Similar love-hate relationship with England is exhibited by a host of Indian writers. Again, on both sides the vision of a union between Hindu and European thought was unconsciously nurtured. When both the sides recognized the superiority of each other's conflict. It is worth noting in this context that Britain, despite a century-and-a-half-old contact with India has been little affected by Indian values. The Britishers confined their fabulous gains to material level alone.[11] The contact is thus unilateral economically as well as culturally, though bilateral politically.

Thus the contact of English with Marathi has been of long duration, continuous and increasing till the last decade of the nineteenth century. English as a language of the dominant group gained unusual prestige in the linguistically divided country. The educational policies created a class of urban elite bilinguals through whose consciousness the new culture values penetrated into the Indian psyche. The historical role played by English in India has been a subject of heated controversies, though all linguists agree that English alone was responsible for rejuvenating the national life during the renaissance in nineteenth century.[12]

Linguists and anthropologists have attempted to classify the types of linguistic contact on the basis of the nature of culture contact in which they take place.[13] As mentioned earlier the type of contact would always vary according to the varieties of cultures confronting each other. The contact of English with Marathi is sudden, stable and continuous. It is *literary* rather than *social*, as it affects the upper stratum of society only. It is of textual or written type rather than live and oral. Being political and colonial in nature, it was forced in the beginning, but later it became voluntary. A number of intellectuals throughout the nineteenth century sincerely believed that it would be permanent.[14] For the entire upper class elite, English was a source of livelihood and prestige. Even with the nationalists, English was a unifying instrument, a symbol of political allegiance. In intellectual activities and in higher education it had no other substitute. Even in literary culture English continued to be a source of inspiration.[15] The entire native tradition of the ancient civilization was made to appear obsolete in view of the permanent need for English in India, so that at the time of Independence it was no longer regarded as a foreign language but one of the 'official' languages of free India. The educational policies of the British after Macaulay were little more than language policies, and their effects were far-reaching. In J. R. Firth's view, "Macualay's Minute, in establishing the use of English in India inaugurated the biggest Imperial language and culture undertaking the world had ever seen."[16] At no stage of the contact Indians exhibited any panic, because they were not afraid of even marginal destruction of their culture. V.S. Naipaul sums up this strange confidence of the Hindus when he says : "India did not wither like Peru and Mexico at the touch of Europe because Hindu India met conquerors half-way and had always been able to absorb them;"[17] and again : "No other country was more fitted to welcome a conqueror; no other conqueror was more welcome than the British."[18]

4.1.2 EFFECTS OF THE CONTACT ON LINGUISTIC SITUATION

The direct and indirect effects of the colonial situation on the linguistic situation of India are of crucial importance. It is difficult to agree with Einar Haugen when he states that "linguistic and social acculturation do go hand in hand."[19] The situation with free immigrants in America he has studied naturally differs from the colonial type of acculturation where a large gap between the two is evident. In many respects the other social counterparts of linguistic borrowings do not exist; as for example, several registers found in fiction, literary criticism, economic and political treatises written during the nineteenth century do not have any social counterparts in India. Therefore no scientific vocabulary could develop in Marathi despite repeated cries against English terms from the Purists.[20]

Still the dynamics of acculturation are always creative;[21] The subsystems of written Marathi existent prior to the contact of English exhibit an inclusive structure on account of the country-wide spread of Marathi speakers from Punjab to Tanjore. Owing to the peculiar geographical position of Marathi on the language map of India, its original *Deshi* structure had been heavily expanded with borrowings from several languages of pre-Dravidian, Dravidian and Indo-Aryan groups of languages and, in the recorded history from the Persian language. The *Deshi* Marathi had been, in fact, a constantly borrowing language. The theory that *Deshi* Marathi is a case of complete acculturation brought about by the Aryan invasion also supports the same hypothesis.[22]

In the kind of situation described in Chapter 3, when the English language was imposed on the Marathi language the system of Marathi became suddenly active in order to absorb the change. The rich verse tradition had been stunted and no major poet wrote in verse after the great Shahirs. The superiority of the English language was accepted not only as a language of the dominant group but also as a rich language. The richness of English was particularly felt in the variety and flexibility of its prose. The natural medium of the spread of new values was prose, especially printed prose. The confrontations implicit in language contact were thus most frontally expressed in the new prose that began its crude course in the first printed books written by Vaijanath Sharma with the assistance of William Carey at Serampore in Bengal.[23] This prose was not known to the first prose writers in Bombay. The new cylce of prose writing, therefore, truly began in Bombay, the Gateway of India (see 3.4).

4.2.1 THE AREAS OF CONFRONTATION

In a contact situation of the type described earlier, no linguistic unity is likely to take place; on the other hand various psychological and sociological processes receive unusual momentum. A. L. Kroeber states that in the process of acculturation, "linguistic phenomena and processes are on the whole less conscious than cultural ones, without however differing in principle." [24] Nothing inside the linguistic system is *sui generis* and the cultural phenomena and processes have to be related to the linguistic phenomena. Since the present study aims at stylistic influences, the areas of confrontation between two cultures are confined to only those systems which are directly related to style. Several other possible extra-linguistic factors which may remotely influence style are beyond the available methodology of comparison.

Ju. M. Lotman, B. A. Uspenskij, V. V. Ivanov, V. N. Toporov and A. M. Pjatigorskij (1975), who define culture as "a sphere of organization in human society", contend that the mechanism of culture is a "system which transforms the outer sphere into the inner one." [25] Both the cultures that confront introduce a number of alien features to each other's systems. Confrontation, in a sense, increases 'the outer sphere' in a sudden type of contact and disturbs the systems of the receiving culture to a great extent. In terms of the present problem, the dominated Indian culture was under great pressure from the dominant culture. The stylistic systems of English forced the Marathi system into new organization. This transformation of the outer sphere into the inner one is precisely the area of confrontation relevant to our study (see 5.2).

Similarly, sociological facts which affect purely linguistic laws in language dynamics are important to us in as much as they serve the users of the receiving language to cope with the increasing complexity of the other conceptual world. Different selective mechanisms work at different levels simultaneously, obscuring the identity of meaning, and creating insoluble stylistic problems. A semiological approach becomes necessary at this stage of stylistic analysis (see 5.4). This fact is stated by Roman Jakobson, who distinguishes between literary-aesthetic features and semi-ological features of style : "Many poetic features belong not only to the science of language but to the whole theory of signs, that is, to general semiotics." [26]

After the exclusion of such features, the areas relating to style are statable in three established systems, namely, literary-aesthetic, linguistic· and cultural-historical.

A detailed apparatus for a closer study of confrontation of two languages in the context of translation is supplied by Efim Etkind (1967), who establishes the following areas of confrontation :

1. The confrontation of linguistic systems of the two languages,

2. The confrontation of stylistic systems of the two languages,

 The Influence of English on Marathi

3. The confrontation of traditional literary styles in the two languages,

4. The confrontation of systems of prosody in their specifically national aspects,

5. The confrontation of cultural and historical traditions of two cultures to the extent that they are expressed in the literary tradition,

6. The confrontation of two separate aesthetic systems, that of the original and that of the receiving language.[27]

Etkind's model is obviously taxonomical and its modification for the purpose of stylistic influence is essential. No. 1 is of prime importance for the study of stylistic influence. However, for this study it cannot be taken as a starting point (see 4.3.5). No. 5 helps in studying contexts of style though it leads to comparative stylistics as a branch of comparative poetics. No. 2 and No. 4 presume an already well-defined picture (or rather pictures) of both the languages in contact, which is not yet at hand. It is true that some elements of style can be active so as to influence the structure of language itself, but if the receiving language had a dormant tradition of style, it will not be so active as to affect the structure of language at the stage of formation itself. No. 3 and No. 6 lead to independent branches of study.

In view of the particular type of contact discussed in 4.1 discussion on the areas of confrontation between English and Marathi will be restricted to the following phenomena :

1. Shift in literary-aesthetic norms : unreality : individualism (4.2.2)

2. Shift in the components of rhetoric : rationality (4.2.3)

3. Revival of linguistic nativism : formation of national prose (4.2.4)

4. Replacement of *supraglossia* (4.2.5)

5. The mechanism of linguistic influence leading to the formation of stylistic norms ; bilingualism (4.3.2) : borrowing (4.3.3) : interference in linguistic systems (4.3.4) : change (4.3.5)

6. Language standardization (4.4)

The formation of period style as a result of these phenomena will be discussed in Chapter 5.

4.2.2 SHIFT IN LITERARY-AESTHETIC NORMS : UNREALITY, INDIVIDUALISM

One of the characteristic effects of confrontation between English and Marathi was alienation of the native aesthetic tradition. The entire tradition of arts in India (including the seven fine arts of European aesthetic conception) shrank under the impact of the new norms. As the social structure was undergoing radical change under western influence, the arts were not only disregarded but also ridiculed by the new generation. This is the result of cultural alienation caused by political domination. Gerald D. Berreman states : "In acculturation situation characterized by directed culture change, where one group is dominant to the detriment of the way of life of the other group, members of the subordinated group characteristically come to value positively many of the norms of the dominant group."[28]

What preserves the arts is the continuity of their systems. The British and western aesthetic norms, conventions in performance and appreciation of art alienated the modern Hindus from their own traditions to the effect of annihilating most of the arts. This observation is made by V. S. Naipaul in the context of Indian sculpture and painting when he states, "The British pillaged the country thoroughly. . . The country had been pillaged before. But continuity had been maintained. With the British, continuity was broken. And the British are responsbile for this Indian artistic failure, which is part of the *general* Indian bewilderment."[29] The general Indian bewilderment is basically the result of interference in traditional systems under pressure of foreign systems. A culture is an organisation of systems. Systems are sets of syntagms and paradigms. Under the pressure of the foreign systems, first the paradigms begin to disintegrate, one by one; then the syntagms are affected. For example, the combed hair replacing the turban in the garment style, gradually bring in the ever-changing trousers. This seriously affects the linguistic associations of culture objects, and gradually disorganizes the syntagmatic relationship.[30] The system then becomes 'ridiculous'. Selection of stylistic features is controlled by the new norms. The writer's filial relation to culture in intercepted by foreign norms (see 5.2).

This discussion is not aimed at reducing the importance of borrowing in acculturation. It is intended rather to point out how English aesthetic norms, which were not even European, destroyed the aesthetic systems in India evolved by large ethnic groups over centuries. It would also support our hypothesis that incoherence in the inter-relationships of literary and aesthetic systems has created serious stylistic problems, which were solved only by linguistic nativism in the Third phase of the influence (see 4.2.4 and Chapter 8).

As discussed earlier in 4.1.1, the early rapport between India and Britain was textual. As the contact matured by the mid-nineteenth century, geo-political awareness gradually introduced such concepts as 'Orientalism', 'Hinduism', 'the East' and 'the West'. This conceptualization distributed itself into aesthetic literary, linguistic, sociological, historical,

                                    The Influence of English on Marathi

and finally by the end of the century, economic and political conscious-nesss of the Hindus. In a textual contact classical values of the culture reflected in its literature dominate. As the more practical side of the contact developed, the clash of eastern and western classical values be-came louder.[31] The Mutiny cured the British of their Oriental taste. The Marathi writers, however, continued to view British Empire as a benevo-lent power, because their contact with England remained textual throughout the century. Nearly all the travelogues written by Mahar-ashtrians visiting England smack of classical values attached to English culture. Literary movements in English literature were taught in Indian Universities without any historical or sociological considerations.[32] Mil-ton was as popular as Cowper or Shelley with the university students, and Dr. Johnson was for them as great a prose writer as Macaulay.[33] Absense of various prose genres in Marathi created a vacuum in the literary culture of the new elite. Moreover, they found that literature participated more directly in western culture than any other aesthetic system. The relevance of the prose writer in the contemporary English culture im-posed notions of the writer as a hero on the new prose writers in Mara-thi.[34] Tho oral culture that had flourished in Marathi arts represented reality in purely mythological archetypes such as Savitri, Seeta, Draupadi, Rukmini, Rama and Krishna.This oral tradition as a medium of communication had outlived its usefulness. It could not meet the demands of the progressive development of civilization.

Writing was by no means new to Indians, but long periods of hostile and often fanatical rulers and the fear of displeasure from the orthodox never encouraged written culture in Maharashtra[35]. With the advent of printing, the new responsibility of the writer as an intellectual addressing the masses made obsolete the primitive role of the writer as an oral composer. Graphic rather than phonetic styles became predominant[36]. The oral forms like the *tamasha* and *Kirtan* had been polarized on the basis of whether they were religious or not. Old prose was not even known to the writers. Music and drama had been traditionally confined to professional artists whose status was occasionally recognized by courtly performances. Many old art forms like sculptures were either obsolete or, like music, fossilized[37]. The Shastris, who were the custodi-ans of learning, did not seem to have read great prose literature in San-skrit and Prakrit languages, such as the prose passages in the *Ma-habharata,* the *Arthashastra* of Kautilya, the `*Kama-sutra* of Vatsya-yana, the *Mahabhashya* of Patanjali, Brahmanas, the *Jatakas*, the Bud-dhist and Jain scriptures, and the *Puranas*. Their favourite models were those that belonged to the decadent Sanskrit tradition of Dandin, Kali-dasa, Bhavabhuti, Bana and Subandhu[38].

The literary culture in the nineteenth century was clearly divided into the English-educated urban elite and the traditional masses. Akhileshwar Jha points out the dichotomy created by western education, something that had never existed in Indian society before the advent of British rule[39]. Under the Influence of English, literary art was identified with social communication of a written type and the entire aesthetic system was modified by means of adaptations at a very high rate. A large proportion of European and English aesthetic forms were borrowed and adapted along with their original contexts in Marathi prose literature. For example, a Pune writer, in his preface, compared conceited readers to Princes gathered at Penelope's court in Ithaca[40]. Another Hindu writer, lamenting the death of his beloved daughter, writes, "Particularly when it is to be considered, that in my peculiar position as a Hindu, I cannot even erect a homely tomb over her lamented ashes as a poor symbol of my mournful affection".[41]

Thus comparative standards contributory to the western norms developed on purely literary lines. Literary criticism, like other forms borrowed from English, developed purely Marathi-Anglican canons of comparative literature. The old Indian poetics gradually became a part of academic Sanskrit studies, and ceased to provide applicability to new literature, though Sanskrit poetics had elaborate classification of prose genres.[42] This tragedy is well summed up by C.D Narasimhaiah : "Our values, it appears, have not been shaped by our tradition, much less in relation to our immediate context."[43]

It should be noted that literary conventions are the medium of a whole generation of writers, a body of the literary tradition of sociey. They are the links between the earlier and the later generations, and also between the writer and his generation. According to Claudio Guillen, they constitute " the systems resulting from earlier, singular, genetic influences."[44] The new conventions borrowed from English literature soon alienated the writers of the nineteeth century from their own aestheic tradition. Reading Shakespeare or Johnson became necessary to write a Shakespearean tragedy or a rhetorical essay in Marathi, but the conventions now demanded that reading Sanskrit or old Marathi or contemporary literaure in other Indian languages was not at all necessary in order to write literary prose. Citing Indian archetypes became a mark of anachronism, citing English aesthetic norms a sign of modernity. The poetic tradition disappeared at the hands of mediocre versifiers. The English literary influences are so deep that they even defy the existing methods of recognising parallalisms in comparative literature. To establish a taxonomy of the relationship between influences and textual similarities would be a fertile area for comparative literary research. The new

                                     The Influence of English on Marathi

prose genres borrowed from English literary tradition, such as the novel, the short story, tragedy, comedy, essay, *humour* and several other varieties of these forms have introduced new aesthetic norms. Glorification of 'white' complexion and depreciation of brown or black complexion, Romantic or premarital love, exotic plots and characters, the unities, the 'love triangle', themes such as adultery, 'virtue rewarded ' and 'vice rebuked', the fall of a tragic hero as a result of his own acts — these are some of the new effects of the shift in literary-aesthetic norms. The ingenious writers created an autonomous literary world of unreality wherin they could conceptualize the freedom they could not realise in society. How this happened would be a fertile area for cultural anthropolpgists to investigate into.

One of the most obvious effects of this confrontation is the rise of individualism first expressed in the Marathi essay and then in other prose genres. The individual in contrast with authority is a western concept wherein individuality is expanded to the full.[45] Hindu aesthetics did not recognise this relationship except in the dormant form, seen in the numerous episodes in the *Mahabharata* and *Ramayana* and in the *Katha-saritsagara.* The new prose, infused by western aesthetics began with social novels and plays portraying rebellious individuals who defied traditional morality. Writers began to employ sociolects and idiolects. The associative effects of these new concepts on literary style were farreaching, especially in the formative stage of the national prose. The imitation of English models and English canons of taste and values brought with them the particular stylistic features. For example, the lyric bombast of Shakespearean soliloquy, in the early historical plays by V. J. Kirtane and Shirwalkar, the Johnsonian complex sentences in Vishnushastri Chiplunkar, Spencer's long-winded clausal pattern in Agarkar, the moralizing paragraphs in *Aesop's Fables* or Berquin's *Children's Friend* in the translations of Hari Keshavji and S.K. Chhatre and several obvious similarities are directly attributable to linguistic influence as a part of aesthetic-literary influence. However, it is important to note that though literature constitutes a number of other systems, the higher rate of influences naturally takes place only in those systems which requires stimulus.[46] In the formative period the influence of English was confined to the linguistic systems, because it was in this area that the need for influence was most felt. Other systems became more active only in the later periods. For example, the middle class morality of English literary tradition as a literary-aesthetic context began to appear in the late nineteenth and early twentieth century in the novels of H. N. Apte, while the themes of individualism were found in the novels of the second quarter of the twentieth century.

4.2.3 SHIFT IN THE COMPONENTS OF RHETORIC : RATIONALITY

All men are rational ; but in some societies, it is the cultural sensibility that obstructs individual's choice to be rational.[47] For want of evidence it is difficult to explain why the Hindu tradition of mathematics, astronomy, medicine and critical discourse was not transmitted from Sanskrit and Prakrit languages to the new Indo-Aryan languages. In any case the non-rational character of Indian literary (and cultural) tradition had become conspicuous by the time of Al-Beruni's historical account of Hindu learning at the beginning of the current millennium.[48] The Marathi tradition of rhetoric is also characterized by a cultural sensibility of low rational component.

Rhetoric as a means of persuasive discource is intimately connected with rationality. However, in European poetics the term also means ornamental writing, an oratorical extravagance.[49] The latter concept of rhetoric is almost contrary to the former. This dichotomy in the concept had developed owing to the historical evolution of prose rhetoric in English from Ciceronian extravagance through Senecan, Baroque and other anti-Ciceronian movements on the one hand, and the rational-empirical-scientific revolution in the late seventeenth century on the other. Modern English prose style as a close, precise and clear instrument of expression is largely the outcome of an organized movement against European Ciceronian tradition of extravagance.[50] This tradition had entered English literature when it was the protege of Europe in the sixteenth century. In T. S. Eliot's phrase, 'attempts to write English with Latin syntax ' have been a regular strain in English prose even after the scientific-rational revolution.[51] R. F. Jones shows how the scientific movements and the various rationalist schools in the latter half of seventeeth century has successfully retarded the oratorical direction of English Prose.[52] Bishop Sprat's principle of "so many things almost in equal number of words," vehemently put forward in 1667 was, in spirit, a nativistic attempt to end ' the battle of the books', the raging controversy of ancient and modern learning. Deductive reasoning and experimental philosophy were the guiding principles of the revolution in prose. By the early nineteeth century these elements of rationality had been firmly established as a base of all prose genres in English, despite reactions from the school of Johnson, the eighteeth-century revivalists and the Romantic essayists of the early nineteenth century. The English conviction that intellectual element is essential to art and particularly to prose genres had greatly encouraged enforcement of rationality in English prose.[53] Otto Jespersen's observation that ' the English language is a methodical, energetic, business-like and sober language that does not care for much finery and elegance, but does care for logical consistency" is only a recognition of the strong native tradition of rationality in English rhetoric.[54]

When such a well-developed prose came in confrontation with Marathi the two strains in English tradition became amply evident. The British policy-makers asserted the rational element in English prose, while the Shastris who learnt English were more attracted to the rhetoric of ornamentation which was closer to the Sanskrit tradition of verbal superfluity (see Chapter 8).

The other strain of rationality found very large patronage among the educated young men who found no incentive in learning the traditional subjects by memorizing and recitation. Therefore they had little or no background of Sanskrit. Since this class of prose writers rapidly grew in size (see 3.3.2 and 3.3.4) and since they had many opportunities to use the newly-acquired instrument of plain persuasive prose style, rationality became the dominant principle in new Marathi prose (see Chapter 7). It gradually became the base of the new prose. The changing social needs too demanded it. With the new base of rationality provided by the contact of English prose, Marathi writers were suddenly in possession of a powerful instrument. The formation of any prose sentences requires a rational base.[55] The larger units of sentences are also elements of a certain rational system and as the sudden dislocation of political and social structure of the ancient civilization demanded reconstruction, the prose writers could also use the prose of rationality for creative action. Since the oral verse tradition was inadequate to express the new needs, the only alternative was the new intellectual prose for this action. The linguistic system of Marathi was thus put to express new needs for which they were not yet ready as finished instruments or expressions. The absence of good scientific and technical terms, too loose a word order, and the non-standardized syntax were suddenly made to express the rational component of rhetoric. This sudden pressure of rationality on Marathi linguistic systems created a totally strange pidgin in the First phase (see 4.5 and Chapter 6).

Rationality is perhaps the most significant component of English learning that the British wanted to induct in the Hindu mind. They had diagnosed the non-intellectual element in Indian tradition as ' the intuitive and unreasonable habits of thinking.' The Hindu learning current in the period was, accordingly to them, 'absurd theories'.[56] C. E. Trevelyan, for example, remarks that "Hinduism is not a religion which will bear examination. It is so entirely destitute of any kind like evidence, and is identified with so many gross immoralities and physical absurdities, that it gives way at once before the light of European science."[57]

Several contemporary British observers have recorded as to how, under the influence of the English language, the minds of native youths were "metamorphosed into the texture and cast of European youth, and they could not help expressing utter contempt for Hindoo superstition and prejudices".[58]

In literary activity this metamorphosis was most evident. L. S. S. O'Mally observes that "knowledge of English language and the study of English literature have done more to spread western culture than personal contact with Europeans in general and the British in particular."[59] As discussed in Chapter 3 the educational policies increasingly overemphasized the literary content of syllabuses. With the expansion of western institutions and channels like schools and associations, periodicals and printing presses there was an unprecedented demand for the new prose genres of skeptical and critical spirit, of controversy and logical argument. In literary-aesthetic terms it meant novels, plays and essays. This precisely explains why new poetry appeared much later, in the last phase of the influence of English (see 8.1). The new activity also led to critical awareness of what is *written*, thus encouraging individual responses to literature. The reader-writer relationship that did not exist in Marathi before, also induced, in the Second phase, the glimmering of literary criticism, a rational response to literature. On the whole, the rational component of rhetoric dominated the prose literature of the century. The intellectual link between the writer and his society came to surpass the purely lyrical-emotional links that dominated in the tradition of Marathi literature before the contact of English.

A kind of Renaissance was on its way. C. E. Trevelyan in 1838 wrote : "Every scholar knows to what a great extent the Romans cultivated Grecian literature, and adopted Grecian models of taste . . . It is a *curious fact* that an intellectual revolution similar to that which is now in progress in India, actually took place among the Romans."[60]

4.2.4 REVIVAL : NATIVISM : FORMATION OF NATIONAL PROSE

Thus the Indian aesthetic tradition was to sponge on English models and large India would be to little England what Italy had been to Greece. The geographical factors and the magnitude of ethnic variety were hardly taken into consideration. The effects of this trend were far-reaching, especially in respect of the treatment of social content in modern Indian literatures. For example, G. S. Amur observes that "the pattern of political and social change in India, as we know, has had close similarities with that of the rest of the Third World and the problems have also been very much the same, but while the representative African writer is generally a committed writer, the representative Indian writer is essentially an uncommitted writer."[61]

                                    The Influence of English on Marathi

Confrontation with alien systems giving rise to nativistic consciousness is not a new feature in Indian hisitory. Such confrontations had led to linguistic nationalism on the one hand and linguistic influence on the other. Linguistic nativistic movements had taken place in Maharashtra in the thirteenth century against Sanskrit bilingualism and again in the seventeenth century against Persian bilingualism—both being literate types of bilingualism. Confrontation with English in the nineteenth century revived nativistic consciousness again with greater force, because the influence phenomenon was also of greater magnitude. The anthropology of several peoples in the Americas and Great Britain including Ireland shows how, when the language of the dominant culture group is not confronted in time, the native culture is totally annihilated.[62] Linguistic nativism is an instrument by which resistance is built up against growing bilingualism which may lead to disappearance of the native language. Knowledge of a second language often outgrows its function and leads, in extreme cases, to the elimination of the first language. In a contact situation where fundamental cultural values of the dominated group are threatened, linguistic nativistic movements play a multiple role by associating themselves with several emotional issues like religion, nationality and literary-aesthetic traditions of the dominated group. Ralph Linton defines a nativistic movement as follows :

> "Any conscious, organized attempt on the part of a society's members to revive or perpetuate selected aspects of its culture . . . Conscious, organized efforts to perpetuate a culture can arise only when a society becomes conscious that there are cultures other than its own and that the existence of its own culture is threatened."

So, culture-consciousness precedes linguistic consciousness. But the process of language change being unconscious, it all the more becomes a sensitive issue for the languge group whose culture is under the pressure of a dominant group. The unconscious nature of linguistic change associated with the process of linguistic nativism is a more difficult problem to study as compared with purely sociological processes of nativism. However, Edward Sapir, while admitting the unconscious nature of the process of change states : "linguistic changes do not proceed at the same rate as most cultural changes, which are on the whole far more rapid. Short of yielding to another language which takes its place, linguistic organization, largely because it is unconscious, tends to maintain itself indefinitely and does not allow its fundamental categories to be seriously influenced by changing cultural needs.[64]

As discussed before in 1.1.1, 3.2.3 and 3.5, a nativistic consciousness in various forms was taking roots among the Hindus, and when the culture contact matured this consciousness developed a loud clash of cultural values. The feeling that East and West are irreconcilable identities expressed by Rudyard Kipling, or the acclamation by Neo-Hinduists that the East is spiritual while the West is material indicates the cultural fact of nativistic identity. On the linguistic plane, this identity was expressed most forcefully in the prose literature of the period. The movement manifested itself wholly in prose, and can be viewed as having two intertwined objectives : 1. use of prose as a substitute or complement of action; and 2. formal restoration of Sanskrit features with Puristic motivation. Both the strands, at different levels, helped to form a national prose.

As discussed in 4.2.3, under the influence of English the Marathi prose writers borrowed the rational base of prose writing along with its functions. Language was identified with the whole community, a single communication system. Earlier, caste compartmentalization had not only created distinct communicative spheres but also maintained casteist literary taste.[66] Literary culture based on western pinciples, namely, strong reciprocal relationship of three types between the artist and the critic, the critic and the public, and the artist and the public took roots in the literary milieu.[65] It stimulated indigenous efforts to start printing presses, periodicals, public forums and other channels necessary for the rapid dissemination of rational ideas in written prose under increasing textual contact of English. It also encouraged the rise of professional writing. The prose writers were also leaders of important nativistic movements of non-literary and semi-literary types (see 3.2.3). B. G. Jambhekar and Bhau Mahajan were editors, among other periodicals, of *Darpan*, the first periodical in Marathi which was bilingual. Lokahitavadi started a campaign against caste system. Dadoba Pandurang, honoured as the Panini of Marathi, was one of the founders of Paramahansa Sabha, a reformist secular forum. Vishnushastri Pandit, editor and translator, fought for widow remarriage. Moroba Kanhoba married a widow and as a result met unnatural death. Jotirao Phule was the founder of the first mass movement in Maharashtra. Krishnashastri Chiplunkar, editor and translator, led the anti-missionary movement. Vishnushastri Chiplunkar, the pioneer of the new brahmanical nationalism, was the founder of Chitrashala Press and editor of *Nibandhamala*. B. G. Tilak, editor and scholar, was the father of Indian unrest and leader of the National Congress and of Swadeshi movement. Agarkar was editor, translator and leader of social reforms. Baba Padmanji, novelist and scholar, represented the anti-Hindu thought. V. R. Shinde, M. G. Ranade, G. K. Gokhale. V. K. Rajavade, R. G. Bhandarkar, K. T. Telang, and several other prose writers of the period were also the leaders of important nativistic movements. Indeed, the nineteenth-cen-

                              The Influence of English on Marathi

tury prose is a creation of social reformers, politicians, statesmen, printers and editors, neo-Hinduists and scholars. The prose literature of the period is a faithful record of the distressing fluctuations in the people's response of political subjugation on the one hand and spirit of social reform on the other. Above all, it was the expression of linguistic nativism.

The prose of this period expresses, for the first time in the history of Marathi, the entire psychogram of the people. Thus the concept of the language community as an organic whole was reflected by the prose writers through the voice of linguistic nationalism. The cultural impact was felt from the top downwards.The leaders tried hard to introduce widespread diffusion of new ideas and influenced the thinking, feeling and behaviour of the masses. The movement of prose was aimed at revitalizing of society as a cultural need. Despite the busy life these leaders lived, their creative affiliation to literature and language, both English and Marathi, was intimate. Their reading of English classics was the source of their inspiration, which is the reason for the rational content of their prose.[67] In harmony with the type of culture contact (4.1.1), the linguistic nativistic movements in Maharashtra were rational and never permitted puristic conservatism to increase.

However, the growing bilingualism added to the anglicization of Marathi and gave rise to another agitation aimed against the putative 'annihilation of the vernacular'. Pidginzation of Marathi was vehemently resisted by the Purists, who intensified their resistance as the influence of English increased. The important result of the Puristic movements was the growing Sanskritism in Marathi prose. The role of the Puristic movements has to be recognized in so far as they prevented further development of Pidginization. Analysis of the prose passages written at different phases of the nineteenth century shows that more Sanskrit features have entered into Marathi during this period of English influence than they did before the contact of English. The borrowings from Sanskrit were, however, mostly at the lexical level. English features, on the other hand, were found entering at all the levels (see Chapters 6, 7 and 8). The Purists' insistence on Sanskrit features was more emotional than rational, and their recommendations were mostly confined to linguistic discussion rather than to what was useful. Utility is a guiding principle in most linguistic borrowings, and the Purists could not proceed beyond emotional arguments. However, the role of the Purists in checking the erosion of Marathi that started in the First phase cannot be denied. The analysis of the prose passages written in the First phase of the influence also shows that erosion of the prosodic systems of Marathi had almost pidginized the written Marathi. It is discernible first in the loss of sentence ryhthm (see Chapter 6). With the nativistic movement gaining strength in the Second phase, this erosion is largely checked (see Chapter 7). However, even in the Third phase the original rhythm of Marathi prose had not been restored (see Chapter 8). Since sex balance was in favour of monolingual behaviour and the rural masses had not been touched by English, there was a hope of the losses caused by this erosion being completely restored at some future stage. This can be deduced from the natural rhythm, in the writings of Godse bhataji, Valangkar and others who had no knowledge of English. In any case this factor itself was enough to prevent creolization of Marathi, as the number of English-knowing persons never exceeded beyond two percent of the entire population.

The national language of a country has always been used as an instrument of strengthening patriotism by associating it with emotional issues such as culture or religion or ethnic integrity.[68] It also adopts conspicuous symbols from its own history : these may be myths, heroes, great writers or archaisms. The prose writers of the period therefore turned to Sanskrit and borrowed extensively from Sanskrit in order to be able to check the encroachment of English features. Puristic movements began their attacks on the pidgin Marathi prose. The contemporary journals regularly exposed the hybridization of culture via anglicized features.[69] Their concern was mainly with particular elements of English, never with the language as a whole. Stable bilingualism which was giving rise to a new *supraglossia,* namely, English, did not permit this movement to grow.

4.2.5 SUPRAGLOSSIA[70]

One of the modes of operation of language is cultural-written-literary as against social-oral-conversational, and one of the spheres of its utilization is communication among persons and groups possessing different languages.[71] The socio-linguistic situation in India is such that it required, at every stage of its long history, a kind of written creole, evolved from pidginized old Indo-Aryan speech, an Indian *Sabir* that could cut across language boundaries. We may also note in this context an important observation made by John J. Gumperz that "from a linguistic point of view the local dialects form a continuous chain from Sind to Assam, the speech of each area shading off into that of the adjoining one."[72]

Historical facts reveal that mutual intelligibility was never a problem for Indians in everyday life as well as in country-wide intellectual movements. Sanskrit as a written creole was a great vehicle of culture and it performed the role of this superior medium of communication above all the spoken dialects and languages, whether Aryan, Dravidian or Tibeto-

Burman. Sanskrit seems to have been the historical and geographical need of the subcontinent from the time of the period of Aryanization. The *shrutis* and *smiritis*, the *itihasas* including the great epics, the *dharmashastras* and the great commentaries, drama and poetry, prose literature containing belletrist forms and sciences—in short, a variety of intellectual and creative modes of expression is available in Sanskrit which had a countrywide patronage from Kashmir to Kerala. Thus it can be deduced that the multilingual unicultural Indian society must always recognize one national creole, a *supraglossia* for inter-societal and inter-language communication in addition to the hundreds of spoken dialects and diglossias. A cultural-written-literary creole has been the need of the country through changing ages. As discussed earlier in 1.4, this kind of creole has also been a geopolitical need of the subcontinent from ancient times. The cultural homogeneity of the Indian peoples was amply strengthened by Sanskrit, though it was replaced by Prakrit creoles between 300 B.C. and A.D. 100 and partially by Arabic and Persian after the thirteenth century. The revivals of Sanskrit after each long break and its survival as a language of learning in the south and at several centres of traditional learning all over the country even during these periods of supercession supports our hypothesis that Sanskrit was existent only as a written creole, a super-language.[73] It is true that Prakrits like Pali, Ardhamagathi, Paishachi and Persian had played equally important roles and that their influence on the New Indo-Aryan language is deep.[74] But these *supraglossia* do not seem to perpetuate the deeply rooted Hindu literary-aesthetic traditions. Nor were they revived after once becoming obsolete. On the other hand, Sanskrit seems to have developed a system of consolidating the processes of creolization, so that no change of epoch would affect its organic supraglossial structure. With the fantastic range of varieties of its written styles, scientific and technical registers, and an equally fantastic range of lexical systems, its flexible word order, Sanskrit gives the impressions of a continental creole. Historians have admitted that it could not have been a spoken language of any group at any stage of its development.[75] Its omnivorous gigantic framework capable of absorbing into its systems almost any feature of Dravidian, Tibeto-Burman, Proto-Austro-Asiatic and other non-Aryan language families also suggests that it was a standardized creole. No structure of a *spoken* language could possibly contain such a variety of semantic differentials in its lexical-syntactic sub-systems. It had maintained a system parallel to and distinct from the spoken as well as written Aryan and non-Aryan languages of the subcontinent.[76] Though the comparative aspect of Sanskrit and other Middle Indo-Aryan and New Indo-Aryan languages has been amply studied by Indologists and Indian linguists, this aspect of the languages has not received adequate attention. It may be hypothesized at this stage that the spoken *dialects* of India including the *apabhransha* dialects contstituted the sub-stratum of the Sanskrit *supraglossia*. Research in this unique phenomenon would be a valuable contribution to world linguistics, since it is an important feature of the ecology of language neglected in the Atlantic linguistics. Language planning in the U.S.S.R. and Isreal in recent years, however, reveals several features contrasting to the Indian phenomenon of change in *supraglossia*, a peculiar result of the colonial situation.[77] (See Chapter 9.)

This brief review of *supraglossia* as the most characteristic phenomenon of the socio-linguistic situation in India was essential at this point, because it is specifically related to the place of English in Modern India as a product of the confrontation between English and all the modern Indian languages. It is difficult to state whether this phenomenon of English replacing Sanskrit as a *supraglossia* is a feature of acculturation or deculturation, since the role of English in many contexts of Indian culture has been, at least, uncertain. For example, R. B. Patankar, citing the language problem of the Indo-Anglian writer, states : "An Indian desirous of writing in *good English* should have English as his mother tongue; however, if he desires to create *good* literature, English becoming his mother tongue would not help. Such is the dilemma."[78] No linguist would approve the use of a foreign language as a medium of expression and of instruction, yet English has been serving that role in India under various titles of 'second language', 'library language', 'international language', 'foreign language', 'official language', 'language of higher education', 'a window on the west' and so forth. The fact, however, is that all the manifold prestige of English lies in its role as a *supraglossia* , the Indian creole.

The exclusively Brahman monopoly of Sanskrit had, at the advent of English, become a disadvantage to the revival of Sanskrit as *supraglossia*. The growing influence of English had been a serious concern of all Marathi writers in the nineteenth century.[79] When English as the language of the dominant group, with the added advantage of being the language of new learning, confronted Marathi and other vernaculars, nativistic consciousness was absent. By the time nativistic movements gained strength, English had already firmly established itself as a clear substitute for Sanskrit. Like Sanskrit, English was the language of the upper caste elite, of knowledge and prestige, of economic advancement and, most important of all, the only medium capable of inter-societal communication. However, English had, unlike Sanskrit, an additional advantage which strengthenend its status as *supraglossia* in that it could be available to all, irrespective of caste, class and region. The non-Brahmans in Maharashtra, paradoxically enough, preferred English to

                    The Influence of English on Marathi

Sanskrit solely on the basis of the so-called democratic nature of English education, although, in reality, it had only served the urban upper classes. As Dilip Chitre observes, "English is a pathetic necessity for most Indians" as Indians are resigned to its use in all social spheres, although this class is "a tiny minority thinly spread over the entire nation, controlling its administration and commercial networks or serving those who control them."[80] Socio-political needs of the different ethnic and language groups in India demand a neutral language which should be above the possession of any of the groups, so that 'equality of disadvantage' is maintained. An Indian *supraglossia*, whether Sanskrit, Prakrit, Arabic, Persian or English, being elitist in its patronage has never recognised the need of a common man.[81] Its features can be stated briefly as 1. specialization, 2. prestige, 3. literary-aesthetic medium, 4. standardization, 5. Elitism and 6. neutrality in respect of all ethnic-linguistic groups.[82] It should be noted that these functions are such as would naturally protect the spoken dialects and various sociolects of the bilinguals which are left uninterfered by the use of a *supraglossia*. In a multilingual situation overlapping of roles is thus avoided. *Supraglossia* also contains rigid norms and allows multiple choices to the bilinguals who use it, because it promotes cultural or written bilingualism which is largely stylistic. John J. Gumperz points out this characteristic of a *supraglossia* and states : "Because of the elaborate linguistic etiquette and stylistic conventions that surround them, classical, liturgical and administrative languages function somewhat like secret languages. Mastery of the conventions may be more important in gaining social success than substantive knowledge of the information dispensed through these languages."[83]

It should be noted that the early founders of English education in India, Indians as well as European Orientalists, never considered the claims of any of the vernaculars as a *potential lingua franca* or an official language for the whole of British India. The earliest controversies regarding the medium of instruction were confined to Sanskrit or Arabic as against English (see 3.3.8). Thus it is clearly evident that English in India was treated as if it were a 'classical' language, a rival to Sanskrit as the language of learning. For example, a letter, dated 1st December 1827, by Jagannath Shankarshet and others representing the native community, addressed to George Jervis, Secretary to the Bombay Native Education Society, provides a concept as to the place of English vis-a-vis the vernaculars. It reads as follows :

> "Your Society will be pleased to bear in mind what the Natives have desired us particularly to express, that, by the study of the English language, they do not contemplate the superces-

sion of the vernacular dialects of this country, in the promotion of native education; but that they regard it merely as a help to the diffusion of European arts and sciences among them ... and as *a branch of classical education* to be esteemed and cultivated in this country *as the classical languages* of Greece and Rome are in the Universities of Europe."[84]

The lack of competing literary traditions in the vernaculars made each of them helpless against the increasing influence of English. The entire nation was made to rally round the new *supraglossia*, which became a permanent necessity for generations to follow. The entire national culture including the holy scriptures had to be 'translated' into English, in order to be known to the educated Indian as the following generations could not absorb both Sanskrit and English systems. English literary-aesthetic system separated the people from their own heritage.The vanishing oral tradition alone remained accesible to the later generations. The upper classes took pride in their foreign (meaning only Western) degrees, and aping the white man became a virtue. The lower classes in turn aped the Brahmans. The effects of this trend on the vernaculars were far-reaching. The homogeneity of literary culture was disturbed. Impoverishment resulting from multilingualism was aggravated by the foreign language (see 4.2.2) and thus Martin Joos's hypothesis as to the origin and modification of pidgins became applicable to the Indian writer's predicament. Joos states : "Hypertrophy of literature (including technical texts) leaves lacunae in personal competences; this tends towards degeneration."[85] Language would, according to this hypothesis, degenerate into pidgin or further become extinct. The degeneration is clearly seen when we apply this hypothesis for verification to the prose written in the First phase (see Chapter 6). English as a new *supraglossia* has given insipid solidarity to the writers' competences, because, unlike Sanskrit, it could not infuse native traditions into their writing. By infusing traditions into idiom, Sanskrit had converted its creolization into mature written styles. The referent of any Sanskrit feature involved a native tradition, but with the establishement of English as *supraglossia*, semantic categories or in Joseph H. Greenberg's term *linguisememes* of the new prose are seen clearly divided into two categories—Indian and western.[86] Pidginized phonological systems further accentuated this distinction into two incompatible sets, especially in technical prose, and affected the syntactic system (see Chapters 6 and 7).

The Puristic movements mentioned in the previous section had recognized this degeneration of the vernacular into a pidgin increasingly in the First and Second phases. The Sanskrit *supraglossia* is, for any vernacular, an extension of its *langue*, a strorage of features, and it can always be

                                    The Influence of English on Marathi

used in *parole*. The Purists therefore borrowed extensively from Sanskrit to replace English borrowings. However, they could not implement their measures consistently. Their measures only accentuated unique features in the vernaculars. Owing to isolated individual efforts, most borrowings from Sanskrit were only at the lexical level. The analysis of prose passages written in the Second and Third phases shows that Sanskrit could successfully fill the semantic holes created by the changing syntax of Marathi under the pressing influence of English. It could also supply the most accurate equivalents for any English jargon (see Chapters 6,7 and 8). The most urgent need of Marathi prose of the period was technical and scientific vocabulary. Sanskrit, having genetic relationship with Latin and Greek, the so-called 'English' technical terms had exact equivalents in Sanskrit. But the pressure of language planning was consistently in favour of English (see 3.3.3, 3.3.4 and 3.3.5), and the permissive bilinguals certainly outnumbered the active nativists. Sanskrit therefore lost its claim of being the language of learning for ever.

The Purists in the Second and Third phases made desperate attempts to restore the erosion caused by the influence of English. Some of them employed social dialectalism as for example in Kunte's *Raja Shivaji* and Jotirao Phule's works; archaic features as in Christian Marathi works and in the works of Kramavant, Mundle, S. A. Lele, Mahadevshastri Kolhatkar and Krishnashastri Chiplunkar; neologisms as in Lokahitvadi, Vishnushastri Chiplunkar; regional dialectal features abundantly used by S. K. Chhatre and Jambhekar—all these experiments led to specialization of prose and gradually eliminated the anglicized variants. However, many dialectal variants were also discarded because they were being used for the first time in Marathi. Major Thomas Candy, the man most responsible for standardizing Marathi prose writing, during the period from 1832 to 1876, has categorically remarked that "if the translators . . . will avoid writing Marathi in English idiom, and will renounce Concanisms and barbarisms, they will find me quite ready to report favourably of their works."[87] However, no contemporary Marathi writer could confront Major Candy successfully. The Purists' arguments were prompted by piecemeal nativistic attitudes rather than by utilitarian and dispassionate study of the phenomenon. Their efforts were rarely confined to regulating the vernacular language as a whole. Actually the remedy was not in regulating the verncular, but in restoring the *supraglossia*. The Purists could not stop the floodgates to bilingualism through which English was bursting in upon the old *supraglossia*. On the other hand they correctly diagnosed the fact that Sanskrit alone could prevent the influence of English.

4.3.1 MECHANISM OF LINGUISTIC INFLUENCE LEADING TO FORMATION OF STYLISTIC NORMS

The different phenomena discussed in the preceding sections have a direct bearing on the formation of new norms of prose style, because in Marathi prose they arose simultaneously with other linguistic processes leading to stylistic norm formation under the influence of English (see Chapter 9). The actual mechanism involved in the formation of a period style has to be constantly related to these phenomena; otherwise there is a danger of our slipping into purely linguistic processes of influence. Linguists have noted the limitations of studies even in this area of linguistic influence (see 1.3.1 and 1.3.2). John J. Gumperz and Robert Wilson, for example, specifically admit that "there has been almost no direct investigation of the actual mechanism involved" as regards how language contact in the past period of history takes place.[88] It is comparatively easy to trace the historical origin of particular items of lexicon, phonology or grammar, but tracing of stylistic features above the level of these items is possible only if we develop a multi-level approach to the problem. On the basis of our investigation, there is evidence to say that stylistic influence differs from purely linguistic influence not only in degree but also in kind. The most important reason is that stylistic influence involves interference of various kinds—cultural, literary-aesthetic, rhetorical, generic and perhaps many more. All these interferences are, however, systematized in the written form of language through purely linguistic processes (see 4.3.5 and Chapter 5). After this systematization which we call *change,* standardization is said to have been accompolished. The operation and interaction of all the phenomena discussed in the preceding chapter, together with socio-linguistic processes that follow, combine to make period style in a phased manner which is evident from the analysis of passages written in the three successive phases of the development of Marathi prose (see Chapters 6, 7 and 8). Prior standardization is the pre-requisite of stylistic norm formation because the mechanism of linguistic influence up to the point of standardization is aesthetically indifferent, neutral or in some cases even unaesthetic. Neither the source language nor the receiving language provides aesthetic norms in the actual process of confrontation and influence (see 4.3.4).

4.3.2 BILINGUALISM

The contact of Marathi with English first occured in small cultural groups in urban centres. There is a general agreement about the fact that bilingualism is the first discernible symptom of confrontation between two languages. The concept of bilingualism has become so broad in recent years that we can safely use the term *literate* or *textual* bilingualism in the context of stylistic influence of one language on the other.[89] The bilingual situation in India with English as one of the two languages is unique and therefore needs to be conceived in totally new dimensions. Uriel Weinreich has, on the basis of census reports, developed a geographical distribution of bilingualism in India.[90] Einar Haugen distinguishes four situations in the period of contact : 1. Bicultural bilingual, 2. Bicultural monolingual, 3. Monocultural bilingual, and 4. Monocultural monolingual.[91] Of these, 1 and 2 did not exist in Maharashtra except in a few communities like Parsis and Anglo-Indians whose mother tongue was not Marathi; the last two are relevant to our study. The dominant minority of monocultural bilinguals constituted the elite of society and most prose writers came from this class. The vast majority of monocultural monolinguals were those who naturally preserved the conservative spirit of tradition. This large class accepted passively the new standard evolved by the bilinguals (cf. 3.4). Jyotirindra Das Gupta and John J. Gumprez have seen the possibility of 'discrete subdomains' of Indian sociolects ' each set off from the others by sharp grammatical and even ... by lexical and phonological features' owing to the barriers of ethnic origin, caste and occupation characterizing Indian society.[92] Such distinct spheres of compartmentalization in the verbal interaction of small groups among the monolinguals did not interfere with the new Anglo-Marathi registers developed by the bilinguals, because they did not confront the speech behaviour of the monolinguals. On the other hand, the bilinguals developed an independent tradition of English learning for themselves. As Ashok R. Kelkar observes, there exists an 'autonomous system' of 'Marathi English' among the 24 million people of Maharashtra because "the teaching [of English] is in the hands of Indians, who in turn have most probably acquired the language in a similar manner." Kelkar further states that in such a situation the 'original' or standard English pronunciation is regarded as 'affected if not incorrect'.[93] These observations by linguists can be applied *mutatis mutandis* to written prose, and it can be said that the twin phenomena of English as a *supraglossia* and its teaching by Indians to Indians have conciliated to a large extent the confrontation of English and Marathi in the bilingual behaviour.

The basis of literate bilingualism is mainly literate or stylistic, especially in a language contact of textual type. The borders between the concepts of *foreign language* and *second language* are never clear in the linguistic situation of India.[94] English had established its links with the literary milieu of Maharashtra so firmly that literate bilingualism flourished without any obstruction and restraint. The communication flow from English into Marathi was never intercepted by any other foreign or

Indian language. The registers of old Marathi literature, of dialects and Sanskrit were adjusted smoothly in the bilingual systems. The balance of literary culture wholly in favour of monocultural bilinguals who alone participated in the literary production of the nineteenth century, is an important factor in the actual mechanism of the influence of English on Marathi prose (cf. 3.3.4, 3.3.5, and see 4.4). Primary sources of the nineteenth century reveal that nearly all the Marathi prose writers learnt, read and wrote English (see 3.3.4). Some of them even carried on their personal private correspondence in English, wrote diaries and important documents in English.[95] Some of them announced their emphatic statements, maxims, which we may call speech acts only in English.[96] The public performance in English of teachers, scholars, authors, journalists, statesmen, jurists, politicians and civil servants is abundantly in favour of their sound knowledge of written English.[97] Many of them like M. G. Ranade, G. K. Gokhale, K. T. Telang and R. G. Bhandarkar wrote and made highly oratorical speeches only in English. However, it is worth noting that the cases of Indians praising Indians' command over English are more frequent than those of Englishmen making patronising understatements about the Indians' use of English. Some of these bilinguals like Gokhale became legendary figures because of their mastery over the dominant group's language to the extent of even surpassing the Englishman. This is an interesting phenomenon for cultural anthropologists to investigate into. As for spoken English British linguists have recognized a distinct 'coloured variety' of English style, a pidgin of India.[98]

Hans Vogt doubts as to whether hundred per cent bilingualism exists, since the use of either language in any situation with the same felicity and correctness and with the same proficiency as the native speakers is not possible. He believes that if such a thing ever exists it would hardly be of any interest to linguists, because then the phenomenon of interference in bilingualism would, by definition, be excluded.[99] Individual cases apart, on the socio-cultural level we have to rule out the possibility of native-like control of two literary styles in view of the low status of Indian writing in English in world literature. Despite a hundred and fifty years of record it can still be safely ranked below vernacular literatures as well. A period style, being a socio-cultural phenomenon, implies that it is more than individual. We have to assume that bilingualism in its essence is a result of confrontattion of two languages as institutional wholes taking place in a mass of individuals, groups of individuals, elites and whole communities.[100]

In a colonial situation, some degree of biculturism is inevitably associated with bilingualism. This factor is implied in the areas of confrontation discussed earlier. Accordingly, it would also mean less than two

                                    The Influence of English on Marathi

complete semantic systems at the bilingual group's command. In the early phase of the nineteenth century, as the records show, English was taught in schools by double translation method.[101] But after the establishement of the University of Bombay, neglect of the mother tongue became a feature of educational system. As S. Nagarajan states, "a pass in the examination signified only that the student had been lucky and had memorised well."[102] The effect of rote habits of learning two languages together cannot be underestimated. Moreover, increasing supercession by a foreign language affected student's conceptualization (cf. 4.2.2). The intellectual remoulding of reality in the minds of the educated generation was done by English. In Einar Haugen's words, "bilingualism is not merely an addition but also an elimination of the first language in certain vital functions."[103] These vital functions in the Indian society meant even private correspondence. Some linguists have stated that bilingualism affects the natural originality of the bilinguals and hampers their development especially in creative faculties.[104] The relation between linguistic signs and reality or in Chomsky's phrase 'underlying language competence', which gives the native speaker the unique ability to create new sentences, certainly suffered in the biligual situation of the Indian type. Though cognitive enrichment was abundantly done through learning English, cognitive fulfilment was impossible. The prose writers' ambivalence regarding the role of English in India is increasingly evident as we approach the end of the ninetenth century. It also affected the healthy learning of English in Maharashtra. According to S. Nagarajan, "English declined in India because we tried to acquire a different personality instead of a supplementary personality."[105] In writing, as in speech, code-switching and code-mixing became stylistic devices.[106] With several writers writing English prefaces, exhibiting the knowledge of English as a bilingual code became a status symbol.[107]

4.3.3 BORROWING

The bilinguals initiate borrowing, which, in the context of stylistic study, may be of two types : *1. Written-textual,* i.e., from the literary texts of the source language direct into the literary texts of the receiving language through various processes of borrowing such as loan words, loan shifts and loan blends. The *written-textual* variety has largely affected the rhythm of sentence in Marathi, but enriched the graphic level. 2. *Oral-textual,* i.e., from the source language through the spoken media into the literary texts of the receiving language. Linguistic evidence for borrowing of this type is detected only in the written occurrences of various types of loans, but the process has been already completed in the spoken varieties of the language. The *oral-textual* variety of borrowing has enriched the language without affecting the ryhthm of sentence, and internalized the borrowed elements more aesthetically than the *written-textual* type (see Chapter 5.2). Since we are dealing with the written use of language more than the spoken, only those occurrences which are clearly discernible on the graphic level will be attended to.

Several linguists regard borrowing as a historical fact of culture relations and treat it as a part of historical comparative linguistics.[108] Comparision between earlier and later states of the receiving language helps as far as detecting the borrowed features along with innovations. On the descriptive level of stylistic analysis, these features may also point to individual writer's innovations. On the level of period style they are treated in this study as variants borrowed for the sake of variety, richness, exactness or just to fill the holes created by other contiguous features. Survival or non-survival of features depends on the relationship of these features to other variants and their respective norms. Sometimes stray English features which do not develop any such relationship in the Marathi system are also found, but such features are neutral as regards the influence on the formation of prose style in the period. Rejection or retention of borrowed features appears to have been decided by several motivational factors such as need, utility, rhythm etc. A complete taxonomy of borrowings and of the motivational factors will be too premature at this stage, but on the basis of the analysis of representative passages, a rough sketch can be drawn as follows :

Stylistic motivation　Borrowed stylistic features

Need	Sentence linkers, sentence structures, loan words, coinage, loan blends
Utility	All graphic features, syntactic features, loan translations
Rhythm	Most Sanskritisms from loan translations
Urge	Features of individual and genre styles
Humour	Loan words with distortion
Imitation	Unique or stray features of syntagmatic nature
Compulsion	Unique or stray features of paradigmatic nature
Fancy, prestige, etc.	Formalistic features like pronunciation and grammatical borrowings

It is important to note that most borrowings were accepted in the system through conscious selective processes on the ground of cultural need of the bilingual group, while comparatively few entered the system under pressure of the foreign language. The features motivated by fancy or prestige are a large quantitative class. However, statistical methods alone would decide the exact proportion of all these features. Again the stamp of the bilingual group who wrote the prose, and the political cultural focus of Marathi in the nineteenth century will have to be taken into account while carrying out the statistical tests. Categorization of borrowed features would then show the specific aspects of Marathi system most influenced by English.

Some of the important effects of borrowings from English may be noted here. The large-scale borrowing necessitated the production of dictionaries, grammatical studies and grammars of Marathi, as the concern for stylistic merit of the newly borrowed features as against the native features assumed serious proportion in the First phase of the Influence. The synthetic structure of Marathi imposed restriction on borrowing verbs, as English verbs could not be inflected with the elaborate grammatical system of Marathi. Sanskrit substitutes were preferrred to English verbs. All Sanskrit substitutes are not necessarily connected with borrowings from English, but Sanskritisms which are purely lexical (see 4.2.4 and 4.2.5), are largely loan translations and hence connected with the influence of English. Some of them are the results of stimulus from English influence. English nouns were borrowed more easily than verbs. Loss of old *Deshi* features due to the introduction of new features is one very noticeable effect of English borrowings. While borrowing is related to extra-linguistic factors, purely literary-aesthetic factors were equally important. Borrowed jargon of the sciences and technical subjects are the most conspicuous. The sudden and speedy expansion of the semantic system of Marathi necessitated such large-scale and indiscriminate borrowings that much of the borrowed vocabulary has remained outside the stylistic system of Marathi. In fact there is a secondary subsystem of this vocabulary in 'academic' Marathi. The pidginized form of materials used in higher learning is rather a superstructure of features borrowed from English, which had a higher semantic development, built upon the grammatical system of Marathi. Often this superstructure does not reveal the deep structure of the semantic base, and the semantic fields of borrowed features are insufficiently differentiated. The Christian literature in Marathi is another example of borrowed features which remained outside the stylistic system of Marathi (cf. 3.5). Intake of borrowed features in the First phase was as high as drop-out of features in the second (see Chapters 6 and 7). In the Third phase borrowing was stabilized and was mainly confined to lexical and syntactic features as stylistic devices only.

In language contact, as in culture contact, content is more readily transformed than form.[109] Therefore on the level of language there is maximum borrowing in content features like vocabulary, graphic categories and genres rather than form features like sentence structures, grammatical features, syntactic patterns, prosody, morphemes and phonemes. However for the analysis of stylistic influence content features are as important as form features because style involves synthesis of both content and form features. It is worth noting here that Persian features have been more deeply synthesized in the stylistic system of Marathi than the English features.

4.3.4 INTERFERENCE IN LINGUISTIC SYSTEMS

The most valuable contribution to the study of interference in linguistic systems as part of the linguistic influence are made by linguists interested in the study of bilingual and multilingual phenomena.[110] Unfortunately, the area most relevant to the study of style, namely, the sentential and near-sentential, has remained uninvestigated as yet. As J. B. Johnson states, "the investigator is left with a false appreciation of the extent of lexical changes and phonetic patterning without being able to perceive and demonstrate concomitant changes in other phases of the language.[111]

Interference caused by borrowing in the subsystems of the written language is the focus of our study. For our purpose, the definition of interference would be the use of features belonging to one language while writing another[112] (cf 4.2.1). At this stage we have reached the border between purely linguistic and purely stylistic norms and also large overlapping areas between language and style. As it will be seen in Chapter 6, under the influence of English a new code of stylistic norms was under formation. At the initial stage, interference in systems caused a sharp break in transmission of culture (1818 to about 1840). Then an oversimplified, pidginized code, which is superimposed by the influence of English appeared in Marathi (1830-47). The new features certainly increased polyvalence, i.e., language expressing itself in so many different ways. André Martinet states :

> "At every stage the structure of language is nothing but the unstable balance between the needs of communication which require more numerous and more specific units . . . and man's inertia which favours less numerous, less specific and more frequently occurring units."[113]

The interference caused by English-based features in the subsystems of written Marathi—from the graphic to grammatical, was directly related to the diversity of functions suddenly imposed on written Marathi under new needs (see 1.1.4). This interim expansion during the First

                                        The Influence of English on Marathi

phase was, in Andre' Martinet's phrase, systematized by the Marathi writers' inertia. Structural constraints on change (4.3.5) eliminated a number of borrowed features in the Second phase (1847-1874) and interference, was fairly regulated in the Third phase (1874-1890).

In the confrontation with a foreign language, the arena is the receiving language's *parole*, a battlefield where new features and old systems relevant to the features, such as phonological, morphological, lexical, syntactic or sentential clash. It is after this intial skirmish in *parole* that a feature is adjusted in the *langue*. The aesthetic test is the problem of *parole*, the quality of performance is the problem of *langue*.The selected features of the dominant language enter the *parole* of the receiving language. However these features are subject to change and other structural restrictions of the receiving language (see 5.1.3).

English and Marathi as sub-branches of the Indo-European family ؍ languages have a distant genetic relationship. Farthest removed from each other, the two languages show distinct structures. However, if we accept Johannes Schmidt's wave theory, dialectal peculiarities crossing each other and resulting in common features shared by both the sub-branches cannot be underestimated in linguistic acculturation.[114] The influence of the *autochthones,* meaning the common prehistoric or protohistoric links, cannot be ruled out during the period of confrontation. This would also explain the growing Sanskritisms parallel to the increasing influence of English. In such cases of intuitive revival of the autochthones, the foreign features often work as catalyst and stimulate the proto-historic links at the substratum of the language structure.[115] The correspondences between Sanskrit and Germanic-Greek-Latin provide the linkage that accelerated loan translations during the period of influence. The semantic roots of many features being genetically related there is a possibility of a large class of borrowings being actually a part of the autochthones. In such cases the influence of English is to be treated as interference phenomenon. Some features of syntax and several basic stocks of words may fall in this category of revived substratum elements. They de-pidginized the language system by replacing the alien features with those stored in the *langue*, forced readjustment of borrowings in the systems and stylized the system eroded by sudden intake of foreign features (see 5.1.3). This is evident from the passages analysed in Chapters 7 and 8; not only dormant features but also dead features are found appearing in the prose for the first time in the history of Marathi.

Interference also caused modifications of one element in a subsystem in order to accommodate another in the same or the related subsystem (see Chapters 6, 7 and 8). Thus new patterns of this adjustment helped new stylistic combinations or in Hans Vogt's words ' trigger effect ', in the development of language[116] (see 5.5). In this process some of the old features are lost if they are not agreeable to the new ones in terms of rhythm. However, all these aspects, strictly speaking, relate to change rather than to interference.

4.3.5 CHANGE

In the mechanism of stylistic influence change plays a crucial role in that it absorbs, patternizes and rearranges indiscriminate and unplanned borrowings on the one hand and transforms the disorganized linguistic interference into the system of the language on the other. It also causes the creation of totally new features in order to fill the holes in the system. At this stage language standardization is said to have been accomplished, although standardization may also entail other socio-linguistic factors and motivations such as planning and nationalism (cf. 4.2.4 and 4.4). It is important to note that change needs a direction which is supplied by cultural motivation.

In relation to written language, the interpretation of change has to be worked out afresh. Change has been differently defined by linguists. In most cases it has been confined to lexical level only. Most often linguists connect change to social phenomena.[117] Explanation of each individual item of change would demand a full-fledged essay because it is related to social values, psychological processes and historical background. Again there is a thin line of division between inherent changes and changes due to borrowing. According to Edward Sapir, there can be no hard line of division between the two, because "every individual's language is a distinct psychological entity in itself, so that all inherent changes are likely, at last analysis, to be peculiarly remote or subtle forms of change due to contact."[118]

Change as the result of the influence of one feature on another, or of one subsystem on another, whether phonological, grammatical, semantic or any other is relevant to our study in so far as it involves stylistic influence.

As discussed before in 4.3.3 and 4.3.4 borrowing gives rise to pidginization on the one hand and stylization on the other. The difference between these two types of linguistic influence is more of quality than of degree. Pidginization is simplification of borrowed features; it is rather rapid; it lacks contextualization totally or partially; its conventionalization lacks scales of delicacy (see Specimen Passages in Chapter 6). Stylization on the other hand presupposes complete structural reorientation of each borrowing. Even loanwords are given new contexts in the receiving language. Loanshifts including coinage are structurally oriented. Pronunciation borrowing is asociated with nativistic values (see

                          The Influence of English on Marathi

Vishnu shastri Chiplunkar's passage in Chapter 8). Stylization also reflects group sensibility (see Chapter 7).

A diachronic perspective of a language under influence like Marathi reveals two systems in confrontation and the resulting merger, either in a pidgin writing (see Specimen Passages in Chapter 6) or standardized growth. For example, change in the norms of pronoun usage (*tu* vs *tumhi*) is pidginization (see Chapter 6), while nominal constructions replaced by verbal ones is stylized standardization[119] (see Chapters 6 and 7). Change in this way presents a choice of development both ways.[120] As a regularizing process, it also means a context of standard, a process of norm formation, a process of systematizing borrowed variants into stylistic features.[121] Borrowing can be erratic, but change is always systematic. The capacity of the oral system of language in storing change is limited, but it is the written system of polysemy in the language that qualitatively helps stylization.[122]

A notable feature of change in Marathi is a wide range of loans. In view of the establishment of English as a *supraglossia*, we have to account for several English features which exist in the stylistic system of Marathi as extensions not of Marathi but of English. Such features can be said to have caused *zero change*. An English feature which is borrowed thus as a stop-gap adjustment is not a part of the system of Marathi, but a guest-feature. Slight phonological changes in the features are expected in their use, but this does not affect the system of Marathi. Such features are not variants of the norms of Marathi prose style. These may be regarded as *zero stylistic features,* exercising no influence on the system of the receiving language.

The motivations behind change are supplied by the contact situation itself and by bilingualism and borrowing (see 4.3.8). According to James M. Anderson, "to establish a psychological basis for change or an explanation for specific kinds of change may not be empirically justifiable."[123] This is true especially when the entire group is motivated to linguistic change. These motivations are made clear by social historians and educationist. The range of motivations therefore can be very wide, from political to plagiaristic. Change in linguistic and stylistic subsystems of Marathi, graphic as well as structural, is so multifarious that it can be explained only as an act of will of the whole language community. As Otto Jespersen says :

> "There may be periods in which the ordinary restraints on linguistic change make themselves less felt than usual, beacause the whole community is animated by a strong feeling of independence and wants to break loose from social ties of many kinds . . . of linguistic authority thrown overboard."[124]

As discussed in 4.2.4, there is evidence that linguistic **nativism along with** this kind of group motivation prompted linguistic **change in the** nineteenth-century Maharashtra. Edward Sapir's view that the vested interests behind such a phenomenon resist critical enquiry is **worth** keeping in mind before attempting any generalizations in this regard.[125]

4.4 STANDARDIZATION

There is general agreement on the essential nature of language **standardi-** zation.[126] The development of standard Marathi is characterized **by the** following socio-linguistic stages :

1. One of the dialects, namely, Pune variety was superposed **on** others.

2. It was a medium of discourse in education to begin with.

3. Then it served as the voice of the entire speech community.

4. It spread with the growth of literacy.

5. For the whole century, it was used by the literate bilinguals, mainly in writing but also gradually in speech.

6. It was closely developed under the influence of English **with** minimum of intermixture from other dialects.

Thus the prespective and literate nature of the **Marathi standard** is the natural consequence of the peculiar course of its development. Standardization of Marathi is also the linguistic corollary of modernization of society. Linguists have defined the characteristics of standard language as efficiency, economy, rationality, adequacy, clarity, commonality, acceptability and aesthetics.[127] The experiments carried out by the standard variety, under the influence of elite bilingualism, formed the permanent writing habits of monolinguals at the successive stages. Change in the standard thus became part of the historical development of the language. The borrowed features together with the native features constituted themselves into norms. Since most writers of the nineteenth century belonged to a few urban castes in Bombay and Pune, standardization in Marathi was comparatively speedy. Owing to its caste affiliation, standard Marathi had by the end of the century a puristic aura.[128] The long years of planning under the leadership of Major Thomas Candy had given it the form of the *evaluatory* and selected variety of 'pure' type.[129] It will not be an exaggeration to say that standard Marathi differed little from literary Marathi.

In an influence study such as this, the standard holds a contrastive perspective of the pressure of two languages, beginning with bilingualism. Borrowing and change are the intermediary stages of this mecha-

                                    The Influence of English on Marathi

nism. When change is converted to stability, the standard is formed. Variance of the standard continues to interfere for some time, but it is either discarded or adjusted, through variants, to the norm (see 5.3). Stylization may be said to begin with the formation of the norm along with its variants.

The most important factor in the speedy standardization of Marathi was the switch-over to written expression. Writing is by nature prescriptive and expedites standardization more than the spoken variety. The rapid graphization of Marathi features into one single *balbodh* script marked the switch-over from the oral to the written style. The written form is the most potent force in the acceptance, propagation and preservation of the standard.[130] The written standard being the carrier of basic cultural values of the people serves as the basis of literary prose.[131] It also reflects the relative cultural stability of society. As Punya Sloka Ray observes, "the important thing to note is that developed prose is truly possible in a written language. As a correlate of this, written signs have, in any language, a communicative function which exceeds that of the spoken signs.[132] The reason of written systems contributing to prose formation is said to be their reversibility and precipitation of an external record, uniformity of pronunciation, unification of dialectal variations in pronunciation due to fixed spelling and flexibility in the arbitrary alteration of the meanings of its words. Since the standard in Marathi was selective, it was also socially exclusive and restricted.

When Marathi came into contact with the English language, variation in spoken as well as written Marathi posed a number of problems for the first generation of English-educated writers. Caste, professional, dialectal and subsystemic varieties which were impervious to the formation of period style had to be eliminated. Molesworth, the first Marathi lexicographer observes, "The Marathi is not a language of well-marked boundaries : the amount therefore of foreign words—words Sanskrit, Persian, Arabic, and Hindustani—current in the language will fluctuate, and the standard by which this currency is determined will differ . . ."[133] Absence of a public educational system perpetuated the variation. When Marathi became a literary language, its fixed institutionalized norms became complusory for all the members of the literary group.[134]

Standardization is linked with a number of paralinguistic factors. With the western contact came better physical conditions connected with writing, such as smooth paper, pen and pencil, duplicating facilities such as printing and well-bound books. The use of Marathi for written purposes on an increasing level expanded the functions of writing in the First phase of the contact with English.[135] The caste-profession links were broken as the old concepts of literary community underwent radical change. The rise of a national language (see 4.2.4) is closely linked with the progressive tendency of the wider concept of literary community. As Otto Jespersen observes," it is an advantage to anybody to give up his small parochial dialect and adopt the national standard language by which he is enabled to get into touch with an infinitely greater number of people—not to mention the greater intellectual horizon offered in this way and many social advantages . . ."[136]

Another important factor in the speedy standardization of Marathi was the rigorous planning of the early British officials. The British worked out a master plan for the standardization of Marathi. Standard orthography and printing types greatly helped uniformity in phonological as well as morphophonemic elements. Dictionaries and grammars preceded the numerous translations in the First phase. Elaborate rules of punctuation were framed after exasperating consideration of Marathi syntax.[137] The discipline of writing was taught to Marathi writers by British officers who had a considerable background of Marathi, and the educational officers sent out from England had to acquire 'a competent knowledge of a native language in two years' which was rigorous and hard for the British.[138] This gave them an adequate contrastive perspective. The demand for standardization was partly a result of British training of the late eighteenth century.[139] Marathi was made to mould itself into a new style of writing, under the pressure of these influences. George Jervis's Translation Notice which stipulates minute details regarding the new standard of writing is rightly called the 'dawn of Marathi writing' (see Chapter 6.)[140] The insistence of Major Candy on uniformity in spelling, grammatical forms and syntax caused heated controversies (see 4.2.5 and Chapter 7). Marathi prose writers consciously expanded their sphere of use and tried the new standards profusely in dictionaries, grammars, textbooks, translations, periodicals, oratorical speeches, creative and critical literature. For all these substyles, English literary tradition provided a discipline as they rose mostly through the adoption of various forms of English literature. The new channels and forums created a new class of writers. With the gradually extended literacy of the masses, need for reading materials increased. The need to produce books on various subjects for academic purposes required uniformity in writing styles acceptable to the conservative officials of the British bureaucracy. They had also to be written in a style intelligible to the ordinary student and naturally, therefore, there was little scope for originality as well as creativity. Standardization was the only possible accomplishment for the ambitious prose writers. New coinage that echoed English concepts, and loan translations dominated this prose (see Chapter 6). Pidginization

                    The Influence of English on Marathi

was another result. It was, in a way, inevitable because, in social fields British planning was advancing without public participation or consent. The new western objects and concepts found little cognitive response in the people's minds. But the very existence of the written materials, which were secular, for all classes and castes, created a need for a common linguistic standard. As Kalyan K. Chatterjee observes, "The Indian psyche has been touched by English at a wide range of stops, and not always harmoniously, so that often instead of music we have only noise."[141]

The rise of great towns is another important factor involved in standardization. The cities of Bombay and Pune grew as centres of learning where the upper castes dominated (cf.3.4). As there were no political-communal conflicts, there was no social destruction to vitiate the smooth progress of prose movement from the natural course of development. The register of the upper class bilinguals became ascription. The shift in the centre of literary activity from Bombay, where several communities participated, to Pune where only one major Brahman community dominated was a change extremely favourable to the.growth of the standard. The language of Pune Brahmans was accepted as standard.[142] Nearly all the school teachers belonged to particular Brahman castes and were educated in Pune and Bombay. After their training in ' Normal schools ' they were posted at district places in rural Maharashtra.[143] These teachers wielded their urban stylistic clout and imposed their register on the language of the new generation. As nearly all the new prose was produced by the bilingual writers imitation of the excellence of great writers led to imitation of their idiom. In short, the situation was ideal for the growth of period style, because the fixed writer-reader relationship helped quick acceptance of the norms.

Of all the borrowings, loan translations are seen playing a greater role in standardizing the structural system of Marathi. As the available resources of Marathi were inadequate to the sciences, where language had to be used as a precise instrument, loans from the vanishing *supraglossia* were taken as substitutes to English terms. As a result there was a lexical subsystem of Sanskrit words in Marathi. The translators also established a new syntactic subsystem. A role similar to that of translators was played by grammarians. The first problem they faced was which variety was to be taken as standard for description. This they solved by adopting the speech of Deshastha Brahmans of Pune. They applied grammatical systems derived from English and Sanskrit to Marathi.[144]

Uniformity of the usage develops norms against which all varieties of language are adjusted to form a period style (see 5.2). In Marathi prose the standard did not exist before it came in contact with English (see

Chapter 2). The standard was formed and speedily consolidated by the last quarter of the century, when dialectal and other varieties began to receive the status of stylistic variants. The first eminent grammarian of Marathi, Dadoba Pandurang was of the opinion that in 1836 "the Marathi language has not had any standard." Another grammarian, R. B. Joshi, admitted in 1889 that "the form of Marathi has been fast changing nowadays." But in 1911 M. K. Damle, the most outstanding grammarian of Marathi admitted that Marathi had been 'sufficiently standardized '.[145]

CHAPTER FIVE

A MODEL FOR THE ANALYSIS OF STYLISTIC INFLUENCE

5.1 THE STYLISTICS OF LINGUISTIC INFLUENCE

5.1.1 INTRODUCTION

In the previous chapters we examined the linguistic influence of English on Marathi in the historical and socio-linguistic framework. We now propose to construct an analytical model necessary for the investigation of stylistic influence that took place simultaneously with the linguistic influence. It should be evident from the case study conducted so far that when new social and communicative needs are forced by historical events on a receiving language, the inherent potential of the language can enable it to develop a mechanism capable of absorbing the intellectual remoulding of the world by means of socio-linguistic processes (Chapter 4). It remains to be verified how language standardization affects stylistic mechanism of a written language and promotes its literariness.

It has to be kept in mind that we are constructing a heuristic model for the purpose of detecting contact stylistic features which are to be distinguished from purely linguistic features. Stylistic influence is seen in the creation of language patterns over and above those which had been in existence in the receiving language prior to the contact, or which had been developed internally irrespective of the process of change described in 4.3.4 and 4.3.5. Since style is the area of integration of linguistic influence, it has always been a difficult task for students of contact comparative linguistics to distinguish clearly the two sets : 1. language patterns developed under foreign influences and 2. those developed internally. The present study intends to confine itself to investigating language patterns of the first type. These include 1. features of Marathi which have been developed under the influence of English, and 2. the consequent gains and losses in the stylistic competence of the language, resulting from this influence. The findings of this study may be useful data for the development of linguistic studies concerning language variation, evolution and acculturation (see Chapter 9), though the primary intention here is to point out and illustrate the nature of stylistic influence.

Several stylisticians and linguists have pointed out the diversity in the definitions of style. Some of them have attempted classification of the definitions of style in order to find common elements regarding the medium and content, means and ends.[1] All the definitions of style have some validity or the other; they should therefore be regarded complementary and not mutually exclusive. As Robert Adolph puts it, "our total conception of style is probably an amalgam of them all."[2] Nevertheless, the fact remains that though stylistics has gained enough ground to exist as an independent science, it has not probed far enough into the specific nature of style. That style signifies several pairs of polarity is perhaps the only common discovery. The inevitable dilemmas every stylistician meets in the study of style have their source in the comprehensiveness of the term style, which ranges from its graphic-visual aspects to the phonetic-musical. The vague feelings we have about the literariness of language are so elusive that they defy any linguistic definition of style. Again, the paradox of language use, both as communication and experience, leaves several loopholes in the actual analysis of style.[3] Aestheticians and linguists concerned with the phenomenon of pure style seem to regard it as an abstraction of our experience of language as a creative medium. For example, Seymour Chatman regards it as a formal quality of a text, while Croce believes that the study of expressions is the task of aesthetics and linguistics.[4] Ashok Kelkar goes one step ahead by calling stylistics ' the aesthetics of language' which, according to him, is the link between linguistics, literary criticism, and the extrinsic study of the literary culture of a community.[5] Rene Wellek includes several additional areas in style besides linguistics.[6] Several linguists like Lubomir Dolezel and Richard W. Baily, David Crystal and Derek Davy, G. Herdan, John Spencer and Michael J. Gregory admit the phenomenon of the ' intuition of the native speaker ' in the recognition of style. Theroretically, linguistic stylistics and literary stylistics may form different branches of stylistics. It is doubtful whether any one theory would provide criteria for all the features of the full stylistic analysis of a text. In the abstract notion of 'Style' we may have to include several styles, including styles of text-production (creative processes) and of text-reception (readers' perception of text). The term *text* also suggests paralinguistic connotations.[7] According to Roland Barthes, a text is multiple containing many forms. Being an autonomous semiotic structure it contains structures other than the lingusitic.[8] Ju M. Lotman, B. A. Uspenskij, V. V. Ivanov, V. N. Toporov and A. M. Pjatigorskij define the text as a sequence of signs and also an integral sign.[9] However, since stylistic facts are apprehended only in language, which is their vehicle, it would be sufficient for this study to regard style as system at all levels of the text. Linguistic stylistics studies such system at the linguistic level only (cf. 5.5).

5.1.2 LINGUISTIC INFLUENCE AND STYLISTIC INFLUENCE

For the purpose of this study a stylistic feature is recognised when a semiotic code is related to the literary-aesthetic contexts of the text. A linguistic feature is recognised on the other hand when a unit of content fully dominates the semiotic code without showing any relation to extra-textual contexts. The content of the stylistic feature indicates alternate code choices within a family of related features. The linguistic feature indicates purely grammatical values of the code, while a stylistic feature indicates organization of textual units besides indicating purely grammatical values. In other words, grammatical value is compulsory for both the types but stylistic value is optional, and therefore, differential. We may, however, grant some interplay between purely stylistic and purely linguistic features in textual systems, which depends on the type of culture that envelops the text. In the literary culture of the Elizabethan age it was very high; in modern English it is low. Another important difference between non-literary language and the language of text (or literary language) is that the content of non-literary language is to a large degree previously shared experience.[10] On the other hand, literary language is made to function in areas where semantic content can refer to purely fictitious contexts stretched to the whole textual space. The content of literary language thus need not be a previously shared experience, though familiarity with linguistic features is to a large extent essential. Since the aim of the present analysis is to point out borrowed elements that are demonstrably reflected in the written diatype of the language of a given period, our task is to develop a purely linguistic framework which will be fairly adequate for the analysis of stylistic influence. Semiologically a linguistic code is not distinct from the literary code, except that the latter is extrapolation of the former. They may differ in function, but not in structure.[11] Without being dogmatic about any theory of style, a fundamental difference between non-literary and literary language can be established. Unverifiable hypotheses based on the elusive elements of style which cannot be traced back to linguistic causality have to be excluded from our model. The paralinguistic aspects of style entering into the receiving language independently or along with borrowed linguistic features will have to be excluded from our stylistic model. They can be more properly studied in comparative literature. The major thrust is therefore to observe and describe within Marathi texts the growth of stylistic subsystems over a given period.

According to Edward Sapir, the most important linguistic influences are those of meaning patterns across linguistic frontiers. He states : "A type of influence which is neither exactly one of vocabulary nor of linguistiic form, in the ordinary sense of the word and to which insufficient attention has so far been called is that of *meaning patterns.*"[12] What Sapir calls *meaning patterns* can be converted to stylistic influences in semiological terms. Roland Barthes provides a semiological model which can also be used as an analytical model for the investigation of linguistic influence. The two poles of linguistic influence according to Barthes's model are : 1. the syntagmatic pole of juxtaposition of borrowed features with the original features of the receiving language, and 2. the systemic pole of the set of linguistic features fully amalgamated in the stylistic system of the language. Chronologically, the former would precede the latter, though historical reconsntruction alone would create corresponding pigeonholes in the structure of the receiving language which can be studied independently (see Chapter 9). A weakly synthetic language like English is likely to create more of such pigeonholes in the structure of a strongly synthetic languages like Marathi. Michael Riffaterre's concept of stylistic device (SD) as an emphasized linguistic element placed in opposition to two types of stylisitic contexts—micro-context and macro-context—is a step in the direction of tracing the relationships of the borrowed features to the native ones.[14] Widdowson's model of two sets of relations—extra-textual, between language items, and intra-textual within the context itself—is a variation on Riffaterre's model.[15] When an innovated feature happens to be a borrowed feature, it is stylistically 'unpredictable' in Riffaterre's sense, because it is placed in the context of 'predictable' native features. The native features N which precede and follow the borrowed features B and which remain exterior to them become the macro-context of the borrowed features, thus creating macro-contxtualization of the following types :

1. B - N, where the borrowed feature precedes the native
     feature.

2. N - B - (N), where the borrowed feature follows the native
     feature or occurs medially.

3. (N) - B starting a new context — B again, where borrowed
     features macro-contextualize each other.

Micro-context which, according to Riffaterre, "consists of the other constitutents which remain unmarked" does not help much in influence study.

Thus a constant reference to the stylistic system (systemic pole) of the receiving language as a whole will be a useful guideline to transform subjective reaction to stylistic influence (syntagmatic pole) into an objective tool (see 5.4). A non-stylistic feature is contextually free or neutral, while a stylistic feature is contextually bound to the systemic pole of the text. In the text, both types of stylistic and non-stylistic (including purely linguistic) features among the borrowed features form concentric spirals tending toward meaningful order. A borrowed feature at the initial stage, whether stylistic or non-stylistic, supersedes the internal processes of macro-contextualization described earlier. Thus style becomes the area of their integration. When they fail to integrate, the result is pidginization or non-style (see Chapters 6 and 7). A borrowed stylistic feature is in interrelation with individual and/or genre use, and 'unpredictable', while a borrowed linguistic feature may be merely in interrelation with the grammar of the language, and grammatically quite 'predictable'. A gap between the two is gradually reduced with standardization. In other words, when norms become cliches, style tends to become non-style (see 5.3). It is for this reason that the stylistic quality of a borrowed linguistic feature becomes obvious only when the receiving language has developed its own norms and is standardized. Stylistic meaning patterns of borrowed linguistic features may be thus late to emerge. In the process of language evolution, internal processes of macro-contextualization supersede the emphasis inherent in the borrowed features.

5.1.3 STYLE IN RELATION TO LANGUE AND PAROLE

The aesthetics of borrowed features can be explained by the test of performance of the features. Initially all borrowings have 'fictitious' contexts in the system of literary style as they differ from the familiar contexts of language. This element of familiarity or conventionality, strictly speaking, belongs to the area of *langue*. The unfamiliar innovations or deviations from the norm are naturally the area of *parole*, because they spring from the individual writer's experiments with the selected elements from *langue*. These innovations are stored in *langue* only after they are tried in *parole. Langue* is therefore a product of *parole* , a systematized set of elements which include selected borrowed features. According to Jan Mukarovsky, *langue* is aesthetically neutral, having its source in style.[16] Thus *langue* exercises the test of performance in respect of new or borrowed linguistic features. The innovated elements whose performance in the *parole* system is 'poor' are eliminated. In other words, innovations, in order to be accepted in *langue*, must be aesthetic.

In a contact situation, the idiosyncratic behaviour of borrowed features can be recognized as a new variant which, when it enters the structural subsystems, receives a code sanction, and becomes a part of collective consciousness. The stable uniform system of language or *langue* is then said to be influenced by the foreign system. Such entries from *parole* into *langue* are easily detected in the lexical and semantic sphere. W. P. Lehmann, however, admits that the result of the influence of other subsystems like syntax is likely, but "the evidence is not conclusive."[17] William Mackey (1962) has attempted a bifurcation of influence under two heads : 1. Borrowing, which according to him is a feature of *parole,* while 2. Interference, which is a feature of *langue.* Elsewhere, the same author (1972) attemps further description of bilingualism on the basis of the four skills, *writing* being one of them, and also adds a classification of contacts, namely economic, administrative, cultural, political, military, historical, religious and finally, demographic.[18] Apart from the obviously wide area that the contacts would provide, such a classification would not help in explaining the inner sphere of stylistic influence. However, the division of borrowing as a feature of *parole* and interference as a feature of *langue* needs more attention, because it has an important bearing on comparative linguistics. Influences of one language on another resulting in changes in *langue* become the permanent property of the receiving language and enter into its historical development. Once the borrowed elements become part of *langue* it is difficult to separate them from the original elements. They present a problem to historical linguists as regards their genetic identity. Such an analysis is even more difficult as regards period style where the dividing line between *langue* and *parole* is often blurred (see 5.2). The problem can be studied more usefully on the levels of individual or genre styles rather than of period style, because period style is a supra-individual and supra-generic *parole*, a half-way house between *parole* and *langue.*

In the colonial situation the aesthetic and the utilitarian needs are often inseparable. As a result, several superfluous borrowed features exist by force of socio-linguistic circumstances (see 4.1.1 and 4.3.2). However, as discussed earlier, the receiving language of a period absorbs only those features which are useful for its development. Thus language standardization precedes aesthetic norm formation and generally the latter depends upon the former.[19] The discovery of an influence does not modify our appreciation or valuation of a work of art. Therefore the order of the aesthetic has to be only one of the considerations in the domain of stylistic influence.

                    The Influence of English on Marathi

During the period of influence the receiving language becomes unsually active, especially in its *parole* aspect. Selection, acceptance and adaptation as well as reaction and resistance are clearly evident in several structural elements. Several old features in the reservoir of the *langue* are revived and adjusted newly with the newly borrowed features. All these constitute the total stylistic competence of the individual authors, the *parole* of the language. Thus the beauty of the borrowed stylistic feature lies in its being an 'exotic' and 'new' language element trying to settle down in the system of the *langue*. Most borrowings are selective, therefore more literary. They have a more special and purposeful existence in the language than the contiguous native features. They are the indirect need of the *langue;* so they are supra-idiolectal, less personal.[20] The supra-idiolectal *parole* becomes the period style (see 5.2). It is for this reason that prose style, being a collective impact of meaning patterns in the text, precedes the poetic style in receiving the influence of a foreign language (see 4.2.3). According to Croce, the two forms of cognitive spirit of man, namely, intuitive and intellectual are both contained in prose; therefore prose style gradually perfects poetic features. After such a perfection, patterning of non-stylistic and stylistic features becomes fairly self-explanatory and poetic style comes under the influence of a foreign language. This is also the reason why prose style covers numerous variations of styles below the umbrella of "everything written that is not verse."[21]

5.2 PERIOD STYLE

A period style is the collective use of written language evident in both good and poor works of a given period. The literary-historical concept of period style is notional and imprecise, because literary history does not adopt explicit or fixed methodology.[22] It denotes the historical stage of the development of the literary language but connotes other characteristics partially reflected in the names given to the period such as Elizabethan period, baroque period, neo-classical period etc. Heinrich Wolfflin calls style as "expression of the temper of an age," and equates it with the element of historical progress in the concept of style itself.[23]

A period style is reflected in the overall patterns of the period. According to Douglas A. Russell, "Artists contribute to these overall patterns, some directly, some indirectly, and some by working in an opposing direction . . . A period style is not an absolute, and it is almost never fully operative in a poem, play, painting or theatrical production . . . The compilation of all the creativity of an entire era is what finally gives us an overall sense of a period style."[24] Thus the notion of a period style is inter-subjective, supra-idiolectal and dominant as a cultural type. It is only through the analytical prism that the spectrum of period style becomes visible and reveals the parameters of individual styles, genre styles and other variations of linguistic diatypes like slang, diction, registers, modes, types, smaller periods, movements, schools and literary cliques. These are parts of the whole, yet they may not be homogeneous in a society like the Indian Society of the nineteenth century, the linguistic repertoire of which was structured in caste-and-profession-specific varieties, and where the parts of the whole could remain unintegrated (cf. Chapter 2).

A linguistic definition of period style carries two tags with it, national and psychological, controlled by tradition and changing usage, viewed as a deep structure beneath a national literature. A period, being a culturally definable traditional type and a stable context category, implies correlation with a certain temper of the language. Our enquiry into the influence on a period style therefore becomes, to a large extent, automatically subservient to the non-linguistic processes. Samuel Johnson states : "I believe there is, in every nation, a stile which never becomes obsolete, a certain mode of phraseology so consonant and congenial to the analogy and principles of its respective language as to remain settled and unaltered."[25] In the sense that Johnson understands it, a national style is an abstraction of period styles in continuous succession over the nation's history, spread over time and space. Even after radical change under foreign influence this 'succssion of period styles' still distinguishes itself by its genetic relation to all the writers in some way. According to Meyer Schapiro, it is the activity of a whole society, a national character of collective thinking and feeling.[26] In comparative literature this inner national tradition becomes clearer in the quality of the thought and feeling made operational to the writers by the language.

In an influence study the general temper of the language also makes psychological impact on the receiving language. For example, Mario Castelnuovo-Tedsesco, a famous European song-writer states : "To be sure, English does present some remarkable difficulties to the song-writer. One, for example, is its great number of monosyllabic words, which it is difficult to distribute over . . .correct accentuation. But, on the other hand, it is perhaps just this—its very lack of 'sonorous substance' that lends English its charm, and makes it one of the most 'spiritual' and transparent languages I know."[27] Foreign experts of English linguistics like Otto Jespersen have also recorded their 'judgements' regarding the temper of the English language. According to Jespersen, "English is more masculine than most languages," and "the English language is a methodical, energetic, business-like and sober language . . . As the language is, so also is the nation . . . "[28] Von Humboldt was the first linguist who believed that 'a different world-view' is expressed by a respective

                          The Influence of English on Marathi

language.[29] Edward Sapir remarks that language is "a self-contained, creative symbolic organization." [30] Benjamin Lee Whorf has hypothesized that "the picture of the universe shifts from tongue to tongue."[31] Similarly philosophers, translation theorists and semiologists, while admitting that there are universals of language, and that the structure of memory image is the same in all cultures, specifically believe in the differences pertinent to each language. Thus the genius of languages in contact constitutes an important element which is useful in the construction of the analytical model, though it has to be kept in the background since, strictly speaking, it is the factor of *langue* rather than *parole*.

A linguistic description of period style may be attempted at this stage. A period style is a set of stylistic devices held together by the interrelations between constitutent units like individual and generic diatypes of language. At a developed stage of style it can be a larger configuration embracing several sets of such diatypes. It is "a time selection defined by a system of norms embedded in the historical process and irremovable from it."[32] The inter-subjective   acter of language phenomena in period style is implicit in their i: .ependence from the individual style. Their being intersubjective also suggests the hypothetical objective character of period style, though little can be said about the relationship between individual and period styles at this stage of research (see Chapter 9). It is for this duality that literary works appear to be unique, and at the same time, universal, classifiable into larger genres, schools, movements and trends. A period style is a more statable expansion of the stylistic system of the national literature, because it is a single whole of the parts in the various phases of its development (in the case of the nineteenth-century Marathi prose style, it is seen in three phases).

In a contact situation, both the origin and the result of an influence can be seen as involving a group of writers or a movement so that their scope is clearly circumscribed by the potentials of the stylistic range of the source language. Dependence on the foreign language is absolute unless nativistic languistic movements intervene. A single writer cannot be the transmitter of the influence to period style though he can be the transmitter of influence into smaller units of period style such as generic features, individual style or literary conventions. The prose style of a period, by virtue of its being under formation (as is the case with the nineteenth-century Marathi prose style) is open to all kinds of irregular sets of borrowed stylistic features, and tolerates unfinished and heterogeneous syntagmatic juxtapositions which may be termed as *variants* (5.1). These juxtapositions create pidginized styles which, when regularized, lead to sysetmic standards, or *norms* (see 5.3). Linguistic influence in a period style implies specificity of linguistic phenomena in the space-time dimension of linguistic acculturation (Chapter 4). Initially, all influence in period style is foregrounding. It moves from the individual to the collective, from the individual works to the literary milieu systematized by successive generations. It reveals the struggle of the language for order, and at the same time, in Jan Mukarovsky's term, *the stage of automatization.*[33] The dimension of literary-aesthetic confrontation involved in linguistic acculturation is implicit in the individual writer's acceptance of the period style. No individual style can contain the entire source of its own strength, because a large part of it is covered by the period style.[34] Therefore, as Karl Kroeber states, "for the student of style, artist is subordinate to his work," and by the same logic, the work is subordinate to the period.[35] This concept of style would also make style social rather than individual. A period style is a corpus of prescriptions common to all the writers of the period. All varieties of style are dominated by period style, which sets the tone for all of them and exercises an unquestioned control over the mode of expression. It is a collective of what Richard Ohmann calls "multifarious *urchoices*" in which the writer finds the origin of his personal rhythm.[36] Style for a bilingual writer thus becomes a choice of variants available in the two languages. The grammar of the earlier stage of the influence is therefore extremely difficult to formulate. Later generations may develop simpler grammars which eliminate the multiple choices, as it has happened in Marathi from Dadoba Pandurang's attempt to write a grammar of Marathi in 1836 to M. K. Damle's *Shastriya Marathi Vyakaran* in 1911.

The term 'nineteenth-century prose style' used in this study signifies the emergence of a distinct set of stylistic devices borrowed from English. It has made the most obvious point of departure in the literary tradition by creating a shift from the oral and manuscript culture to the print culture in the early nineteenth century. From the first printed Marathi text, *St.Matthew* (1805) to *Pan Lakshyat Kon Gheto ?* (1890), the first novel by Hari Narayan Apte, the three phases reveal the gradual maturing of stylistic devices simultaneously along with the process of standardization. The First phase, 1818 to 1847, is a period of experimentation; the Second, 1847 to 1874, from the publication of Lokahitavadi's essays to Phule's *Gulamgiri* (1873), marks the introduction of several new literary genres; and the Third, 1874 to 1890, from the publication of Vishnushastri Chiplunkar's essays in *Nibandhamala* (1874) to H. N. Apte's novels in the last decade of the century, marks the perfection of stylistic devices for purposes of self-expression. The body of texts written and printed during the period presents unique data for the student who wants to study the formative nature of linguistic influence. The oral style (normally characterized by the accompaniment of kinesthetic move-

                                    The Influence of English on Marathi

ments) was on the decrease and is seen being replaced speedily by purely written techniques of self-expression. The oral and manucript culture of the old and medieval Marathi came under influence of English textual culture, which demanded fixed writing and emphasized the closed nature of a print culture.[37] A steady increase in the reading public also ensured, for the first time in the history of Marathi, the growth of literary milieu, owing to greater communication between writers and readers.[38] The impersonal quality that results from the writing which has no particular reader in mind further characterized the prose style of this period.

Although the period is marked by a speedy standardization on the linguistic plane, it was characterized by gradually multiplying individual styles and genre styles. It would be rash to maintain that the style of this period is homogeneous, but the prose writer in the nineteenth century Marathi was not a deviant type.[39] The individual competence of the writer to operate successfully within this culture had affected his linguistic performance. The rule-governed rather than the rule-forming creativity therefore dominated over the individual styles of the period. Most prose writers seem to avoid their own dialectal features in favour of the foremost need of the period — standardization. This further restricted the choices of the writers. Initially, the most favourite genre was the discursive essay. Plays and novels appeared later. Travelogues were rare, humour almost absent. The essay attracted most writers because it was more suited to the less personal variety of prose style. Maturity of different genre styles within a period style is possible when norms have been firmly established. Josephine Miles's argument that the writer's medium comes to him from the past and is the individual author's own peculiarity does not apply to situations like the nineteenth century Marathi prose.[40] Similarly, Louis T. Milic's objections to the models of period style as a classification "false and unnecessary" seems to be dogmatic.[41] On the contrary, the principles of typology of style gains strength in the light of the case study of Marathi prose style in the nineteenth century. It can be emphatically said that owing to an almost unanimous desire of the writers to expedite standardiztion, there seems to be a complete surrender to period style and that even *foregrounding* was done in the direction of the standardization. Thus, however important and complementary it is to the understanding of period style, the study of individual and genre styles does not offer encouraging prospects in the contexts of the influence of English on Marathi in the nineteenth century.

5.3 CRITERIA OF COMPARISON : NORMS AND VARIANTS

Norms and variants are the concrete statable concepts which help manipulating the investigation of stylistic influence more readily. [42] Stylistic influence can be recognized in terms of stylistic features in a text. These develop in the receiving language as elements of a stylistic system that corresponds to the different stages of linguistic influence : bilingualism, borrowing, interference, change and standardization (Chapter 4). A few definitions may be attempted at this stage of the study in order to pinpoint the discussion on stylistic influence.

A *stylistic feature* may be a norm or a variant (see 5.2). A *norm* may be stylistic or purely linguistic (see 5.1). A linguistic norm is already formulated in a language capable of producing literary texts. A stylistic norm has the dimension of text.

A stylistic norm has *variants*. A norm without variants is not stylistic, but non-stylistic or purely linguistic. The non-literary language may contain several stylistic variants, but in the absense of norms, the variants cannot be functionally differentiated. A norm has autofunction. The variants have a deviating and/or a reference function.[43] Norms and variants have multiple relationships, such as weakning, intensifying, enlarging, narrowing etc. The relationship may also be ambiguous. These can be better outlined in aesthetics.

Norms in the textual space enter into vertical, horizontal or oblique relationships with each other, such as super-imposition, parallelism and opposition. The reasons are again aesthetically bound. They are made to serve a system of correlative factors in the literary text.

The relationship between variants is fixed and static. Choice, frequency, surplus, dynamics, tonality and duration are some of the positive qualities of norms in the text; deviation is their negative quality. These qualities are also imposed on the variants of the norms. Often the relationship between the norms changes according to the level of analysis we adopt (5.5).

The norms and the variants keep each other alive. A *cliche'* is a dying variant of a live norm. When norms become cliches, style tends to become non-style, because the variants of the norms have been subjected to an inherent process of decay. The test of this decay is that the variants lose distinct relationships with each other. An *obscure feature* (found only in the dictionary) is a *dead variant*. *Archaism* is a revived variant with or without a norm. *Loan words* are new variants. A *calque* is a revived variant. *Coinage* is a new variant.

Within a period style norms may be common to many genre and individual styles. Variants are restricted to certain genres and certain individual styles. They can be only stylistically differentiated.

Linguistic influence, as seen earlier in 4.3.4, is linguistic interference systematized by the laws of change into standardization. Norms and variants are the most crucial test of stylistic influence, because they are elements of the system to which they originally belong. When new stylistic features enter the receiving language at the point of first borrowing they show vacillating uses in the text until they become part of the system. The historical method is fairly adequate to detect this point of entry in the language. The new features are converted into norms and variants after some time, but till then they confuse the general patterning of the stylistic system of the receiving language. Style is the area of their integration, where unifying forces are at work. Style being selective, there is a controlled import of elements into the receiving language. In cases of continuous contact, such as between English and Marathi, fresh features are tried at each phase. Some of the old ones are eliminated after having been tried. It is obvious that linguistic forces work behind the retention or deletion of these features. It is only in the study of period style that such processes are seen in the proper perspective. When a borrowed features has succeeded in becoming a norm, it has also succeeded in establishing its realm of variants in the *parole* of the receiving language (5.1).

The complete taxonomy of stylistic borrowing, when reduced to norms and variants, would show total exclusion of norms at one end of the scale (which does not concern influence proper), and a total inclusion of all the norms of a foreign language at the other end (in which case the stylistic system of the receiving language can be said to have been totally annihilated). Such a taxonomy can be presented schematically :

0. Complete exclusion of norms.
1. Complete exclusion of some variants while borrowingn whole norms.
2. Obligatory inclusion of a norm.
3. Varying degrees of inclusion of a specific variant without complete elimination of competing variants in the language, thus enriching the language by different shades of synonymy, parallel constructions etc.
4. Norms and variants tried and eliminated at later phases owing to various socio-linguistic or aesthetic reasons.
5. Norms and variants accepted as they do not exist in the receiving language.
6. Norms and variants appearing to be gains at one level of language but resulting in loss at another level. (The replacing of an existing feature by a foreign feature at the same level is not possible, though temporary replacement of this kind in parole is possible.[44])

7. Complete inclusion of norms.

As discussed in 5.1.3 the value of influences would pose a difficult problem for stylisticians. Since stylistics cannot avoid the question of values, it can be said at this stage that, whether on the ground of utility or aesthetics, the value of a stylistic feature may be judged on a three-point scale, namely, gain, loss or zero.

Behind every influence, there is a definite rearrangement of earlier variants, which positively increases the expansive capacity of the language by stimulus and encourages hitherto dormant processes like adoption of language features, dialect features, features from dormant *supraglossia* like Persian or Sanskrit or from neighbouring languages. This also results into the exploitation of the possibilities of the native resources of language. The unconscious desire of the language community to weed out unwanted (non-structural, non-prosodic, cacophonous and unsuitable or surplus) semantic norms and variants for better, shorter, suitable rhythmic features is thus fulfilled.

Influences increase the structural complexity and encourage new meaning patterns quantitatively and qualitatively.

During the formative period, as in the First phase of the nineteenth century Marathi, variants are borrowed without norms. The period style can be said to have been accomplished when both norms and variants are found having a constant form. Only a developed prose permits variants of norms.[45]

A borrowed (and new) norm or variant in the language essentially shows deviation from the existing contiguous norms or variants in the system.

Because the borrowed feature is the need of the *langue* (5.1 and 5.3), the functional flexibility of a borrowed feature establishes priority of use in the individual *parole*. In a sentence therefore a borrowed stylistic feature creates a nonsymmetrical balance. It carries more semantic load and emphasis than native features. At this point, stylistics merges into literary criticism. Therefore, mere recording of the feature as 'influence' would be enough at this stage of influence study. It should proceed by recording parallelisms between the source language and the receiving language without attaching any values to the process of borrowing, because at this initial stage mostly all the borrowed features are vacillating until their macro-contextualization values are fixed in the written system. The question of gain or loss often transcends the limits of period style.

                    The Influence of English on Marathi

Having fixed the criteria of comparison, the next task is to establish levels of comparison corresponding to comparable subsystems of textual styles in the two languages. The actual process of investigating the influence of English on Marathi begins with comparing stylistic features of Marathi texts written before the contact of English with those in the nineteenth-century texts written after the contact. The two points—One fixed at the eighteenth-century set of norms reconstructed as a workable base-line from which to triangulate the change, and the other moving towards the end of the nineteenth century—provide the first data for the study.[46] Some hypothesized norms may need verification by internal reconstruction, but all the old features need not be reconstructed; synchronic descriptions of old Marathi texts is adequate for the purpose. Broad stylistic features statable in norms can be obtained to begin with and more detailed variants may be left for further research. A hair-splitting search does not help because word order in Marathi has been fairly loose and several borrowed features may find formal similarity with old Marathi constructions (see 5.5.3-C). Stylistic variations are infinite and a formal structure of a stray feature is likely to be found in the past records. What is important is to see whether a feature can be related to the process of internal change, i.e., whether norm or variant is developed internally as a part of the stylistic system of the period. In other words, we should ascertain whether it is *actually* borrowed, with the help of another comparison, namely, with the feature in the system of English.

The second step, therefore, is to relate and correlate the innovations in the first data to the two phenomena of linguistic change :

1. Change due to borrowing.

2. Change due to other factors including internal development, irregularity etc.[47]

The third step is a comparison of the seemingly borrowed features with their originals in the source language. Change due to borrowing can be established with comparison on the basis of a full understanding of the structures of both the languages. The model can be presented diagrammatically as follows :

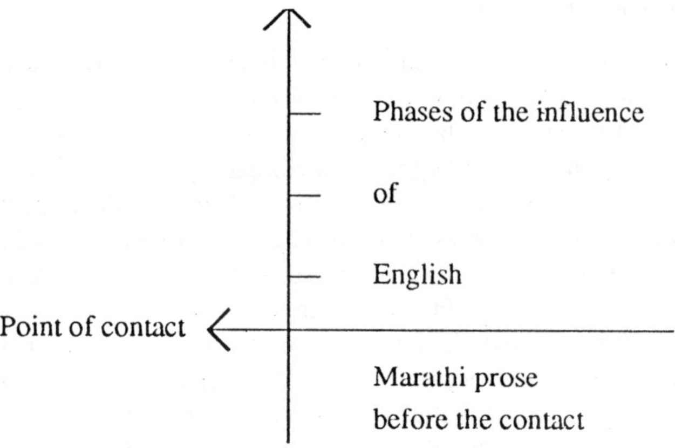

It should be noted that we are not comparing two languages, but sections of the languages which we call stylistic subsystems within the languages, the adequate knowledge of whose structures is assumed. In general, each subsystem in Marathi should be formally treated in comparison with the same level in English. However, since the two languages have different structures, every feature need not assume one to one correspondence, because every parallelism does not always proceed from an influence. When an innovated feature investigated by historical comparison shows a high degree of overt formal agreement with the suspected source feature and is isolated in the system, especially at the initial stage, such a feature can be safely assigned to influence. At a later stage such features are regularized in the system of the receiving language, but their mode of entry needs close observation.

The model is primarily constructed for the macro-linguistic categories in period style. Comparisons of minute variants and less obvious and unidentifiable features should be left for further research. It is worth mentioning here that as an enquiry into the stylistic influence, comparison should also mean comparison for trying out the model.

5.5 LEVELS OF COMPARISON

The problem of accuracy and precision in stylistic analysis of the text seems to defy linguists and stylisticians alike.[48] To the extent that the levels of analysis are firmly rooted in their corresponding linguistic categories, the structural subsystems are well taken care of. The present provisional base developed in comparative descriptive linguistics, however, needs to be modified in relation to the textual content under investigation. As pointed out in 1.3.2, a microlinguistic focus is inadequate for the purpose of stylistic analysis, because it leaves out the most important subsystem of the style of texts, namely, the sentential, which is the kernel

The Influence of English on Marathi

of textual system in prose style. A data-oriented model rather than a purely theoretical one, which will cover a broader range of levels that allow occassional reference to micro-levels as well will be more convenient for the investigation of stylistic influence. Again, the levels of analysis should be so devised as to give scope for emphasis on the comparison of two systems belonging to different cultural traditions and reflect the different stages of influence without violating the frame of reference. Further, the levels of comparison must not deviate too much from the categories of general linguistic theory.

The model constructed for the purpose of this study is based on the concept of linguistic text as a writing system. A text is a semiological structure, a system of subsystems not all of which correspond to clear-cut structural categories of language. Categories like sentence-linkers, paragraphs and sentence-rhythm often belong to the borderland of various structural categories. According to Tynianov, "the system is not a co-operation based on the equality of all elements."[49] Again, in a contact situation some elements are found to be more dominant than others. Our model therefore has to modify the stock of categories established for the analysis of single-language texts and include a few other significant levels of analysis. Imprecise categories may be provisionally ignored or formally related to other contiguous categories for the purpose of adequacy, so that we can establish the homogeneity of statable and precise categories.

In the actual analysis of texts, it is found that relationship between norms changes according to the level of analysis we adopt. Modification of one feature in one subsystem causes accommodation of another in the same or related subsystem, because what belongs to grammar in English may belong to syntax in Marathi, or a syntactic device in English is reflected by lexical devices in Marathi. Also, a feature may enter simultaneously into relation with similar features belonging to other levels,or a feature may demand treatment at more than one level simultaneously. Cross-references, therefore, will have to be made at each level. In some cases, a borrowed stylisitic feature may have to be described at one of the levels, usually the earlier in serial order, or at the level which is the most dominant. This may be done for the purpose of economy and clarity and not to emphasize the prominence of that level.

The model constructed for the purpose of analysing stylistic influence and applied to specimen passages in Chapters 6, 7 and 8 can be described as follows :

1. The extra-textual level which includes statable literary-
        aesthetic substance in relation to period style.

2. The graphic level which includes

        (A)   Script,

        (B)   Graphology,

        (C)   Punctuation.

3. The structural level which includes

        (A)   Inter-sentential linking,

        (B)   Sentential structure,

        (C)   Syntactic structure including word order,

        (D)   Micro-linguistic categories.

5.5.1 THE EXTRA-TEXTUAL LEVEL

The level is employed to point out stylistic influences determining the direction of change in period style. Self-contained contexts exclusively internal to text are inssuficient to account for all the stylistic phenomena. The cultural function of a text is linguistically not always relevant, though in acculturation studies it is crucial and extremely relevant to structural changes. As seen in 4.2, literary-aesthetic substance with reference to individual and genre styles in a particular phase of the period style often becomes instrumental to foreign influence. The extra-textual level would also serve as an introduction to other levels as it refers to language planning, important literary movements and activities and literary milieu as already discussed in the previous chapters. The treatment of data at this level has to be ultimately dependent on the contexts of period style (see Chapter 3 and 4.2.1).

5.5.2 THE GRAPHIC LEVEL

As seen in 2.4.3 the writing system of Marathi prose before the contact of English was most impervious to reasoned thinking, and consequently to growth of stylistic norms. The influence of English effected a shift from oral to written tradition, from verse to prose and from manuscript culture to print culture. Since writing became the sole medium of expression of the new age (see 1.1.4) the communicative function of the textual system dominated the thinking process of the whole period, especially in the First and Second phases. The graphic level is essential for the analysis of influence not only because it marks the beginning of the period style but also because it records the entire process of linguistic influence from borrowing to language standardization (see 5.6 for its limitations). It offers concentrated and uniform visual response to stylistic features as written signs. As a storage of social memory, it is particularly conducive to large-scale borrowing from a foreign language.[50] The

        The Influence of English on Marathi

influence of English on Marathi at the graphic level can be viewed at three sublevels :

(A) Script : meaning a set of letters used in writing. It would be seen how script is standardized in relation to speedy growth of uniform pronunciation throughout the language community.

(B) Graphology : meaning formats and typographical arrangements of textual features, like norms of line-length in different prose-genres, spacing between words, sentences and paragraphs and insetting, margins etc. It would be seen how these norms borrowed from English affected the structural levels also.

(C) Punctuation : Since nearly all punctuation marks are borrowed from English, the effects of these including intra- and inter-sentential spacing, will be studied in relation to logical standards introduced by the English punctuation system—its effect on the structural level, especially in respect of sentence prosody, sentence types, syntactic patterns, and other categories.

5.5.3 THE STRUCTURAL LEVEL

The structural level being too wide in its implication, the area covered by this level has to be restricted to the following sublevels which are most significant in respect of influence study :

(A)	Inter-sentential linking : To study features of linking two or more successive sentences.

(B)	Sentential structure : To study sentence prosody, sentence length, types of sentence and clausal structures. Qualitative changes are to be particularly considered.

(C)	Syntactic structure : To study change in word order. Though syntactic changes are presumably numerous, their investigation will be difficult and in many cases almost impossible because, as stated earlier, Marathi word order is so loose that a particular pattern cannot be readily assigned to borrowing. Syntactic influence will therefore be investigated to the extent of broad categories which exhibit clear evidence of borrowing from English. Moreover syntax, unlike sentence, has direction, and therefore it cannot be treated as a static category in influence study.[51] Borrowing of phrasal and clausal patterns and syntactic punctuation will need more attention, because these two features go contrary to the nature of Marathi word order. Gains and losses effected by the analytical structure of English categories in the synthetic structure of Marathi also need attention.

(D)	Micro-linguistic categories : For practical purposes, the lexical and grammatical levels are merged because independent treatment of words and grammar is found to be repetitive and over-lapping. However, a limited reference to these two categories will be made in the next few chpaters. A full treatment of loans could be covered in independent semantic studies. Quantitatively, the area covered by lexical borrowing in period style is so vast that it would require a full-length study. It would even require an independent model. Where a gammatical feature affects a broader category, like syntax or sentence, it will be discussed in relation to these features. Losses and gains in lexical and grammatical categories in general will not be noted.

Phonic substance is distributed at different levels : the nonsegmental is treated at the sentential level and the segmental at the graphic, because both phonological and graphological levels deal with the same substance in the text. Most influences in respect of pauses and accent can be treated at the punctuation level.

Phonological and morphological borrowings are the fewest in Marathi, and they are of little relevance to our study. However, specific cases of importance in these categories will be noted at the lexical level, since the lexical subsystem is the nearest to these features.

                                        The Influence of English on Marathi

CHAPTER SIX

The Early Phase : 1818—1847
Advent of a New Standard

6.1 A GENERAL NOTE ON THE PROCEDURE IN CHAPTERS 6, 7 AND 8

At this stage of the present study, we turn to the actual analysis of stylistic influence by linguistic stylistic method. The analysis attempts to furnish a cross section of the evolution of period style under the influence of English.

As the points of contact were numerous in the sudden exposure of Marathi to English in the First phase (1818—1847), Marathi texts written in this phase exhibit unique features at all the subsystems, from the graphic to the phonological. The area of analysis, therefore, in this phase is extensive. As the contact matures in the later phases (Chapters 7 and 8), the borrowed features of the graphic and micro-linguistic categories are found to be stabilizing in inter-relationship with the native ones in the texts written during these phases (1847-1874 and 1874-1890). So the focus of analysis is gradually turned toward the innovations at more active subsystems. The principles of norm formation in other subsystems are more or less stereotyped in these phases and therefore do not deserve special notice. Repetitive observations are thus avoided, though occasional reference to the graphic and micro-linguistic categories is made when a major change is reflected at these levels.

As stated in 1.2.3, this analysis makes no attempt to furnish a complete picture of the entire sets of stylistic features at different subsystems. Statistical tests in future research alone would be able to provide such data regarding individual features in period style.

The passages in Chapters 6, 7 and 8 arranged generally in chronological order, are representative and are selected according to the criteria suggested by the analytical framework adopted for this study (1.2.3, 1.3.3 and 5.4).

The passages also represent the spectrum of various genre styles, styles of individual works and of individual authors belonging to different castes, classes, dialects, sexes and age groups. Observations regarding graphic categories (script, composition and punctuation) are based on original editions available in the libraries of Marathwada university, Aurangabad; Mumbai Marathi Granth Sangrahalaya, Bombay; School of Oriental and African Studies, University of London, the British Museum and India Office, London. It should be noted in this context that it is extremely difficult to relate the chronological evolution of Devanagari printing with the writing system of Marathi for lack of original manuscripts written in the nineteenth century.[1] Both lithography and typographic printing continued simultaneously until the last quarter of the century. Lithography being strongly idiosyncratic in style defies any generalization regarding graphic norms. It would be necessary to undertake an independent project to study the progress of the orthographic system in the period.

We have confined ourselves here to the graphic level only as a correlative of structural level within a system, and not treated it for its own sake. Though there is evidence to believe that the authors' punctuation was different from the printers' we have no access to the authors' manuscripts and the only data that we have is the printers' version, and therefore not much can be said about this aspect of graphic style. However, there is evidence to suggest that both authors' and printers' graphic styles were variations of the English punctuation system until the end of the nineteenth century. Until the mid-nineteenth century, even in English the graphic norms were still wavering and English punctuation system was not fully settled to distinguish clearly between oratorical and syntactic pauses.[2]

The graded scale designed to show degrees of completeness or incompleteness of sense in each component of sentence in English began to operate in Marathi in a full-fledged form only toward the end of the Second phase. Major Candy's *Viramchinhanchi Paribhasha* (1850) is the first detailed guidebook of Marathi punctuation, and it reveals a total ignorance of Marathi sentence prosody.[3] Even grammarians were not sure of their punctuation norms. The controversies regarding 'pure writing' in the last quarter of the century also suggest the irrational principles behind the imposition of English punctuation system on Marathi.

    The Influence of English on Marathi

Thousands of words and phrases were graphized for the first time. As Molesworth put it, "our work . . . was to reduce to order a boundless chaos."[4] Texts in the First and Second phases are either over-punctuated or under-punctuated or irregularly punctuated. We have therefore taken the printer's graphic system as the period standard and presented some photocopied passages from the more widely read books to facilitate the discussion of the purely graphic aspect of writing system in the period. The other passages included in Chapters 6, 7 and 8 are reproduced from the original or standard printed editions.

The following abbreviations are used in the footnotes to the specimen passages in Chapters 6, 7 and 8 :

E   :   English

M   :   Marathi

Skt : Sanskrit

6.2 INTRODUCTION

From the first documentary evidence of the exposure of Marathi to the norms of English writing system in 1805 to a laborious pidgin leaning heavily toward a willing acceptance of English norms in the 1840s, this phase reveals full exposure of all its subsystems to English. With the increasing contact of the English textual system through ever-expanding bilingualism in the first generation of English-educated Maharashtrians, the texts in this phase reveal various degrees of interference phenomenon caused by indiscriminate and unplanned borrowing.

The first English-knowing Marathi authors, translators and employees of the East India Company on the one hand and the Marathi-knowing Englishmen and Anglo-Indians on the other do not seem to have been aware of the tradition of Marathi prose, though the Shastris had a strong background of Sanskrit learning, especially of the traditional scriptures and pseudo-sciences (3.3.3).

Till the first generation of bilingual authors took over literary leadership in the 1850s, the prose exhibits a complete disorganization of structural categories, though at the graphic level it has absorbed all the subsystems of script, standardizing punctuation and composition (5.5.2). The irregular punctuation betrays the wide gap between the indigenous substance and the foreign norms. Though the printed word became open to all, reading and writing was hardly a habit of social inter-communication (1.1.3 and 3.3.3). However, despite the lack of practice in reading and writing, literacy was growing in all sections of society.

Bombay being the centre of the new print culture, several communities found easy access to the new prose which was in fact encouraged by American, Scottish, Welsh and English missionaries and by the liberal section of the Company's civil servants. There was shortage of printed materials. M. G. Ranade lists a total of just 43 books published during this whole phase. Since most early writers belonged to the Konkan region of Maharashtra, they introduced local dialectal features as substitute to English features. The new bilingual writers faced a number of odd problems—from the choice of script to the prejudicial public opinion regarding printed books, which were regarded as contaminating and anti-nativistic. Lack of printing machinery, absence of native models to suit the new needs, the dual standards in orthography —*Modi* and *Nagari*, lack of rationality in the social milieu, a general unawareness of the concept of national prose and a state of overwhelming bewilderment at the initial stage of western influence—these are some of the factors that characterize the poverty of prose in this phase. Total absence of readership further increased the impossibility of new prose being born indigenously.

In such circumstances Missionaries in Tanjore, Serampore and Bombay had found a new way of literary communication by inaugurating modern prose. In Bombay the prose standards were set by secular Englishmen in the 1820s. It is in their whole-hearted support for vernacularization of education that we find the roots of modern Marathi prose. The moralistic tone that persists in most of the prose written in this (and also the following) phase indicates compromises arrived at between the Christian proselytizing and the Romantic-Utilitarian ideals for educating the Hindus in English learning (3.2.1, 3.3.3 and 3.5).

In schools *writing* skills were given more prominence than those of reading or speaking, a fact recorded by a number of contemporaries. For example, Balshastri Jambhekar, in his report on Village Native Schools in 1841 to the Secretary to the Board of Education writes : "Great pains are bestowed on writing, but not so much on reading . . . No printed books of any kind are as yet used in any part of the country."[5] It is to be expected therefore that the graphic level should be the focus of borrowing at this stage.[6] English education was in ever increasing demand. There was hardly any controversy regarding language use, content of books, the vanishing Sanskrit learning or the changing values in society during this phase.

The passages selected to represent the prose written in this phase show an overall imposition of a foreign writing system on the native one, as discussed in Chapter 2 (see 2.4.4 and passages in Chapter 2 : Annexures A to F).

6.3 SPECIMEN PASSAGES WITH ANALYTICAL NOTES

1. 1805: Vaijnath Kanphade and Dr. William Carey; "Devnagari Lipitil Pahila Mudrit Granth", *Dr. Kolte Gaurav Granth*, ed. Madhukar Ashtikar (1969), pp. 139-40.

The passage on the following page represents the highly anglicized or pidgin tradition of Missionary prose. It is dominated by Varhadi dialectal features. Its original is *Matthew* 1 : 16—23 of *the Authorised King James Version*.

१६. तथा यांकूबान युसफास् जन्म[1] दिल्हे ते[2] मारियाचे स्वामी ज्याचे[3] पोटात् यिशु जन्मलेत् ज्यास्[4] म्हणतेत् ख्रीष्ठ[5] ।[6]

१७. याकरिता[7] आबराहामावधि दाउदापर्य्यन्त्[8] अवघे चौदा पुरुष आणि दाउदावधि बाबेलीं घेऊन जाणे पर्य्यन्त्[9] चौदा पुरुष ।

१८. यिशु ख्रष्टाचे[10] जन्म या रीतीचे होते । त्याहांची माय[11] मारिया यूसफास् वाग्दत्ता[12] होन त्याहाचे संसर्गां[13] पुर्व्वीं ते धर्मात्मा क (डे) न्[14]

१९. गर्भवती झाली होतीत । त्याहांचा स्वामी युसफ याथार्थिक[15] मनुष्य होऊन आणि प्रकाशी[16] त्याहांस् अपयशी करवायास इछा न[17] करून् ।

२०. गुप्त[18] त्याहांस रूपी त्याग करायाचे मनात केले[19] परन्तु[20] या विषयीं चिन्ता करिता[21] २ ईश्वराच दूतान त्याहांस स्वप्नात् दर्शन् दिल्हे आणि बोलतेत्[21] अहो दाउदाचे सन्तान युसफ तुम्ची जाया मारियास्[22] ग्रहण करायास्

२१. भीत नका होऊं कां[23] किं जे[24] त्याहाचे गर्भीं धृत आहेत् ते धर्मात्मा कडून तेही पुत्र प्रसव होतील आणि त्याहाच नाव तुम्ही यिशु ठेवाल कां किं

२२. त्याहाचे लोकांस् त्याहाचे[25] पापाहून[26] ते उद्धार कर्त्तिल् । पाहा[27] एक कन्या गर्भवती होऊन पुत्र प्रसव होईल्[28] आणि त्याहांच नाव ते

1. Verbalization is transferred to M. nominalizaton, for E. *begot.*

2. Pronominal determiner; backward definitization of note 3 below.

3. Relativization of 2, insertion downgrading following components.

4. Branching within relativization, creating unbalanced predicate.

5. Non-standardized graphization, (see variant at 10).

6. Full stop mistaken for the traditional end of verse line; this irregularity persists in the following units, disturbing sentence pattern.

7. Sentence linker substitute for E. *so.*

8. Variant of E. *from . . . to* with M. oblique forms.

9. Variant of E. *until,* gerundivization after E. norm.

10. See 5 above.

11. Variant from dialect, non-standardized.

12. Skt. nominal variant for E. verbal *espoused*; stimulus to Sktism.

13. Nominal for E. verbal *come together.*

14. Non-standardized feature for E. *causing pregnancy by.*

15. Calque for E. *just.*

16. Substitute synonym for E. *public.*

17. Nominalization, negative + verb participle after E. *not willing.*

18. Adverbial use of adjective, substitute of E. *privily.*

19. Verbal variant narrowing E. *minded.*

20. Sentence linker downgraded as conjunction for lack of punctuation mark.

21. Mixing of tenses ; simple past + simple present for E. present participle *saying,* causing need of connective.

22. Case inflexion causing unbalanced adjective + Noun apposition.

23. Connective for E. causal *for* + traditional Persian connective.

24. Relativization is suspended owing to M. place of subject in the following passive construction.

25,26 For E. *from their sins,* pronominal repetition according to E. norms.

27. E. vocative ineffective in M. for lack of punctuation.

28. E. Verbalization *bring forth* transferred to Noun + copula, nominalization.

29. E. clause *which being interpreted* is substituted by Skt. word.

ह्या देशांतील जे इंग्लिश भाषण शिकायास इच्छितान त्यांस शि
कविणारावांचून समजायास ही लाहान पोथी केली आहे व जे इंग्लि
श लोक मराठी भाषण शिकायास इच्छितान त्यांस ही उपाय आहे॥

ह्या पोथीची योजना ऐसी आहे कीं

१ शब्दावळींसारिखा एके एके शब्दाचा अर्थ वेगळा वेगळा सं
गीतला आहे॥

२ तेच शब्द गोष्टींत मिळवून दाखविले आहेन॥

३ जीं प्रयोजने उद्योगांगांत उपयोगी पडतात व बुद्धीस वाढवि
नान व अंतःकरणास शुद्ध करितात नीं निवडलीं आहेन॥

ह्या योजनेप्रमाणे ही सर्व पोथी बहुधा घडली आहे॥

प्रथम शिकणाराने जे शब्द वेगळे वेगळे सांगीतले आहेन ते फार पाठ
करावे आणि मग जसे गोष्टींत मिळविले आहेन तसे शिकावे॥ ला
हान जों वाक्यें नीं फार पाठ करावीं आणि भाषणाची शुद्ध रीत स
मजायासाठीं प्रत्येक वाक्याचा अर्थ समजून घ्याबा॥

शिकणाराने याप्रकारें ही सगळी पोथी शिकली असतां इंग्लिश भा
षण एवढें समजेल कीं बहुत प्रयोजनाविषईं आपली कल्पना म्हणू
बोलूं सकेल आणि शब्दावळीचे साह्य करून इंग्लिश भाषणांतील सा
धारण गोष्टया वाचायास आणि समजायास सकेल॥

ह्या दोह्या भाषणांत जे निपुण आहेन ते असें पाहानील कीं दो
न्ही भाषणे जोडिल्यामुळें वाक्यें क्वचित अगत्य साधारण पडलीं आहेन॥

ह्या देशांतील सर्व ज्यांस विलायती लोकांशी कामाकरितां प्रसंग
पडतो आणि जे बुद्धीस अभ्यास करायासाठीं विलायती कळा विद्या
समजायास इच्छितान त्यां सर्वांस ही पोथी फार उपयोगी पडेल असा
अभिप्राय धरला आहे॥

2.   1818 (?); Gordon Hall'; *A Help in acquiring a Knowledge of English* (1818 ?), preface p.2.

The script is fairly uniform in most of its characters except that the conjucts esp. constituting श, र and य as one of their components are still non-standardized and irrational. The adoption of Nagari in place of the more popular Modi (5.5-A) is a drastic change in Marathi writing system (cf. Chapter 2: Annexure F 1, 2 and 3). The *anusvara* and the length grapheme are still irregular.

Punctuation according to English norms has far reaching effects on the structure of Marathi. The traditional vertical bars used as full stop still survive. The full stop as a norm of English textual system is being imposed with its full logical value, though its rhythmic value is missing in Marathi texts. In the absence of other punctuations marks, esp. the comma, the early 19th century texts show complete dependence of the sentence on the full stop. The graded scale of comma, semi-colon, colon and full stop was absent in Marathi prose until 1840s. Capitalization was imported into Marathi but was found to be superfluous and therefore abandoned, which made the full stop an absolute sentence marker. In the absence of the comma, sentence length is always moderate, though sentence connectors are seen pressurizing the sentence length making the sentence longer than the traditional one (2.4.3). Compositional features such as the format, paragraph and section have revolutionized the arrangement of logical units. Indenting, margins and numbering are some of the new features. Other books published in this phase show that compositional and other graphic features in typographic as well as litghographic printing are stabilized in a comparatively short period. For example, the dash to indicate the end of the paragraph and other irregular punctuation features have undergone speedy changes so that by 1847 these features have been fairly standardized under the influence of English punctuation system.

3

ह्या देशांतील जे[1] इंग्लिश भाषण शिकायास इच्छितात त्यांस शिकविणारावांचून समजायास ही लहान पोथी केली आहे व जे[2] इंग्लिश लोक मराठी भाषण शिकायास इच्छितात त्यांस ही उपाय[3] आहे ॥[4]

ह्या पोथीची योजना ऐसी आहे कीं[5]

१ शब्दावळीसारिखा एके एके[6] शब्दाचा अर्थ वेगळा वेगळा[7] सांगीतला आहे ॥

२ तेच शब्द गोष्टींत[8] मिळउन[9] दाखविले आहेत ॥

३ जीं[10] प्रयोजने उद्योगांत[11] उपयोगी पडतात व बुद्धीस[12] वाढवितात व अंतःकरणास शुद्ध करितात तीं निवडलीं आहेत ॥

ह्या योजनेप्रमाणे[13] ही सर्व पोथी बहुधा घडली[14] आहे ॥ प्रथम[15] शिकणाराने[16] जे शब्द वेगळे वेगळे सांगीतले आहेत ते फार[17] पाठ करावे आणि मग जसे गोष्टींत मिळविले आहेत तसे शिकावे ॥ लहान जीं वाक्यें तीं फार पाठ करावीं आणि भाषणाची शुद्ध[18] रीत समजायासाठीं प्रत्येक[19] वाक्याचा अर्थ समजून घ्यावा ॥

शिकणाराने याप्रकारें ही सगळी पोथी शिकली असतां इंग्लिश भाषण एवढें समजेल कीं[20] बहुत प्रयोजनाविषईं आपली कल्पना शुद्ध बोलुं सकेल आणि शब्दावळीचे साह्येकडून[21] इंग्लिश भाषणांतील साधारण[22] पोथ्या वाचायास आणि समजायास[23] सकेल ॥

ह्या दोहों भाषणांत जे निपुण आहेत ते असें पाहातील[24] कीं दोन्ही भाषणें जोडण्यामुळें वाक्यें[25] क्वचित अगत्य[26] साधारण[27] पडलीं आहेत ॥

ह्या देशांतील सर्व ज्यांस[28] विलायती लोकांसी कामाकरितां प्रसंग पडतो आणि जे बुद्धीस[29] अभ्यास करण्यासाठीं विलायती कळा विद्या समजायास इच्छितात त्यां सर्वांस ही पोथी फार उपयोगी पडेल असा अभिप्राय धरला[30] आहे ॥

3. 1818 (?); Gordon Hall; *A Help in Acquiring a Knowledge of English* (1818 ?), preface p. 2.

The passage is a preface to a most popular bilingual grammar which ran into several editions during this phase.

1. Relativization, making relative pronoun as subject of the clause, but suppressed as indirect object owing to M. word order and impersonalization of the subject of the sentence.
2. Relativization with relative pronoun. used as determiner in the latter part of the compound sentence.
3. Variant for E. *facility.*
4. Traditional full stop converted to E. norm as a logical device; it has a little more value than discontinuity device in the following discourse.
5. Overparagraphing owing to absence of comma, semicolon or colon.
6. Frequentative lexical device used in absence of norm, see 7 and 9 below.
7. Adverbial frequentative device.
8. Vague variant for E. *composition.*
9. Vague variant for E. *explained.*
10. One correlative premodifier used for three successive clauses joined by additives to a simple-sentence clause to make it a complex sentence.
11. Ambiguous variant for E. *business.*
12. Noun in dative forced as substitute to prepositional phrase in E. *improving to the mind.*
13. New variant for E. *plan.*
14. Passivization converted to M. impersonal construction making inanimate object as subject.
15. Ambiguous use for both adjective and adverb.
16. Verbal noun after E. *learner*; a word formative device.
17. Wrong variant for E. *thoroughly.*
18. Variant for E. *correct use.*
19. See 6 above.
20. E. co-ordinator *so as. . . to* merged into M. *ki.*
21. E. phrase *by the help of* reverted.
22. Vague lexical variant for E. *ordinary,* overlapping semantic value with 27 below.
23. M. compound verb grammatically distorted participle for E. *to be able to understand.*
24. Inclusive semantic variant for E. *observed.*
25. Rhythm of word order is disturbed by postposed subject.
26,27. Juxtapositioning of traditional adverb and irregular variant for E. *necessarily impaired.* (See 22 above).
28. See 1 above.
29. See 12 above; variant due to lack of adjectivization.
30. For E. *it is hoped,* passivization restructured in active construction; impersonalization is retained by making abstract noun as subject.

4

वर्णांत भेद दोन आहेत.[1] स्वर आणि व्यंजनें.[2] आतां त्यांचीं स्थानें त्यांचे उच्चारणें[3] करून[4] जाणिजेताहेत. केवळ स्वरां चा उच्चार होतो. उदाहरण.[5] अ. आ. इ. ई.[6] तसा[7] केवळ व्यंजना चा सुखाने[8] उच्चार होत नाहीं.[9] तर त्यास मागें अथवा पुढें स्वर असावा. कारण.[10] स्वरसाहित्यावां चून व्यंजनां चें च[11] यथास्थित उच्चारण होत नाहीं. उदाहरण.[12] अकस्मात् या शब्दांतील प्रथमवर्ण अकार आहे. त्यां चें उच्चारण सुखाने होतें. अ. तसें क दुसरें अक्षर.[13] यांतील अकार टाकून केवळ ककार व्यंजन या चें उच्चारण होत नाहीं.[14] आणि तिसरें अक्षर स्मात् यांतील आकार टाकून राहिले सकार मकार तकार हीं व्यंजनें यां चें च केवळ उच्चारण होत नाहीं. त्यांत स्वर आहे तर सुखानें[15] होतें. स्मात्

4. 1822; Jagannath Shastri Kramavant, Gangadhar Shastri Phadke and Bal Shastri Ghagave; *Maharashtra Bhasheche Vyakaran,* ed. A. K. Priyolkar (1954), p. 2.

The Shastris who wrote one of the first grammars of Marathi, from which this passage is taken, had to follow English punctuation system. The result is the total breakdown of the sentence ryhthm. The abrupt ending of sentences., too frequent a use of the copula which is sometimes el- lipted, and uncertain sentence length — are some of the major effects of the imposition of English punctuation system.

1. Copula is unnecessary, but exists for lack of colon.

2. Copula is dropped, as full stop serves its purpose.

3. Verbalization is adjusted with the nominal term.

4. Dots to indicate dental series of affricates; this proved to be a shortlived variant despite Dadoba Pandurang's persuasive use of this feature in his most influential grammar.

5,10,12. Full stop for colon.

6,9,13,14. Full stop for commas and semi-colon at the end.

7,9. Linker necessitated by preceding full stop.

8,15 Variant for E. *ease.*

11. Emphasis misplaced after E. word order.

5

गोविंद - थट्टा नाहीं मुली, मी हें खरेंच सांगतों.

वेणू - तर[1] मला आठवत नाहीं तें ?

गोविंद - तें खरेंच, पण हा हिंदोळा[2], मीं दारीं कधीं टांगला ह्याची तुला आठवण आहे ?

वेणू - कां ? तो सदां[3] आहे तसाच आहे.

गोविंद - तसें कसें होईल मुली ! तूं ह्या लाहान्में[4] बाळा एवढी होतीस ते वेळेपासून हा हिंदोळा टांगला[5] आहे.

वेणे - खरेंच काय ! तर तें माझ्या लक्षांत कसें राहिलें नाहीं ?

गोविंद - बाळें लाहानगीं असतात तेव्हां जवळ काय होतें[6] तें त्यांस समजत नसतें. हा तुझा लाहान[7] भाऊ तुझ्या एवढा होईल तेव्हां तूं त्यास आजच्या गोष्टी पूस कीं " [8] मी त्यादिवशी तुला नाव घ्यायास शिकवीत होतें, त्याची तुला आठवण आहे ?" मग तुला समजेल त्याला आठवतें कीं नाहीं तें.

वेणे - काय ?[9] आणि मीही असेंच आईचें थान[10] पीत होतें ?

गोविंद - होय ह्यांत काय संशय ?[11] तुजकरितां[12] काय काय श्रम पडले आहेत मुली ! तूं अशी अशक्त होतीस, कीं तुला कांहीं खाव्वत[13] नसे; आह्मी प्रतिक्षणीं भिऊं, कीं ही आतां मरेल[14]; तुझी आई ह्मणे[15], "अगे माझे बापडे[16], तुझे प्राण धाबरे होतील." असे ह्मणून तिनें तुला मोठे श्रमानें थोडथोडें थानचें दूध प्यावयास शिकविलें.

वेणू - आह्मागे माझे बये[17], तर मला खाव्यास तूं प्रथम शिकविलें नाहीं बरें ?

गोविंद - होय माझे लेंकरा[18], तुझें आईनें तुला थान प्यावयास शिकविलें, तेव्हां तूं तुष्ट आणि पुष्ट झालीस. असे श्रम तिनें तुजकरितां दोन वर्षे पर्यंत रात्रदिवस केले. कोणेसमयीं भागवटघामुळें तुझें आईस अंमळ नीज लागली असतां तूं रडून तिला उपद्रव[19] करावा, मग तिनें गलबलून[20] उठून तुझ्या पाळण्यापाशीं येऊन ह्मणावें[21]. " वेणे वेणे, बेटा, उगी राहा; तुला भूक लागली असेल, माझे बये." मग तिनें तुला थानाशीं धरावें.

1849; S.K. Chhatre; *Balmitra-1* 2nd ed., rev. by Major T.
Candy (1849), pp. 5-6.

The gap between written prose and conversational language is clearly demonstrated in this passage. 'Konkanisms', a dominant feature of this phase, are frequent. The original of Chhatre's *Balmitra* is the English translation of Berquin's French *L'Ami des enfants*.

1.   Linker for E. *but;* variant unsettled.

2.   The comma is superfluous.

3.   Variant from traditional poetic register.

4.   Adjective + noun, oblique form of adjective, dialectal; variant unsettled (cf. 7 below).

5.   E. perfect passive modulation converted to M. compound verb.

6.   Distance in tenses maintained according to E. tense system : simple past + habitual present.

7.   Adjective without oblique form + noun, see 4 above.

8.   Direct speech beginning without a comma, juxtaposed with traditional (Pers.) *ki* for E. *that*; feature substituting comma.

9.   Forced borrowing; M. question word followed by E. question mark; superfluous.

10.   Dialectal feature; an example of stimulus borrowing after E. *breast;* non-standardized.

11.   Variant combining question with exclamation.

12.   Poetic register, traditional.

13.   Script : consonant conjunction non-standardized.

14.   The semi-colon is superfluous.

15.   Comma before direct speech; non-standardized. (See 8 above & 11 below.)

16,17,18.   Vocatives; an example of forced borrowing evident in two contrasting situations : one reported and the other direct.

19.   Variant of semantic enlarging, non-standardized.

20.   Adverb + verb, adverbial use to indicate nuances.

21.   Frequentative use of subjunctive mixed with habitual past after E. *would*-construction.

6.4 CONCLUSION

This phase reveals an interesting feature of linguistic acculturation in that it initiates a permanent borrowing relationship with English. English is introduced as a *supraglossia* replacing Sanskrit. Since the rational basis of prose is introduced through a planned programme of translations, educational textbooks and journalism, the entire focus of borrowing is on English literary texts. The borrowing relationship is so firmly established that the traditional native features remain dormant throughout the phase, allowing the points of contact to increase at all subsystems, though at varying degrees. This phenomenon results in an unequal proportion of influence at different subsystems. It is most complete at the graphic level, fairly high at the lexical, and moderately advancing at other subsystems. Several borrowed features are haphazardly adjusted in the subsystems. Blank holes created by the unequal influence at different subsystems have to be filled up temporarily by approximated semantic features, creating variants which are not rigidly demarcated. The bilingual Marathi writers, therefore, develop a general mechanism of linguistic borrowing which affects the whole stylistic system of Marathi prose during this phase.

Specimens of individual and genre styles in this phase are extremely rare—a fact which can be related to several socio-political and sociolinguistic factors (4.2.2 and 4.2.3). When the period style is absent, it is difficult for the writers to find their personal styles which depend on the overall relationship with the norms of period style. The prose in this phase is dominated by an impersonal tone as no specific readership exists for the new prose. The slow-moving and laboured prose is dominated by two extremes : 1. A style altogether remote from the colloquial Marathi, and 2. A style which merely graphizes the syntagmatic interference caused by English norms in Marathi subsystems. Nearly all the prose works of this phase reveal a graded influence of English structures which can be spread between the composition of type 1 and type 2. This is partly the result of the lack of writer-reader relationship. The writers working under the Western value system create a psychological gap between the text and the reader.

Numerous experiments in graphic subsystems are for the first time introduced. This is the greatest gain of the prose during this phase. Numerous lexical and syntactic innovations are noticeable. Most of these innovations are supported by the introduction of English punctuation which affects the length of sentence in the main. The frequent use of the new types of sentence, namely, interrogative, negative and exclamatory, shows a noticeable departure from the 18th century syntactic structures and discourse cohesion (2.4.4 B). This feature is facilitated by the importation of new punctuation marks—especially the comma, the question mark and the exclamatory mark. However, the graded scale of English punctuation system is not yet fully established in Marathi writing system. The rigid full stop does not allow any rhetorical overflow of the grammatical sentence. Most sentences therefore need time and place linkers and most frequently have abrupt ends. The balance between the subject and the predicate is most often disturbed by the imposition of superfluous syntagmatic elements borrowed from the English structure.

Another important gain is that the new norms of writing system are established according to English compositional norms. The pronunciation of Deshastha Brahmans of Pune gains prominence over other dialects owing to the standardized script used universally in the prose works of this phase. However, the Bombay community consisting of several other communities still maintains its hold on the language. 'Konkanism' is fairly noticeable. The Nagari script replaces the Modi and the characters of the script, except a few consonant conjuncts, are fully standardized.

The lexical subsystem undergoes a major change, a fact which can be measured quantitatively as well as qualitatively. The traditional word formation processes are reduced by loans of various kinds from English. The loss of Sanskrit as *supraglossia* has created a vacuum in the process of substituting English loans by native features. There is little writing in this phase which is not anglicized and affected. The general notions of English syntactic patterns are obviously seen affecting Marathi word order, though the borrowed patterns have to work out details by allocating the old and new variants their respective roles in the new writing system. The sentence structure remains basically unchanged from the traditional simple sentence which was composed of subject + verb as its kernel. The new norms create formal patterns which overlap the simple rhythm of the traditional short sentence. Modifications in the sentence structure are seen taking place at the subject side, i.e., additions of linkers, adjective clauses, noun clauses and also adverb clauses which often come at the beginning of the sentence. The subject side is further overloaded by connectors and several lexical devices which sunder the verb farther away from the subject. This destroys the rhythm of the sentence considerably. Another reason for the loss of sentence rhythm is the multiple autonomous elements borrowed from English sentence structure, supported by the newly borrowed comma and semi-colon. These elements, namely, relativization, serialization, insertion, parenthetical clauses and correlative subordination increase the length of

Marathi sentence with little regard to its subject-predicate concord, increasing the burden on the main verb beyond its capacity to bear it. The verb remains weak in comparison with the other elements, though the impact of English verbalization is increasingly felt in the growth of the verbal structure. The sudden expansion of the simple, compound and complex sentences demand a more powerful verbal system which the traditional writing system did not possess. Borrowing of verbs from English is blocked, because the concepts of action and movement that the verb connotes are not as easy to borrow as the concrete concepts of nouns. Again the elaborate conjugational structures of the Marathi verb defy the borrowing of English verbs. The only possible way out therefore is that the nuclear semantic structure of Marathi verb should develop internal modification.

The syntax reveals multidimensional growth, because borrowed syntactic features of the well-developed English writing system are tried all at the same time. The syntax therefore moves too far from the conversational idiom. Often the writing system shows all variants and no norms. Since the prose of this phase is composed in an artificial situation, with little readership and totally hew concepts to deal with, the syntax loses its direction. In Marathi sentence the verb comes last and all other components become left-handed. On the contrary, in English the verb comes in the middle of the sentence with a more proportionate distribution of its left-handed and right-handed members.[7] The impact of the English construction on Marathi increased only the left-handed elements, leaving the verb to develop its compound forms and participles at the end of the sentence. The pressure of the English verbal structure on the personal verbal forms is already evident toward the end of this phase. Thus the compound verb in Marathi which had already shown noticeable development before the 18th century is seen functioning under great pressure to accomodate the features of English verbalization.

Traditionally, Marathi word order is not as highly organized as the English word order. With the imposition of the rigid English SVO order the ideas in Marathi sentences become fragmentary. The spontaneity of Marathi sentence has already been affected by the shift from oral to written tradition and from manuscript to print culture. Prosodic features suited to the new medium of textual space are not yet developed. The written prose therefore is at the mercy of numerous interferences in different subsystems. Since this phase is marked by a great vocabulary shift and the resulting pidginization, the lexical subsystem is being enriched speedily. However, increasing reliance on purely lexical devices like lexical linkers and lexical connectors rather than rhetorical devices destroys the rhythm of the new sentence.

     The Influence of English on Marathi

The Missionary prose written during this phase is a characteristic variety which deserves independent treatment (3.5). It is mainly in the form of Biblical translations, the semantic fidelity of which is more to the English lexical and syntactic subsystems than to Marathi. The Missionary prose has an independent tradition which was never absorbed in the mainstream of the nineteenth century prose. Though the Bible in English promises great stylistic equivalence in translation, it does not make noticeable impact on the nineteenth-century period style despite numerous translations. On the other hand, it becomes an object of ridicule which is not wholly prompted by religious bigotism. All these translations exemplify a process of pidginization owing to their anglicized syntactic structures, purely logical relations between sentences, and their lexical subsystem, partly colloquial and partly calque-based. This prose shares many of the properties of the prose in the First phase. But it is being stratified and continues to be aloof from the period style even during the later phases.

In general, the prose of this phase develops a secondary subsystem of grammar within the main system. However, it crosses the stage of obligatory inclusion of norms and begins to adopt several nativistic norms and variants which compete with the purely borrowed norms toward the end of this phase. Thus the stage of creolization is by-passed by increasing Sanskritisms of the English-educated Shastris. This trend is soon to become dominant in the Second phase. The Sanskrit learning of the Shastris avoided over-translation and anglicization by transferring English structures to Marathi with the help of new sets of stylistic patterns. The newly written grammars of Marathi begin to reduce chaos to rule by the English and Sanskrit norms. Borrowing is being given a new direction of refinement under motivations other than mere need and utility. The tendency of most Marathi writers to convert ready-made English constructions suggests that the thinking has been done for them. However, this trend is changing with new writers motivated by the urge to communicate and express. The tendency to use prose creatively can be clearly noticed in the prose written toward the end of this phase (see Chapter 7 : Conclusion).

CHAPTER SEVEN

The Middle Phase : 1847-1874
Stabilization of the Standard

7.1 INTRODUCTION

The prose in the Middle phase (1847-1874) is marked by increasing anglicization at syntactic and sentential subsystems and by a nativistic desire among the writers to build native lexical sets to compensate the loss of prosodic elements caused by the ever-increasing interference in the stylistic system. Increasing bilingualism, spreading gradually after the first generation of English-educated Maharashtrians, intensified the confrontation between English and Marathi. Borrowing was given a definite direction by language planning, resulting in the gradual stabilization of features through linguistic change. English graphic norms had already become a part of Marathi writing system and this phenomenon had far-reaching effects, especially on the sentence structure. The empty slots created by the imposition of the norms of English syntax were filled by a number of stylistic devices — from revived traditional and colloquial variants to Sanskrit lexical features. The new prose can be seen as a part of linguistic nativistic revival, a movement of the prose of action which would become fully noticeable in the Third phase. Both the trends, anglicization and deanglicization are found to be stabilizing in the 1860s. A number of changes are introduced into the sentence structure and the area of influence shifted towards the relationship among larger syntactic as well as sentence units.

Some of the most characteristic events in the literary history of Marathi took place during this phase. The beginnings of several literary genres based on those in English literature are seen in the appearance of the essay, drama and novel as major forms. Individual styles can now be distinguished, and some of their features are traceable to the styles of English writers scattered over different periods of English literary history. The primary sources reveal that the favourite English writers among the Victorian Indians were : Edmund Spenser, Shakespeare, Bacon, Milton, Temple, Dryden, Hooker, Cowper, Bunyan, Defoe, Swift, Richardson, Fielding, Goldsmith, Burke, Johnson, Jane Austen, J. S. Mill, Herbert Spencer, Burton and Macaulay. An English Head Master, who had just come to Surat from England recommended some 'latest' novelists to Dadoba Pandurang in 1843; these were : Scott, Bulwer-Lytton, Marryat and Dickens.[1] The individual styles in this phase therefore are deeply influenced by a wide spectrum of English individual style registers and hence are not sharply distinguished.

The most radical developments in language planning under government patronage began in this phase. The chief architect of this planning was Major Thomas Candy (1806—1877), who was Superintendent of Pune Pathashala from 1837 and Translator and Referee for Marathi books between 1847 and 1876. It is stated in the Report of the Board of Education, 1850-51 that the Board requested Major Candy "to examine *very carefully* each of our Mahratha publications with the view of *removing everything that may be found objectionable*."[2] This role Candy played with a heavy hand. His puritanical spirit and hard work were gratefully acknowledged by most of the contemporary writers. [3] Candy was against writing Marathi in English idiom and he hated 'Konkanisms'. He looked upon non-standardized expressions as 'barbarism'. Several other Britishers, namely, Thomas Perry, E. I. Howard, George Jervis, Molesworth and the Missionary as well as Indian grammarians took keen interest in Marathi book production. European supervisors who possessed some knowledge of Marathi (3. 3.4) and Maharashtrian bilinguals who were educated by 'the double translation method' unitedly exercized a stylistic clamp on Marathi. The coercive English teaching and judicious knowledge of English literature made the influence of English on Marathi all-pervasive. As a result, the rational standard of prose writing, replacing the traditional rhetoric of myths and legends came into existence. The new middle class, mostly of Brahmans residing in the district places of Maharashtra, and the English-educated Brahman teachers spread the new standard all over the Marathi-speaking area (4.4).

The middle-class genres like the novel, drama and the journalistic essay popularized the new narrative techniques and genre features borrowed directly from popular English works. Journalists wrote their editorials after the style of the *Edinburgh Review* and *Quarterly Review*. A number of Government, Missionary and private agencies undertook and encouraged written prose by translating, printing and publishing activities. Indigenous printing presses beginning with Ganpat Krishnaji's press in 1840 were established. Javaji Dadaji's Nirnayasagar type foundry, a landmark in the history of Nagari typographical printing in India was established in 1864. Numerous forums, debating associations, readers' clubs, journals and newspapers encouraged the spirit of controversy. Thus the fields of communication expanded rapidly, and Marathi was put to new uses in Government and private affairs. Easy accessibility to printing gave confidence to Marathi writers during this phase. M. G Ranade lists about 2182 books published in Marathi during this phase as against only 43 books in the First phase. The books published cover a wide area of literary genres such as the essay, comedy, tragedy, the novel, literary criticism, scientific treatises, translations and numerous school books on a variety of subjects.

The newly written grammars mostly modelled on English grammars, dictionaries and the massive translation programmes established comparative literary standards which never existed in Marathi before. Linguistic controversies regarding written Marathi were settled by norms outside Marathi, either of Sanskrit or of English. A large number of these grammatical works acted more as prescriptive norms than as descriptive principles. In general, language consciousness was growing. The large number of publications assured both quantity and variety, which are the prerequisite of stylistic norm formation in prose, because they facilitated experimental use of newly created variants. The writers found ample opportunity to try the new stylistic norms which improved the *parole* aspect of Marathi, in consequence helping stabilization of the standard.

Another significant factor in the speedy standardization was the dominant Brahmanical standards of written prose (3.3.5 and 4.4). Since most of the writers were Brahmans, the standards of writing tended toward conservatism, which can be correlated with the literate Brahmanical tradition of Sanskrit learning. This trend gradually developed into a nativistic movement led by purists who claimed and asserted the superiority of Sanskritism over anglicism. However, the battle between the new and the old traditions which began toward the end of this phase was not clearly discernible during the early years of this phase, and disputes regarding anglicisms and Sanskritisms were amicably settled, the final authority being Major Candy. The Shastris and Candy seemed to have evolved certain Sanskritist-puristic norms as the most effective means of language planning. For example, Major Candy stated in 1851:

                                        The Influence of English on Marathi

"Unless a Hindoo be a good (Sanskrit) scholar as well as acquainted with English literature and Science, we cannot, I think, reasonably hope that he will gain extensive influence as a Reformer and Enlightener of Hindoos."[4]

The first generation of English-educated bilingual writers began to write prose in the 1850s and 1860s. Since the centre of gravitation was shifting from Bombay to Pune, the Pune dialect of Chitpavans who became increasingly dominant in education and journalism, gradually became the standard form of Marathi writing. Their enforcement of what they called 'pure writing' helped to eliminate pidgin features, 'Konkanisms' and anglicized idioms under fastidious rules of correct writing. The need for new rhetorical features as part of involvement in social action increased, because under the new circumstances, the discourse had to be rhetorically rather than formally structured. Toward the end of the phase, most prose writers were seen as great social leaders capable of swaying public opinion. With bitter social and religious controversies such as those between the conservative and the radical Brahmans, and between Christian missionaries and Hindu nationalists (3.5) the prose register began to develop specialization of stylistic features with clearer semantic demarcation. Poetry was still highly Sanskritized while prose tended toward involved anglicization.

The reading public increased and with the increasing participation of readers in literary activity the writers became conscious of their reading public. As a result, the objective of the prose writers changed from mere information and instruction to entertainment and expression. After the 1850s, prose came to be increasingly used as intellectual action. This trend can be correlated with the rise of nativistic movements (3. 3.5 and 4. 2.4).

The specimen passages that follow show a marked change from those in Chapter 6 in that the earlier variety of dialectal and caste registers is being fast replaced by the new Brahmanical standard of Pune dialect. Though the circumference of culture contact expands tremendously, the channels of language use become narrower, especially in lexical subsystem and other syntactic features of native tradition (see Conclusion). The sentence structure is particularly under pressure and shows rapid transformation.

7.2 SPECIMEN PASSAGES WITH ANALYTICAL NOTES

लोकिकांचा भाष गोसाय यांचे शापूंनी उधव रीनीमे
बाहेर पडून न्यायाधीशाकडेस घेऊन याबर आरोप
ठेविला, तो आरोप जरी खरा झाला असता तरी तो
काही अपराध असे दुसरे नसते. सोक्रेटीस यांनें स्वप
स्थापन कुशाग्रतेनें केलें, परंतु न्यायाधीशास याचि-
खी दुरात्र होता म्हणून हा अपराधी असे यांनी हर-
ून याला विष पाजून मारुन टाकावें असा याम दंड
नेमला. यापात्रें आजपर्यंत जगाच्या दृष्टीस जे सर्वो-
त्कृष्ट साधु पुरुष झाले आहेत, यांतला हा एक पुरुष वण्या
अपराधाच्या पापें नाश पावला.

शीलेन प्रेम.

आप ... सर्वांचे पोग्यदेखी उणीव करण्याचा भो
स्वभाव आणिघरी शीलेन प्रेम हा गुण राखावयाजोगी
आहे. आपल्यापेक्षा जी कोणी रूपानें व गुणानें व पर्व-
खस्थितिनि निर्धयेकरून कधी याची मात्र ती स्तुति
करिती. ... पापः आश्चर्य मानावासारिखी या अव
त्याख्या गुणाचा हर...र उपायानें अपकर्ष कराःयास
ती पावती, असे काय जाणूं निला त्याचा थोरपणा
सद्भल्मावरून असुखब होतें असतें.

परोपकारबुद्धिविषयी जो सर्वसंमत अमुक एक
पुरुष याची स्तुति निनें केली म्हणजे ती असे म्हणाली
की "तो परोपकारी आहे अर्थात, परंतु मला वार्ने

ख्याख्या जजख्या* नालानें जे बडते तें सर्व ख्याख्या बा-
ख्या हालास समजंने, त्याचे गुप्त परोपकार बुद्धिविषयी
कोणी एकाख्यानें मला सांगावेल काय।

विलेन प्रेम भरे म्हणती की "मारिया हाल इच्छा
तर सर्व चांगलेपणाच दिसतो, परंतु लोक जसं आहेत
तसे ते दिसावे हे माझ्या मते बरे. ज्याचे बाहेरील
आंग सुंदर आणि अंतरंग पोकळ अस्या फळाचा मला
वीट येतो."

"लिखी प्रेस तर आपल्या द्रव्यवान, वृद्ध, मनास
बास येण्याजोग्या भुलख्याचे सेवेत तत्पर झाली आहे,
पण मी वृद्ध, वासक आणि द्रव्यवान चुलख्याचे सेवेत
आहे."

शीलेनास असे वाटतें की ज्याजवर उत्तर झालें
नाहीं तें सिद्ध झालें. आता अमुक एकाचा जो गुप्त
उपकार ख्याजविषयी विशेषतेनें सांगून देणें कठीण आहे.
मारिया हालचां चांगलेपणा तर सर्वांस दिसता आहे.
परंतु ती अंतरंगी पोकळ आहे असें जे म्हणणें तें रद
करणें तोपें नव्हे. लिखीप्रेसचा चुलता द्रव्यवान आहे
ख्याजविषयी नाकार करवत नाहीं, परंतु ती त्याच
सर्बेनें त्याचे सेवेत विशेष तत्पर झाली आहे हे हेले-
न प्रेम वाचून दुसरें कोणाचा बोलायास कधी हिंया

[footnote, illegible] पिखला ख्रास्खात असें वाक्य आहे की जें तुझा वजगन गान करि
न ते करग मानास बुद्ध नेई नको ... त्याचा अर्थ आपल्या चांगल्या
करणाच्या गोषिक ... सांगणी हाख्यादरिना तो लोकांस करग

The Influence of English on Marathi

1.   1846, Hari Keshavji Pathare (trans.); *Shalopavogi Nitigranth*, 2nd ed. (1850), pp. 178-179.

The Nagari script is almost standardized, though conjuncts especially fromed by श and र still show variants. श continues as a graphemic variant of श throughout this phase. Words of Sanskrit origin retain pure consonants. The *anusvara* is now uniformly placed at the right of the *matras*. The English vowel ɔ is not accepted even in English loan words and is either dropped or transcribed as *a* or *o*. The English vowel æ is transcribed as *ya*. The English diphthong *ai* is transcribed as əi, English *E* as *i* or *e* and English ə as a, e or ə. Several other adjustments of English phonemes and allophones are made with Marathi phonetic and graphemic systems.

A fully graded system of English punctuation is introduced. Most punctuation points, especially the comma, are profusely used, though the colon is rare. Double inverted commas are sometimes preceded by a comma to introduce direct speech, but they invariably end with a full stop, comma, question mark or exclamatory mark. Footnotes are indi- cated by asterisks and similar signs. There is a general tendency to over-punctuate.

Oblique forms of English loans are made according to the rules of Marathi grammar, imposing any one of the three genders on the loan words arbitarily.

New norms of paragraphing according to English text formats are fully accepted. Distance between words is shorter than the distance between sentences, substituting the absence of capitalization at the begining of Marathi sentence—a norm which continues for some time in the nineteenth century but is dropped later in the last phase. Paragraphs, sections and titles show a good sense of format.

2

जर[1] गोविंद आणि गोपाळ यांचेंजवळ परस्परें[2] सारिखे दोन चेंडू असले, त्यांतून[3] गोविंदाचा गोपाळाच्या चेंडवा[4] पेक्षां किंचित चांगला[5] असला व जर[6] गोपाळ खोटा दावा सांगूं लागला कीं गोविंदाकडेस चेंडू आहे तो माझा, आणि गोपाळ ज्यास[7] कोण्या समयीं मारीत असेल असा जो[8] महादू म्हणून एक तिसरा लहान मुलगा त्यास तिन्हाइतादाखल गोपाळानें पुसलें कीं मी जें[9] बोललों तें खरें किंवा कसें, त्याजवरून[10] तो चेंडू गोविंदाचा असें[11] महादू चांगलेपणीं जाणत असतां गोपाळाचा आहे असें[11] माराच्या भयानें सांगूं लागला, तर[12] त्या चेंडूचा जो[13] वास्तविक धनी गोविंद त्यास महादूने मोठें मुकसानीचें काम केलें असें होईल[14]. अस्या[14] प्रसंगीं गोविंद बहुतकरून आपला तो चेंडू आपल्याकडेस ठेवण्याविषयीं यत्न करील आणि गोपाळ तर तो चेंडू त्यापासून बळानेंच घेऊं पाहील आणि तो गोविंदास कदाचित् मारीलछी खरा[15]. तेव्हां त्यांची मारामारी होऊं लागेल, त्या क्षणीं जर पंतोजी बाहेर निघून पुसूं लागेल कीं [16] हाणामार कोणी आरंभिली. त्यावरून महादू गोपाळाच्याच भयानें बोलेल कीं[16] गोविंदानें, तर महादू मोठ्या दुष्ट प्रकारचेंही कांहीं[17] बोलला असें होईल, कां[18] तर पंतोजीची बहुतकरून गोविंदावर फार गैरमर्जी होईल अथवा ते कदाचित् त्यास कांहीं वास्तविक शिक्षा करितील. असा तो[19] महादू आपल्यास त्या एका थोंटाच्या धमकीपासून[20] रक्षायाकरिता[20] दोन लबाड्या सांगितल्यावरून मोठ्या अपकारास[21] कारण होईल.[22]

2. 1846, Hari Keshavji Pathare (trans.); *Shalopayogi Nitigranth*, 2nd ed. (1850), pp. 222-23.

The passage represents a large class of anglicized prose and translations written during this phase. Purely grammatical construction, faithful to the original rather than to the receiving language, creates a pidgin form of written prose. Formal rather than rhetorical structure is the sole concern of the writer.

1. Beginning of the sentence with sub-ordinate correlative after E. if-construction destroys the balance of the sentence. M. is still incapable of absorbing E. clausal patterns as the sentence length is not an inherent growth. Premodification in the whole clause creates confusion as the main clause is widely sundered from the beginning clauses and the verb is kept still farther away. The length thus directly affects clarity, increasing the prominence of connectives and too may copulas in each clause.

2. Space between postpositions and preceding words is non-standardized.

3. A connective branching parenthetical clause made possible by the comma. This increases the length of sentence, postponing the logical termination of argument.

4. Single noun common for both adjectival nouns referes to the elliptical one. The feature is made ineffective because of branching. Oblique form is traditional.

5. Innovation E. diminisher+comparative *little better* transferred to M.

6. Cf. 1 above; purely formal parallelism of clauses by means of the same connective, though the condition in this subordinate clause is downgraded.

7. Another downgraded relative clause starting altogether new context.

8. Inserted clause branched to 7 using the same connective again.

9. Another relative clause with the same connective, used to eliminate direct speech.

10. Causal connective deserving to be a linker on the borders of two sentences, both downgraded.

11. Single connective repeated performing two functions, trying to balance the stacked relative clauses.

12. Illative conjunction too weak to initiate the main clause, which is made insignificant by its brevity.

13. Subject obscured by relativization.

14. Predicate blurred at the border of the amorphous sentence; pressure of several interlocked correlatives and relative clauses juxtaposed by weak syntactic links in the chain of sentence units; obligatory inclusion of the norm of E. relativization destroying syntagmatic support of sentence rhythm.

15. Colloquial for E. *even*; placed at the end of the sentence after the verb giving it surplus value in M. word order, though gender is the concord link.

16. Reported speech without punctuation marks; followed by colloquial elliptical phrasing.

17. Determiner substitute for E. *some*, elliptical device.

18. Variant of E. illative phrase, non-standardized.

19. Demonstrative pronoun as discourse reference.

20. For E. *to protect from* E. prepositional structure transferred to M. nominal + verbal (traditional poetic variant) form, too strong as a verbal substitute.

21. Traditional Skt. variant.

22. Compound verb with weak operator ending the sentence abruptly; emphasis distributed unequally owing to the pressure of E. actor-action construction.

3

जर[1] छापखाना व डाक हिंदुस्थानांत असती, तर परकी लोक[2] हिंदुस्थानांत सुलभपणे[3] आले तसे आले नसते; परन्तु[4] या लोकांचें दुर्भाग्य. तेणेकरून[5] छापखान्याचा फायदा त्यांस कळत नाही. व[6] जे ब्राम्हण प्राचीन समजुतीचे[7] अद्यापि पुष्कळ आहेत, त्यांस असें वाटतें[8] की, छापखान्याचा काय उपयोग आहे ?[9] बुकांत पैका घालून काय फळ ? पृथ्वी वरच्या बातम्या ठेवून आम्हांस काय करावयाचें आहे ? आपलें घरांतलें आपण पहावें. आपल्यास मोठ्या गोष्टी कशास पाहिजेत ? अशा ते[10] रांडगोष्टी सांगतात.

असे हे हिंदु लोक शिथिल आणि मूर्ख[11], म्हणून या दशेस आले. जर पेशव्यांचे अमलांत इंग्रज मोठे आहेत व त्यांची काय अवस्था आहे, हें लोकांस कळलें असतें, तर राज्य न घालवते; परन्तु पोटार्थी भट[12], त्यांनी गोड खाण्याशिवाय दुसरें कांही मनांत आणलेंच नाही. गोड खाण्यास मिळालें, म्हणजे सर्व ब्राम्हण[13] एकत्र डोंगळ्यांप्रमाणे[14] जमतात व मग त्यांचे अवधान फार लागतें, कोठे मुक्तद्वार किंवा ब्राम्हण-संतर्पण किंवा उत्साह आहे, अशी वार्ता आली की, ब्राम्हण मोठ्या हौसेने तेथे जमतात. दुसरी कांही राज्यकारभाराची किंवा ज्ञानवृध्दीसाठी सभा असेल, तर हालणार नाहीत. तात्पर्य[15], या जातीची नजर जेवण आणि दक्षणा याहून पलीकडे जात नाही व याहून दुसरा मोठा कारभार पृथ्वीवर आहे, असें या जातीस वाटत नाही[16].

एकास लाथ मारली तर दुसरा 'कां' म्हणावयाचा नाही[17]. इतके तर हे भित्रे, रांड्घे व[18] निर्बल आहेत. यांचेमध्ये साहस, धैर्य, आणि[18] खरेपणा हीं प्रायशः नाहीत. साहस म्हणजे मोठे कार्य डोकीवर घेणे[19]. धैर्य म्हणजे आपल्यावर किंवा दुसऱ्यावर जुलूम कोणी करील, तर न सोसणे[20]. आणि खरेपणा म्हणजे लबाडीचे व्यापारांत न शिरणें.[20] यांपैकी एकही गुण यांजमध्ये नाही. जनावरासारखे[21] हे मूर्ख आहेत.

The Influence of English on Marathi

3. 1849; Lokahitavadi; *Shatapatre*, ed. S. R. Tikekar, 2nd ed. (1940), pp. 296-97.

The passage marks the beginning of individual styles motivated by instruction and urge; The development of syntactic patterns is seen in clausal balance supported by traditional sentence rhythm, sharpening of several syntactic features and controlled sentence length. The syntactic structures of English are seen expanding the simple Marathi sentence frequently.

1. Beginning the sentence with subordinate correlative after E. if- clause.
2. Subject in the middle of the sentence to achieve symmetrical balance; semantic load equally distributed among clauses, subject and predicate, adjective and noun.
3. Adverb to substitute E. insertion; E. idea of action expressed by adverb converted to M. adverbial coinage.
4. Connective followed by downgraded clause with ellipsis of verb; traditional device for emphasis.
5. Linker; Sktism. For E. causal *hence*.
6. Additive linker superfluous, obstructs the swift movement of the discourse.
7. Noun + adjective phrase, synthesis of E. insertion and traditional word order (see Ch. 2 : Annex. D2, D3 and E 2).
8. Simple present tense after E. *think that* followed by serialization of interrogative clauses for enforcement; equal distribution of emphasis realized by short simple clauses.
9. Copula, not repeated in the following clauses but appears again in the third.
10. Subject reinforced by pronoun; traditional device to repeat the predicate for balance after serialization.
11. Copula deleted for emphasis followed by brief predication for emphasis.
12. Copula deleted followed by a longer clause descriptive of the immediately preceding subject.
13. Subject in the middle for distributional balance.
14. Traditional feature revived, adverbial simile; synthesis of E. and native styles.
15. Conclusive linker linking the preceding and the following sentences with the antithetical thematic content.
16. Short sentence tag; formal parallelism with negatives.
17. Overflowing sentence rhythm supported by following conclusive linker.
18. Two additives — Persian and Skt.; variants interchangeable; placed before the last of the series strictly according to the norm of E. word order; deviation from the traditional norm of frequentative use of the additive.
19,20. Gerundivization; synthesis of E. verbalization and Skt. *sutra* style; inanimate subjects and abstract Nouns growing in M.; parallelism with negative gerund, also due to lack of appropriate verbs in M.
21. Strong adverb at the beginning of the sentence; reversion for emphasis; simile as emphasizer

4

यावरून असें दिसतें[1] कीं फिरविण्याचा दांडा जितका लांब असेल[2] आणि मळसूत्राचीं सूत्रें जितकीं अति जवळ असतील[2], तितकी त्या मळसूत्राची शक्ति अधिक होईल[3]; म्हणून[4] या यंत्राचें यांत्रिक[5] सामर्थ्य वाढविण्यासाठीं, जा उच्चालकानें[6] शक्ति लागू होते त्याची लांबी वाढवावी[7], अथवा सूत्रांमधील अंतर कमी करावें[7]. उदाहरण[8], सारख्या परिघाचा दांड्याचीं दोन मळसूत्रें आहेत, त्यांत जर[9] एकाचे सूत्रांमधील अंतर १ इंच आणि दुसऱ्याचे सूत्रांमधील अंतर ३ इंच असेल तर[9], उतरणीचा मूळ कारणाचा विचार केल्याने[10] असें दिसेल, कीं[11] जा[12] मळसूत्राचा सूत्राचे अंतर ३ इंच आहे, त्यापेक्षां[13] जाचें[14] सूत्राचें अंतर १ इंच आहे, त्यापासून[15] तिप्पट नफा होईल. जर दोन उतरणीची उंची सारिखीच आहे, परंतु[16] त्यांतून एका उतरणीचा पायाचा तिप्पट दुसरीचा पाया आहे, तर लांब पायाचा उतरणीपासून जो[17] यांत्रिक नफा होईल, तो दुसरीचा नफ्याचा तिप्पट होईल. परंतु त्या उतरणीचा उंचीवर पोंचण्यास तितका[18] काळ अधिक लागेल हें पूर्वी दाखविलें आहे. कांहीं अवकाशांतून जाण्यास ३ इंच सूत्रांतराचा मळसूत्रास जितक्या वेळा फिरावें लागेल, त्याचा तिप्पट वेळा १ इंच सूत्रांतराचा मळसूत्रास त्याच[19] स्थळांतून जाण्यास फिरावें लागेल, असें[20] वरची गोष्ट[21] मळसूत्रास लागू केल्यानें दिसेल. यावरून[22] जा स्थळांतून गमन घडतें अथवा[23] जो काळाचा तोटा होतो, तो नफ्याशी[24] प्रमाणांत असतो; . . .

4. 1853; Govind Gangadhar Phadke (trans.); *Yantrashastrachi* Mule (1853), pp. 191-92.

The passage is a perfect example of the synthesis of traditional Sanskrit features and the English sentence structure. The challenge of expressing the totally new concepts in a science like mechanics has been fully met with by several devices, the most important being loan translations freely adopted from Sanskrit. Precise clausal linkage, subject-predicate balance and logical relationship between sentences combine to make a steady movement of discourse. English lexical paradigms are being nativized. The text reveals perfect use of the graded punctuation system of English including the semi-colon which was comparatively scarce in the previous as well as this phase. Inanimate objects as actors, impersonal actions suited to scientific writing and growth of abstract nouns appear in good proportion in the text.

1. Impersonal construction.
2. Verbal forms for hypothetical conditions.
3. Verbal forms for fulfilled conditions.
4. A connective in the middle of the sentence preceded by a semicolon balancing several clauses on both sides.
5. Included semantic variant formation.   6. Skitism.
7. Tense device indicating modulation different from 2 and 3 above.
8. Variant for E. *for example,* non-standardized.
9. Three conditions expressed by one subordinator — one left-handed and two right-handed, connected by an additive and having one common verb achieving brevity.
10. Another verbal participle device avoiding lexical connective.
11. For E. *that* in the middle of the sentence, balancing two parts of the argument.
12,13.   E. comparative expressed in one conditional clause, economy device.
14,15.   Similar economy device ellipting implicit nouns and inflecting the pronouns.
16. Branching the preceding condition.
17. Relativization reinforced by following pronoun.
18. Adjective synonymous with E. *proportionate,* traditional words made to function in new context.
19. Demonstrative for economy.   20. Discourse reference.
21. Another discourse reference as booster bringing clarity and exactness to 20 above.
22. Linker for E. *thus.*   23. Sktism.
24. Instrumental case for E. preposition *in proportion to.*

5

परंतु इतकेंच नाहीं तर आह्मा गरीब मांगमहारांस हाकून देऊन आपण मोठमोठ्या इमारती बांधून हे लोक बसले, व[1] त्या इमारतीच्या पायांत आह्मास तेल शेंदूर पाजून पुरण्याचा व[1] आमचा निर्वंश करण्याचा क्रम[2] चालविला होता. आह्मा मनुष्यांस ब्राह्मण लोकांनी गाई म्हसीपेक्षां[3] नीच मानिलें आहे. सांगतें ऐका[4], ज्या वेळीं[5] बाजीरावाचें राज्य होतें त्या वेळीं[5] आह्मास गाढवाप्रमाणें तरी मानीत होते कीं काय ?[6] पहा बरें[7], तुम्ही लंगड्या गाढवास मारा बरें; त्याचा धनी तुमची फटफजिती करून तरी[8] राहील कीं काय ? परंतु मांगमहारांस मारूं नका असें ह्मणणारा कोण होता बरें ? त्यासमयीं[9] मांग अथवा महार ह्यांतून कोणी तालीमखान्यापुढून गेला असतां[10] गुलटेंकडीच्या मैदानांत त्याच्या शिराचा चेंडू आणि तरवारीचा दांडू करून खेळत होते. अशी जर मोठ्या सोवळ्या राजाच्या दारावरून जाण्याची बंदी; तर मग[11] विद्या शिकण्याची मोकळीक कोठून मिळणार ? कदाचित कोणास वाचतां आलें व तें[12] बाजीरावास कळलें तर तो ह्मणे कीं[13] हे महारमांग असून वाचतात, तर ब्राह्मणांनीं कां त्यांस दप्तराचें काम देऊन त्यांच्या ऐवजी थोटक्या बगलेंत मारून विधवांच्या हजामती करीत फिरावें कीं काय ? असें बोलून तो त्यांस शिक्षा करी.

दुसरें असें कीं,[14] लिहिण्याचींच बंदी करून हे लोक थाले कीं काय ? नाहीं[15]. बाजीरावसाहेब तर काशीस जाऊन धुळींत रहिवासी होऊन तद्रूप झाले पण त्यांच्या सहवासाच्या गुणानें येथील महार तो काय ? पण तोहि[16] मांगाच्या सावलीचा स्पर्श होऊ नये म्हणून प्रयत्न करीत आहे.

5. 1855; anon. (a Mang girl student); "Mang Maharanchaya Dukkha Vishayi," *Pune Varnan,* 2nd ed. (1971), pp. 163-64.

The passage represents moderate and indirect influence of English revealed in some features of the sentence structure which are considerably submerged under colloquial and traditional features. Anglicization has become an established phenomenon by this time and several English norms are found percolating through anglicized Marathi prose. The influencing factor, therefore, is a purely internal adjustment of borrowed and native features.

1. A large number of additives and verbal forms in the sentence are the result of anglicization. This kind of combination was missing in old M. prose.

2. Sktism.

3. Morphological variant non-standardized; synonymous with E. *lower than.*

4. Folk style traditional discourse linker followed by correlativization; reader-consciousness.

5. Time connectives, cf. 9 below.

6. Rhetorical questions repeated in the text suggest overdone use of a borrowed feature.

7. Colloquial padding as linker, cf. 4 above; reader-consciousness.

8. Variant for emphasis; ambiguous use.

9. Time linker; sktism., cf. 5 above.

10. Conversion of E. prepositional construction to M. verbalization.

11. Connective necessarily followed by interrogative construction.

12. Colloquial discourse reference for economy.

13. E. conditional construction ellipting subordinator and making explicit *that* - correlative.

14. Enumerative linker.

15. Rhetorical question but followed by the implicit answer.

16. For E. adversative followed by emphasizer.

(१६) शारीरसंबंधीं अपराधांचे बाबदींत.

१. हे ज्यामुळें कदाचित् शिक्षेंत कमज्जबाब होईल परंतु गुन्हेगारींत क्षीणता येणार नाहीं.

२. जें त्या ज्या ज्या वेळेस घडणें त्या त्या प्रत्येक वेळेस तिची खुषी असली पाहिजे. खुषी नसल्यास तें कृत्य करणें अपराध आहे. परंतु खुषीनें त्या कामांत भाग घेतल्यावर एखाद्यानें नाखुषी दर्शविली तर तो अपराध नाहीं. कारण दर्शनानीं खुषी दर्शविण्याचा तिजला मग अधिकार राहात नाहीं. आणि जरी निर्भेळ असेल स्त्रीला योग्य असलें तरी तो त्याचा गुन्हा होत नाहीं.

३. दाहा वर्षांहून कमी वयाची मुलगी असून तिचे योग्य स्त्रीभर्तारीनें निजलाचा हक्क नाहीं अशा पुरुषानें संभोग केला तर तसें करणारा तिला नवरा असला तरी तो जबरीचा संभोग झाला.

४. दाहा वर्षांहून अधिक वयाचे स्त्रीशीं लग्नाचे पुरुषानें संभोग केला तरजरी अपराध नाहीं. तसेंच लग्नाची स्त्री १० वर्षांहून अधिक वयाची असून तिना नाराजी असल्यामुळें नवऱ्यानें उपभोग घेण्यासाठीं निज वरजबर केली तरी अपराध नाहीं. कारण त्याज बरोबर लग्न झालें त्यापेक्षां भारानें असण्याचा तिला अधिकार नाहीं.

५. जबरीं संभोगाचें रवटल्यांत स्त्रीचा पूर्णपणें उपभोग न झाला तरी हरकत नाहीं. फक्त इंद्रिय प्रवेश झाला होता इतकें सिद्ध झालें तर बस आहे.

६. ज्यास पुरुषत्व नाहीं अशा मनुष्यानें उगीच जबरीसारखा प्रकार केला तर योग्य रीतीनें इंद्रियप्रवेश होण्याचा संभव नसल्यामुळें त्याजवर तो गुन्हा न भरे तथापि इंद्रियप्रवेश होण्याचा संस्कार झाला इतकें सिद्ध झालें तरी पुरे आहे. भाग त्यापेक्षां पुरुषत्वांत कांहीं व्यंगपणा असला तरी चिंता नाहीं. असें हें कित्येक लोकांचें मत आहे.

७. इंद्रियप्रवेश होण्याचे रंखूनें पूर्वी फेलेली जबरी किंवा इंद्रियप्रवेश होण्यास इतजबरदाब सबूत न सांपडली तर त्या इसमानें जो जबरीसारखा प्रकार केला असेल त्यावरून त्याजवर फक्त अभ्यासाची व जबरी केली किंवा जबरी संभोग करण्याचा प्रयत्न केला अशा बाजी चालला पाहिजे.

८. इंद्रियप्रवेश स्त्राल्यांवांचून जबरी संभोग केल्याचा गुन्हा होत नाहीं.

९. जबरी संभोग त्या शब्दाचा अर्थ खु इसपर लावाचा स्त्रीनें पुरुषांवर जबरी केली अशा अर्थी लाऊनयें. कारण शब्दनीति रेप त्याला अर्थ केवळ पुरुषार व आहे. म्हणजे पुरुषानें स्त्रीवर जबरी जबरी करणें इतक्याच अर्थीं योजिलेला आहे. सबब अधिक विचार करीत नाहीं.

6. 1863; Ganesh Babaji Mate; *Nyayaratna,* 2nd ed. (1867), p. 98.

This photo-copy of a page from the lithographed book gives considerable idea of the change in writing system and calligraphy. The script, graphology and puncutation in the book show that the graphic subsystem is almost stabilized toward the end of the Second phase.

The script is mostly uniform even in handwriting though some conjuncts show variation. The *anusvara* is uniformly at the right of the *matra/s* as indicated also in the printed passage Specimen Passage 1, Chapter 7 (1850). English allophones and phonemes have been perfectly adjusted with Marathi syllabary.

More frequent use of parentheses, dash and question mark is seen over the years. The comma is being used too frequently and its irrational use has also developed (e.g. — and , + additive). Quotation marks are still rare but they are standardized after English norms such as being preceded by the comma and ending with the full stop, comma or question mark. Sometimes bold letters are used for proper nouns, while single or double quotation marks or underline or both are used to indicate proper names. Uniform spacing between words and sentences is maintained. Footnotes are indicated by several signs at the bottom of the page.

Excellent sense of format with margins and space for independent sections and paragraphs is seen, though breaking of words at the end of the line is arbitrary.

The paragraph usually ends with an emphatic tag or an emphatic conclusive sentence. There is no undue economy of space and the writer seems to be fully at home with the new writing system.

The sentences in the passage are perfectly balanced despite the complicated legal register and interlocking clauses. Passivization has become almost part of Marathi syntax. The lexical subsystem is fully capable of absorbing all types of loans, adaptations and equivalents. Despite complex legal conceptualization there is no ambiguity at any stage. Growth of abstract nouns is accelerated because of strong Sanskrit background of the author. Deviation from the norm as a device begins in specialized features for want of synonyms in Marathi. Lexical accuracy and synonymy are noticeable features.

7.3 CONCLUSION

The outstanding features of the development of period style in Marathi during this phase are love of experimentation and systematic language planning. The area of contact between English and Marathi now covers all the subsystems of Marathi owing to increasing bilingualism. Written Marathi was developing toward a stage of creolization in the 1840s (Specimen Passage 1). The nucleus of this putative creolization was the lexical subsystem and it was gradually spreading to the syntactic subsystem also. Borrowing from English became a standard source of enriching Marathi prose and the bilingual writers seemed to face a problem of obligatory inclusion of English norms. The total absence of genre features in Marathi writing system and the increasing status of English as the new *supraglossia* together increased the rate of borrowing. Although numerous cohesive features from English prose entered into Marathi structure, the abstract base of scientific thinking and rationality remained outside the semantic system of Marathi until the 1850s. When several controversies in social life initiated a rational view of argumentation and instruction, the writers felt an increasing need for rhetorical devices in various fields of discourse.

A new kind of synthesis between the native and English features is seen taking place after about 1850. Both anglicization and Sanskritism reached their maximum levels of influence during the 1860s. The Sanskrit background of the English-educated brahmans gave a new turn to the writing system of the language. The traditional native features from the Bakhar and Pundit styles which had survived in old popular texts were also utilized to compensate the loss of rhythm owing to the influence of English features. Thus Marathi prose of this phase reveals three streams — anglicism, Sanskritism and textual traditionalism. Sanskrit, Persian and traditional Marathi features entered partly to fulfill the need of rhythm and partly as a result of growing linguistic nativism. Colloquialism was also being introduced, though it is still a minor trait.

With different selective pressures working at corss-purposes in the Second phase, each of the three streams claiming its rightful place, experimentation at all subsystems becomes inevitable. The prose in this phase, therefore, reveals fluctuations in the use of stylistic features, most clearly seen in the behaviour of variants in all subsystems. The great vocabulary shift during the First phase caused by the influx of numerous concrete terms, abstract concepts and new ideas had already affected the lexical subsystem. The adjustment of these features in the related subsystems now begins to show interference at the other levels and necessitates modifications in the whole stylistic system of Marathi.

                                    The Influence of English on Marathi

The most significant of these modifications is seen at the sentence level. The new Marathi sentence is allowed to expand according to the needs of its clauses, resulting in the elaborate sentence which is a general feature of prose in this phase. The simple sentence is expanded with the addition of demonstratives, adjective clauses, noun phrases, insertions and verbal participial extensions. The complex sentence is expanded mainly by serialization of clauses supported by commas and connectors and linkers. Consequently, the weak verbal structure of Marathi is particularly responding to the pressure of English verbalization. In short, it is the sentential subsystem which absorbs the major changes, sacrificing its traditional brevity and rhythm.

Another major modification is seen at the lexical level where growth of synonymy caused by unrestrained borrowing from English is systematized by lexical norm formation. Though the native word-formation processes are weakening because of the tendency to borrow either from English or from Sanskrit, different lexical sets are fully amalgamated with the general system of written style. As a result, a wide play of difference of meaning among the variants of general semantic identity is evident. Overlapping and inclusive variants are more frequent, while sharply distinguished variants are rare. With all these limitations, the lexical norm formation is seen to be in process.

Modification at the syntactic level is comparatively a slow process. The fully graded punctuation system contributes largely to the overbalanced syntactic organization of borrowed and native features in the new sentence. The syntactic subsystem is seen at odds with the expanded sentence, as traditionally it was linked with the word order of a short sentence span. The concord of gender, number and person serves a powerful invisible link in Marathi word order and it connects the two separated poles of Marathi sentence, namely, the noun and the verb. This is so rigid that it permits only a few variations in syntactic innovations. The syntagmatic support of the grammatical systems of gender, number, person and case inflexion allows little modification in Marathi syntax. Similarly, the formal relationship between adjective + noun , noun + verb and adverb + verb in Marathi sentence permits little modification. Therefore, it is the verbal structure which is seen developing its flexibility as a co-ordinating syntactic device to meet the new demands of syntactic patterns. The imbalance in the syntactic subsystem, which is mainly the effect of the expanded sentence length, demands new rhetorical devices. Such devices will be seen developing in the next phase.

At the intersentential level, the newly developed sentence linkers as cohesion devices play a crucial role. However, linking devices other than lexical, such as ellipsis, discourse reference and conjunction, are not fully developed. The haphazardly expanded sentences loosely hanging on the invisible grammatical concord are linked with each other in a purely functional way. Paragraphs are rarely architectured. The standardized graphic norms, especially those of punctuation, largely help to achieve formal balance in different units inside as well as outside the sentence. In the absence of rhetorical devices, the sentences have to rely heavily on English rhetorical devices. Different types of the sentence, especially the interrogative and negative, are on the increase. Devices like clausal stacking, modifiers, inversions, relativization, connectors, correlatives, parentheses and sentence-tags of several types are seen employed for holding the sentences together in a paragraph. The paragraph is just beginning to develop a sense of logical relationships between sentences. These modifications naturally increase the semantic load on the predicate side of the sentence, trying to restore the prosody of the extended sentence.

The typical sentence in this phase is usually a long sentence trying to imitate the English periodic sentence. Even in Victorian England, the counterparts of Marathi prose writers regarded the periodic sentence as the ultimate form of good prose, a model of cohesive excellence in discourse. The Marathi writers, while adopting this norm, overpunctuate their sentences and stack the sentence with downgraded clauses. This results in a kind of superstructure of prolonged clausal linkage enveloping the traditional simple structure of Marathi sentence. This can be counted as the most noticeable loss of the Marathi sentence which continues to corrode the sentence prosody in the next phase too. The new syntactic patterns have completely destroyed the spontaneity of the Marathi sentence. The complete subjugation of the laws of rhetoric to the more urgent needs of language standardization and grammatical correctness suspended the growth of rhythmic prose style during this phase. The stylistic need of a sentence is that it has to be rhetorically balanced. The imposition of language standardization supersedes rhetorical norms, giving little scope for personal competences and resulting in failure to use the language aesthetically.

Numerous interferences in the subsystems are seen preventing the rhythmic balance of the Marathi sentence. It is interesting to observe the texts in this phase from the point of view of how the prose writers attempt to accomplish rhythmic balance despite interferences caused by borrowed features. Since most writers have a thorough grounding in English language and literature, they cannot dissociate the interference phenomenon even if they wanted to. In English, the semantic load of the sentence is evenly distributed on both sides of the verb, the verb being in

                    The Influence of English on Marathi

the middle. On the contrary, the Marathi verb, being always placed at the end is often a mere technical necessity and a weak component of the sentence (2. 4. 4 C). With the increasing pressure of English sentence, the pressure of its left-handed elements increases tremendously, exposing the poverty of the verbal structure in Marathi. The English-educated writers find out a way to strengthen the verbal structure by expanding its components. The already existing compound verb in Marathi is fully concentrated upon, and its supporting adverbs, adverb clauses, conjunctions and post-modifiers are made to put their full weight on the predicate side. The rich conjugational systems of Marathi verb are revived in full force. The copula is strengthened by preceding participials, bringing numerous modulations in the verbal structure. The compound verb in Marathi begins to develop numerous reinforcement devices borrowed from the traditional sides and colloquial varieties. The development of a chain of participles is more frequent in this phase.

Secondly, the English devices of using adverbs and prepositions to express the ideas of action and movement are converted to new adverbs borrowed from or blended with Sanskrit or traditional elements. Though Marathi has a tendency to avoid adverbial constructions, the new sentence is made to absorb the new adverbials. Post-modifiers rather than pre-modifiers are given increasing prominence. Sentence-tags of negative and interrogative types are seen more frequently. Traditional and colloquial paddings have increased to cement the gaps between borrowed and native features. Thus the writers in this phase, though not wholly successful in converting the balanced movement of English sentence to Marathi, could initiate devices that recover a part of the rhythm lost because of anglicization. Krishnashastri Chiplunkar's prose is a classic example of this experimentation.

During the Second phase, the prose shows a transition from communicative to expressive competence of language, developed under the influence of English. This results in an important gain of sharpening of different substyles pioneered in several new genres, although these are not fully distinguishable from one another. Individual stylistic variations start appearing during this phase, but it is difficult for the writers to establish their personal styles as the period standard has not yet fully established itself. The pioneers in a number of genre styles during this phase model their prose on English classics and borrow several registers from English genre styles. However, the borrowed registers from oratorical, journalistic and official prose, humour and satire, descriptive, narrative and dramatic prose need specialization in Marathi stylistic system. Over-production of books and massive translation programmes provide ample opportunities for such specialization. The motivation of imitation and of urge combined to make selective borrowing of unique and strong features from both paradigmatic and syntagmatic systems of English. These features are modified, and converted to Marathi substitutes by numerous experiments during this phase.

The stylistic norms and variants borrowed from English into Marathi prose undergo radical changes as the influence matures toward the end of this phase. Therefore, unlike the borrowings in the First phase, the later borrowings fail to correspond categorically to the stylistic tendencies implied in the original English structure. For example, inversion is a popular device of emphasis in English because it causes significant syntactic breaks in the English word order. When this device is borrowed by the Marathi writers of the First phase it created little impact. Inversions like Noun + adjective, verb + adverb, verb + Noun, verb + object + subject, verb + subject + object, object + subject + verb, adverb clause + Noun clause + verb etc. do not result in any stylistic deviation from the norm in Marathi, because the norm implies a certain kind of rigidity and obligatory nature, which did not exist in Marathi word order at this time. It is only after the development of scientific writing in the later phases that some rigidity of word order enters Marathi prose.

There is a clear indication in the Second phase that confrontation of the two linguistic systems now extends to the more contextual areas. In other words, the confrontation of stylistic systems now begins. Simple adjustments work out to fill the gaps created by borrowing selectively and gradually develop specialization of features. Norms which did not exist in Marathi earlier are included as wholes, while inclusion of specific variants from English without complete elimination of native variants is taking place in varying degrees. The influence study, therefore, has to change its focus toward borrowing related to cohesion features, i.e., extra-sentential features and genre features in discourse structure.

A more interesting effect of borrowing from English, on account of its paradoxical nature, is the establishment of English as a new *supraglossia,* replacing Sanskrit in the subcontinent (4. 2.5). Marathi, like other modern Indian languages, was so thoroughly inadequate in respect of scientific and technical vocabulary and registers of several literary genres, journalistic, commercial and official varieties that the influence of English in the new fields was inevitable (1.1. 4). The pressure of the dominant Western culture is destined to be a phenomenon of long duration. In such a situation of putative subjugation to a foreign language, Marathi develops two devices of maintaining its identity, while still changing considerably : 1. Borrowing unlimited lexical sets in all

                              The Influence of English on Marathi

fields of discourse to enlarge its semantic field, and 2. translating in a variety of ways such as loans of all kinds, literal translation, transliteration, transposition, transferrence, substitution or modulation and paraphrasing. Marathi thus develops a mechanism in the form of a subsystem within the main system. This mechanism has continued even beyond the nineteenth century. The restructuring of these new elements has not been perfectly engineered even today. The gap between the main system and this subsystem is clearly evident in scientific writing where most terms have little or no referential value. Even rational discourses like literary criticism and the essay in Marathi reveal whole sets of patterned symbols, transferred straight from English, which refuse to become part of the deep structure of Marathi.

However, at the level of lexical subsystem the strong links between Sanskrit and Marathi can absorb most of the temporary devices successfully. This phase witnesses the phenomenon of the simultaneous growth of Sanskritism as well as anglicism, with the result that the more the language is anglicized, the more it is Sanskritized. The process of Sanskritization, which sets in as a corollary of growing deanglicization is an important characteristic of the linguistic acculturation.

As we proceed to the Third phase, nativistic forces on the one hand and vigorous language planning on the other combine to help regain the lost sentence rhythm of Marathi discourse by adopting a mature attitude to language standardization. Marathi is subjected to rigorous prescriptivism of the new grammarians in this phase, and the dialect of Pune Brahmans is imposed imperiously on the writing system of Marathi, in effect consolidating the written standard.

CHAPTER EIGHT

The Late Phase : 1874-1890
Consolidation of the Standard

8.1 INTRODUCTION

The linguistic contact became largely literary and the cultural type of literate bilingualism assumed full stature during the Third phase (1.1.2 , 3.2.3, 3.3.5, 3.5, 4.1.1, 4.2.2 and 4.2.3). Borrowing had reached a stage of saturation by the 1870s when several subsystems were found unwilling to make further accommodations. The lexical subsystem, however, continued to be active. Growing Sanskritism developed the flexible mechanism of substituting English loan by Sanskrit word formation. The skills of using English no longer remained just passive; on the other hand, some of the best minds of this phase like M. G. Ranade, Jotirao Phule Dadabhai Naoroji, K. T. Telang, B. G. Tilak, Pherozeshah Mehta, R. G. Bhandarkar, G. K. Gokhale spoke and wrote English with full confidence. English became a medium of national political movement. Most Marathi writers wrote English and Marathi and it was customary at the beginning of this phase to write prefaces and introductions to Marathi works in highly stylized English, modelled on the prose of Fielding, Richardson, Johnson and Macaulay,[1] though this 'colonial' trend was severely attacked by Purists.[2] Several writers conducted private correspondence and even wrote personal diaries and memoris in English. As English received great patronage from Brahmans, the dominant class, the new literati used English features as a prestige symbolism (3.3.5, 4.2.2 and 4.3.3), and a kind of anglicized elitism replacing the older kind of Sanskritist elitism was established in Marathi literary tradition. Imposition of the fairly standardized dialect of Pune Brahmans upon the idiolects and dialects of the personal and spoken language of those who were being taught the alphabet for the first time in the newly opened schools all over Maharashtra expedited the speedy growth of the standard literary variety. The first generation of university grduates started dominating the literary scene in the 1860s. These writers received instruction in English grammar and English rhetoric which gave them most of their stylistic devices. They developed a bilingual-bicultural zone in Marathi literary culture. Most of them wrote little in Marathi and revealed schizophrenic tendencies expressed in the numerous controversies that raged during this phase : Anglophobia and anglomania, colonialism and atavistic nationalism, pro-Brahmanism and anti-Brahmanism, Christianity and neo-Hinduism, extremist and moderate politics — in short, no field of intellectual activity remained untouched by these controversies (Chapter 3). This resulted in creating vigorous prose of aggressive oratorical qualities. On the linguistic plane, this spirit of bi-culturism is most visible in the use of anglicized and Sanskritist features, both of which are equally rigorously employed in journalistic prose, novels, plays, essays and criticism. Several nativistic movements asserted themselves in the prose of action (3.3.5, 4.2.4). The linguistic nativisitic spirit boosted up several literary and para-literary activities. The growth of journalism, establishment of indigenous printing presses and publishing houses, printing the manuscripts of old saint-poets and Pundit poets, reinterpretation of Maratha history and publication of historical documents like Bakhars — such activities, mostly politically motivated, reveal little aesthetic discrimination; however, they were symptomatic of the search for roots in the native tradition and emancipation from the literary-aesthetic impact of English (cf. 4.2.2).

The revival of Sanskrit learning was also a part of linguistic nativism, though Sanskrit had already become a dead *supraglossia* (4.2.5). A surprising feature of the literary culture in this phase is that the translations, publications and adaptations from Sanskrit works are more in number than those from English. As discussed in the previous chapter, the English-educated Brahmans had initiated a mechanism of highly Sanskritized lexical sub-system to convert the features borrowed from English. However, the Anglicists had an edge over the Sanskritists in that the study of English classics encouraged rational and secular literary trends in Victorian India. Since the sources of this anglicization were more creative and more liberal, and since they were supported by the rising *supraglossia,* English exercised greater influence on the prose of this phase than Sanskrit. The most dominant feature of the prose of this phase is awareness of social problems and a rational interpretation of man-to-man relationship based on the works of English rationalists like Hume, Locke, J. S. Mill, Spencer and of Thomas Paine. A good deal of prose in this phase is concerned with refutation of the inadequate Hindu notions of man and society. Heated controversies regarding child marriage, widow remarriage, the age of Consent, privileges of Brahmans, rights of the Shudras and social and political freedom increased the potentialities for stylistic devices in the prose of this phase.

A considerable part of the prose of this phase is devoted to such linguistic problems as 'correct writing', stylistic qualities of borrowing from English and purism, a fact which indicates the increasing language consciousness of the prose writers. Even in serious arguments 'incorrect' uses of language, which meant anglicisms and colloquial and dialectal features, are denounced as 'barbarisms'. The faulty usage is pointed out to weaken the rival in argument. The aesthetics of the mother tongue gives rise to emotional attitudes in all those who write in Marathi. These trends are highly conducive to building national prose, and a national style is the natural outcome. The phase is claracterized by an unprecedented activity in book and periodical publications. M. G. Ranade mentions 6967 books published during this phase alone against the background of only 43 books during the First and 2182 books published during the Second phase.[3] This figure of 6967 excludes many other publications such as serialized works, pamphlets, journals, periodicals and miscellaneous works which were also prolific. This overproduction indicates growing confidence in the use of Marathi prose among all sections of society.

Under the influence of the Victorian literary trends in England, the Marathi writers develop a sense of reader-consciousness as a valuable discipline for prose writing. More attention is paid to cohesion in discourse. The influence of the Romantic movement, which was fading in England but was new to Victorian India, cannot be undermined in the context of prose, though it is more crucial in the context of modern Marathi poetry which begins in the 1880s. The Romantic emphasis on individualism, love of the past, and particularly the man-woman relationship new to the Hindus inspires the fiction writers, progressive essayists and poets. The Romantic novel of love-adventure beginning with *Muktamala* (1861) becomes instantly popular during this phase. The prose reveals, under the influence of English Romanticism, a curious admixture of classical Sanskrit romances and the historical-picaresque novel of the late eighteenth- and early nineteenth-century England. Poetry, however, is written in highly Sanskritized register until the Romantic poets led by Keshavsut revolutionize it about 1885 (see 4.2.3). The other forms, namely, drama and the novel, are largely modelled on English examples with transmutation of elements from Sanskrit literature. Borrowing genre features and idiomatic expressions from English literary substyles is a universal trend.

    The Influence of English on Marathi

A kind of *deux ex machina* of English literary devices is a common feature of even the major literary works of this phase. Several formal elements like the serialized Victorian novel and the five-act play divided into scenes are direct borrowings. Aesthetic use of irony is borrowed from the 18th century writers, the persecuted heroine from Richardson, Christian moralism converted to sentiment of pity from Dickens and satire from the Augustans. On the whole, this phase marks a full-blooded stylistic relationship between the two literatures. It is only toward the end of the phase that nativistic stimulant rises from the concern for social problems when the deeper voice of society begins to be heard.

It is extremely difficult to present a complete picture of the full stylistic growth of the period style in all its substyles from the lexical to the generic, though we have occasionally pointed out some of the fresh variants at different levels borrowed from English, during the course of the analysis of specimen passages. More importance has been given to pointing out cohesion features at the sentential and extrasentential levels.

8.2 SPECIMEN PASSAGES WITH ANALYTICAL NOTES

1. 1876; Vishnushastri Chiplunkar; *Nibandhamala* : 44, 3rd ed. (1926), pp. 442-43.

The passage is a review of the **Report of Satyashodhak Samaj, Sept. 1876.** Chiplunkar's prose marks the beginning of a distinct genre style of the periodical essay in Marathi which is sharply distinguished from other genres within period style. Influenced by the oratorical over-decorative individual styles of the English writers in the tradition of Johnson, the author represents the oratorical prose dominant in this phase which is characterized by Macaulayan modes of order, devices of aggressive posture, tight linking of sentences and vigorous use of language shift. The writer's personality is thrust upon the reader. Rhetorical devices, incisive satire and arrogance representing the voice of the communal group are some of the features of the journalisitc essay popular in this phase. Careful beginnings and middles of the sentence are supported by strong verbal structure at the end of the sentence. English features are fully amalgamated with revived native features. Variants are set in clear relationship with each other. This passage shows adversative devices, sharp syntactic patterns, broad sentence span with downgraded clausal structure and the paragraph as an oratorical entity with clearly distinguished ironic undercurrents, features all new to Marathi prose.

1

अजम[1] जोतीराव गोविंदराव फुले[2] हे[3] वर सांगितलेल्या समाजाचे मुख्य पुरस्कर्ते व आधारस्तंभ होत[4]. या गृहस्थांच्या अंगीं अनेक अलौकिक गुण[5] वास करताहेत[6]. ते कोणते ह्मणाल[7] तर हे कवि आहेत, इतिहासज्ञ आहेत, मोठे गहन भाषापंडित[8] आहेत, वक्ते आहेत; आणि सर्वांत विशेषतः सांगण्यासारिखें हें कीं, आमच्या देशांत आलीकडे लोककल्याणाला वाहिलेली जी मंडळी चोहोंकडे आढळते[9] त्यांत तर यांच्यासारखे केवळ तद्रूप बनलेले थोडेच सांपडतील[10] ! हें काम आज पुष्कळ वर्षांपासून ते करीत आहेत असें 'पुण्याच्या वर्णना' वरून व खुद्द त्यांच्याच[11] 'गुलामगिरी' वरून समजतें[12]. मुलींच्या शाळा स्थापण्याच्या कामीं यांनीं मदत केल्यावरून या 'तात्यासाहेबांस'[13] सरकारनें एक शालजोडी आनंदानें बक्षीस दिली.' पण[14] मध्यंतरीं 'भटपांड्यांचें बंड उपस्थित झाल्यामुळें सर्व युरोपियन् कामगार यांस पाहिल्याबरोबर कपाळास आंठ्या घालूं लागले.'[15] ज्या कामगारांविषयीं आमच्या राजनिष्ठ[16] जोतीरावांची[17] इतकी कृतज्ञताबुद्धि होती कीं, 'त्यांचे उपकार त्यांच्या जातभाईंच्या अंगांत खिळून त्याजबद्दल त्यांनीं आपल्या शरीराचे चर्मीं जोडे करून त्यांच्या पायांत घातले तथापि ते उतराई होणार नाहींत[18],' तेही जेव्हां त्यांचा तिटकारा करूं लागले व त्यांस हिडीस फिडीस करूं लागले, तेव्हां मग काय पुसावे ![19] तात्यासाहेबांस परम वैराग्य प्राप्त होऊन त्यांनीं लोककल्याणाची व आपली फारकत करून टाकली[20]. हा जोतिबांचा[21] पहिला अवतार समाप्त झाला ! पण[22] पुनः दहा वीस वर्षांनीं त्यांस स्वस्थ बसण्याचा कंटाळा येऊन ते ग्रंथकर्ते या नात्यानें पुनः अवतीर्ण झाले[23]. तारीख १ आगष्ट १९७२ रोजीं त्यांनीं त्यांचा कुलांतक जो[24] विष्णूचा सहावा अवतार परशुराम त्यास एक नोटिस दिली[25].

The Influence of English on Marathi

1. A variant from Persian to substitute E. *hon'ble;* several native variants are being utilized to replace anglicisms in this phase.

2. Quoting various forms of the rival's name, a device of weakening variants, occurs in this passage (see 13, 17, 21 below). Each variant is loaded with oblique meaning, usually alluding the communal or nativistic undertone.

3. Demonstrative, traditional variant utilized to indicate derision.

4. Doublet suggesting derision followed by a variant of copula suggesting curt period; clear reversion of E. subject - predicate "... is the ... of ..." construction.

5. E. word order : enumerative adjective + qualitative adjective + noun.

6. Pundit style feature used as travesty.

7. Reader-consciousness; device to involve the reader in the horseplay.

8. This serialization of absolute clauses is all ironic; clausal linkage juxtaposed to the following amplifier; syntactic order of 8 : qualitative adjective + intensifying adjective + noun; several Sktisms.; parallelism both formal and syntactic; emphasis on adjectives raising the status of the adjective by distributing semantic load equally among adjectives and Nouns.

9. Device of mockery.

10. Understatement suggesting increasing sarcasm; exclamatory mark reveals the undertone; end of the loose periodic sentence merged into following subordinate clause.

11. After E. reflective-self; synthesis of E. + native (Persian) features.

12. Passivization after E. impersonal construction, subject deliberately suppressed, strengthening verbalization.

13. Cf. 2, 17 and 21; this Brahmanical title of respect used for Phule by another writer, S. R. Gaikwad, is quoted in order to ridicule both Phule and Gaikwad.

14. Linker for use of discontinuity in discourse, inserted to point out the discrepancy between the two quotations. This insertion turns the argument to other side of the antithesis—a typical Johnsonian device of antithesis.

15. Quotations used to expose the pro-British stand of Phule; this becomes clearer later in the discourse. (See 16 and 18 below.)

16. Anti-British sentiment ironically indicated.

17. Cf. 2, 13 and 21.

18. Cf. 15; Phule's quotation juxtaposed to reveal two opposite undercurrents.

19. Exclamation driving the argument to expose colonial British attitude.

20. Compound verb for mockery; strong verbalization by dramatic emphasis.

21. Cf. 2, 13 and 17.

22. Linker introducing another unit of discourse.

23. Pundit style variant used for burlesque.

24. Insertion to emphasize opposition; pre-modifier immediately after the head adjective raising the status of M. adjective; Pundit style feature merged in the new sentence; each of the three components of the sentence has a distinct and individual tone.

25. Synthesis of M. + Persian + E. elements; refers to Phule's own statement in *Gulamgiri* distorted to go against the original intention. This is a favourite device in M. journalism which usually leads to inconspicuous apology by the editor.

2

पूरवी थोरले माधवराव साहेब पेशवे यांचे कारकीर्दींत झाासीस पारोळकर सुभेदार असता[1] त्याचे पदरी कोणी नारायण शास्त्रीबाबा हे[2] धर्मशास्त्र वगैरे[3] सांगण्याकरिता शंभर रुपये दरमहा देऊन पदरी ठेविले असता[4],कोणी येक दिवसी[5] शौचकूपांतून बाहेर शास्त्रीबाबा येतात[6] तो[6] तेथे आपले मातोश्री बराबर भंगिणीची मुलगी वयानी तेरा चवदा वर्षाची होती. तिजला पाहून या[7] शास्त्रीबाबांचे मनांत असे आले की, ही बहुधा पद्मीण जातीची कन्या असावी. शास्त्रीबाबा शृंगार शास्त्रात पुरे होते. ते समई त्या मुलीची लक्षणा पाहण्याकरिता येकीकडे बलावून आणोन पाहिली व[8] सर्व अंगास कमलाप्रो[9] सुवास आहे हेंडी[10] लक्षण मनांत आणोन[11] तिजला प्रथम दिवसी चार आणे पर्यंत खर्च करून खाऊ दिल्हा आणि[12] तिजला असे सांगितले की[13], तूं रोज या वेळेस येथे येत असावे. बहुत चांगले आहे असे म्हणोन[14] ती मातोश्रीबरोबर निघोन गेली. याप्रो रोज तिजबराबर शास्त्रीबाबांनी स्नेह ठेवून तिजला खाऊ व अपूर्व फले वगैरे देतादेता[15] तिचे मातोश्रीस येक दिवस असे सांगितले की, या तुझे कन्येचा बाप तर मरण पावला आहे. आता[16] या मुलीचे लग्न तूं करणार परंतु[17] आम्ही तुजला असे सांगतो की, या कन्येचे लग्न तूं करू नको. कारण[18] मी इजला आपले बायकोप्रो बाळगीन. खाणेपिणे वस्त्र-प्रावर्ण व द्रव्य यास कधीही तोटा पडणार नाही व[19] तुजलाही अन्नवस्त्र चांगल्या रीतीने देईल. परंतु[20] तूर्त ही गोष्ट कोणापाशी सांगू नये असा प्रकार[21] बोलण्याबोोचा करून त्या मुलीस येक साडी दिल्ही व[22] येक चोलीही दिल्ही व[23] तिचे आईपासी तूर्त खर्चाकरता रूो काही दिल्हे.

2. 1883; Vishnubhataji Godse; *Majha Pravas*, 4th ed. (1974), pp. 68-69.

The passage is another example of the indirect influence of English, percolated through the writings of contemporary bilingual writers, on a Shastri. Godse Bhataji does not seem to have read works other than traditional scriptures and old Marathi works, but borrowed features such as connectors, impersonal constructions, logical relationship of sentences, cohesion features, clausal linkage and growing verbalization indicate the indirect influence of English features. The charm of the individual style in this travelogue lies in clear and unornamental prose and unaffected rhetoric which state the experience in a straightforward manner. Synthesis of several traditional native Marathi features including those of folk style and borrowings achieves a rhetorical rather than merely functional effect of the discourse.

1. Downgraded clause.

2. Device to connect subject with the following clause for clarity.

3. Padding from oral style.

4. Downgraded clause linked by Verbal participle creating stereotypy.

5. Initiative linker downgraded as connective, shifted to the middle of the haphazard sentence for balance.

6. Dramatic present introducing another subject; disparity of tenses creating ambiguity.

7. Demonstrative used as linker but misplaced for back reference.

8. Additive with implicit ellipsis.

9. Disappearing graphic variant as short form of words.

10,11,12,13. Demonstrative connective with emphasis + verbal participle + another additive; Persian construction merged into anglicized *that*-construction.

13,14. Speech words as substitute for direct speech; signals indicating technical absence of quotation marks.

15. Colloquial connective device other than lexical.

16, 17, 18, 19, 20, 21, 22, 23. Rich variety of connectives and linkers used for linking downgraded clauses; Persian Bakhar feature mixed with anglicized cohesion.

करितां स्वस्थ राहिले असते. मग ही स्वर्गसम सुखाची खाण पृथ्वी, प्राण्यास नरकसम झाली असती आणि हा संसार असा सुंदरही दिसला नसता. ह्यावरून सिद्ध होतें कीं, आपापले अभाव पूर्ण करून घेण्यास मनुष्यांस पशूंची; पशूंस मनुष्यांची; तेल्याला तांबोळ्याची; त्याला वाण्याची; धनी लोकांस गरीबांची व गरीबांस धनवानांची; किंबहुना सर्वांस सर्वांची गरज आहे. आणि ती आहे म्हणूनच सर्व परस्परांशीं संबंध ठेवून एकमेकांचें हित करून सुखानुभव घेऊन काळ घालवितात. असें ईश्वरी नियमाप्रमाणें जर परस्परांच्या साह्याशिवाय सुख व्हावयाचें नाहीं असें ठरलें, तर स्त्रियांच्या साह्यावांचून पुरुषांस व त्यांच्या साह्यावांचून स्त्रियांस सुख होईल तरी कसें?

आतां तुम्ही म्हणाल, "सुख तर आम्हांस होतें आणि पुरुषांसही होतें; मग आणखी सुख तें कोणतें?" माझ्या प्रिय बहिणींनो, सुख म्हणजे खाण्यापिण्याचेंच असा माझ्या सांगण्याचा अर्थ नव्हे. सुखाचें मुख्य साधन म्हटलें म्हणजे विशुद्ध स्वाधीनता. ही ज्या तुम्हांस नाहीं, आणि तुमच्या आळसानें दुसरीं कामें करण्यास वेळ न सांपडणाऱ्या पुरुषांसही नाहीं, तर तुम्हीं कशाच्या योगानें सुखी म्हणवितां? एका कवीनें म्हटलें आहे—"सर्वं परवशं दुःखं सर्वमात्मवशं सुखं." म्हणजे पराधीनता हें सगळें दुःख आणि स्वाधीनता हें सुख. आम्हां लोकांत स्वाधीनता कोठें आहे? प्रथम स्त्रीजातींत पहा; इनकी पराधीनता कीं, कापड फाटलें तर दोन टांचे कसे घ्यावे, शंभर आंब्यांस मीठ किती पाहिजे, बोहोरी वगैरे लहान लहान वस्तु विकणारे दारावर आले तर किती किंमतीस काय घ्यावें; इत्यादि क्षुल्लक गोष्टी जाणण्याकरितां एक तर आम्हां लोकांस दारोदार जाऊन जाणत्या लोकांच्या विनवण्या केल्या पाहिजेत; नाहीं तर सगळ्या गोष्टीची नासाडी करून उगाच बसलें पाहिजे. रावसाहेब बाहेर गेले आहेत व कोणी माणूस एका

3. 1882; Pandita Ramabai; *Streedharmaniti*; 2nd ed. (1883), p.13.

Pandita Ramabai is one of the scholarly women renowned for her Missionary activities and the struggle for the rights of women. With a good command over Sanskrit, English and Marathi, she translated the Bible, changing the pidginized form of Missionary prose to a more readable variety. Her prose contains numerous innovations at different subsystems. It reveals a typical bilingual syntax synthesizing English, Sanskrit and colloquial Marathi women's registers.

The Script here shows little change after the Second phase except that consonant conjuncts are fairly standardized. Duplicate forms of some conjuncts are, however, still found.

The punctuation system has come closer to the current English system. Distinction between single and double quotation marks is not popular. Double inverted commas of direct speech invariably begin with a comma and end with some relevant point. The graded system of punctuation with , ; . ? or ! and — is common, though : is very rare. There is a tendency to overpunctuation. The *anusvara*, supported by 'Konkanism' and Sanskrit etymology, is too frequent. Spacing is being used as a device to separate words by shorter space and sentences by longer space, since no capitalization exists in Marathi. This norm is eliminated in the later years.

Sections are well marked; the titles and subtitles are printed in different grades of types and a tail-piece indicates the end of the section.

4

30th April 1858	:	Venayak G. Shastree presents Mrs. Kero with a **दुशांची माळ** for my Planetary Tables[1].

30th April 1858   :   Venayak G. Shastree presents Mrs. Kero with a **दुशांची माळ** for my Planetary Tables[1].

20th August 1873 :   Wednesday **श्रावण व ॥ १३ शके १७९५**[2] Govind Ramchandra Bhagwat breathes his last[3] of **कफोदर**[4] according to Marathi **वैद्य** and of Heart disease accoding to European doctors[5].

25th May 1882   :   Waroo-baee, looses her daughter, 2 years old of Measels[6].

17th July 1882   :   Gave up looking over watersupply to the inhabitants of the City of Poona[7].

3rd August 1882 :   Garbhadan Ceremony of my daughter Durga-baee[8].

ता. ३० डिसें. ७६   :   वैसरायसाहेबाचे[9] मुलाकतीकरितां. त्या ठिकाणीं, विलायतेच्या[10] राणीसाहेबांनीं एम्प्रेस आफ इंडिया[11] हा किताब घेतला, याचा स्मरणार्थ एक रुप्याचें पदक मिळालें. वाइसराय[12] याणी आम्हास "रावबहादूर" हि किताब दिला.[13]

     The Influence of English on Marathi

4. 1858-1882; Kerunana Chhatre; *Prof. Kerunana Chhatre yanchi Tipanvahi*, ed. A.K. Priyolkar (1958), pp. 3, 10, 14 and 28.

The extracts from Prof. Kerunana Chhatre's diary reveal to what extent English has penetrated the thinking of the bilingual intellectuals of this period. The phenomenon of interference is seen in a variety of ways in the mixed bilingual entries in the diary.

1. Untranslatable concrete objects are retained in the original M. (Nagari) script.

2. Religious value of days in Hindu calendar defies FL influence, translation as well as transliteration.

3. E. cliche'.

4. Ayurvedic term is retained on the strength of native roots.

5. Contrast between Hindu and European terms retains the M. word with the original script.

6. E. and M. word order mixed up; Transliterating an Indian name into E. with hyphen and superfluous repetition of vowels.

7. Multiple prepositions; overconscious syntax.

8. Translation devices of M. proper names and unique terms.

9. Variants in Nagari transliteration of E. *Viceroy* (cf. 12); interference in syllabary.

10. Meaning *home*; colonial standards accepted for Indian words.

11. Transliteration.

12. Cf. 9 above.

13. Confusion of genders masculine/feminine between the two semantic concepts for E. *title*.

येत नाहीं.) नारायणा, तर तुला ठाऊक नाहीं अशी गोष्ट ह्या लहानशा खोलींत एक निघाली आहे बरें! आणखी अशा कांहीं गोष्टी निघणार नाहींत, असें तुला खचीत वाटतें! नीट विचार कर.

नारा०—(विचारपूर्वक चोहींकडे पाहून उत्तर देतो.) मला ठाऊक नाहीं अशी दुसरी गोष्ट निघणार नाहींसें वाटतें. ह्या खोलींतील बाकीच्या गोष्टी सर्व मला माहीत आहेत, अशी माझी बरीच खातरी आहे.

विष्णु—(भलेपणानें हटकून बोलतो.) संभाळ, नारायणराव, उगीच खातरीचीं भाषणें बोलूं नको.

मामा—बरें तर नाना, त्या पलीकडचे दारास किली घालावयाचें भोंक आहे, त्यांतून वारा पार जातांना शिळीसारखा कां वाजतो! (त्याच्यानें उत्तर देववत नाहीं.) पहा, तुला ठाऊक नाहीं अशी ही दुसरी गोष्ट निघाली आहे. पहा, ह्या खोलींत काय काय चमत्कारिक पदार्थ आहेत! त्यांपैकीं ईश्वरानें पदार्थांचेठायीं जे गुण व ज्या शक्ति करून ठेविल्या आहेत त्यांचे कांहीं परिणाम आहेत, व मनुष्याच्या कलाकौशल्यांचे कांहीं परिणाम आहेत. त्या गुणांचें व शक्तींचें व कलाकौशल्यांचें वर्णन करूं म्हटलें, तर मोठाले ग्रंथ होतील. तुला आणखी विचारितों, त्या चौरंगावर मोहोळाच्या पोळीचा तुकडा आहे, तो कसा केला आहे हें तुझ्यानें सांगवेल बरें! तें पलीकडे उष्णमापक यंत्र आहे त्यांतील पारा कां वर चढतो, व कां खालीं उतरतो, हें तुझ्यानें सांगवेल बरें! विटूनें लांकडें चुलींत घातलीं, तीं तडतड कां वाजतात, हें तुझ्यानें सांगवेल बरें! ती पहा एक माशी भिंतीला धरून चालत आहे, व एक खालीं पाठ करून छतावर चालत आहे, असें त्यांस कशानें चालतां येतें, हें तुझ्यानें सांगवेल काय?

नारा०—(मला सर्व गोष्टी ठाऊक आहेत अशी गोष्टी मिरवीत होतां तिची कांहींशी लाज धरून,) माझ्यानें सांगवत नाहीं, मामा

मामा—ज्या कारणानें किल्लीच्या भोंकांत वारा शिळीसारखा वाजलो, त्याच कारणानें त्या माशांस चालतां येतें, व त्याच कारणानें घडा

नारा०—(भ्रमास तिलांजलि करून) मामा, मला तर खचीत वाट ठीं म्यां उत्तर बरोबर दिलें. हें उत्तर सारसंग्रहाचें पुस्तकांति पाठ केलेलें म्यां आपल्या बापापुढें शंभर वेळ दिलें आहे.

गोपाळ—(लावून बोलण्याच्या स्वरानें) हें तुझें उत्तर ऐकून तुझ्य बाबास ज्ञान झालें असेल, आम्हांला तर ज्ञान झालें नाहीं. (ह्याव बाप गोपाळाकडे रागानें पाहतो.) नारायणराव, इंग्लंददेश राज्यकारभार चालविण्याची रीत कशी आहे, हें कृपाकरून सां

नारा०—तेथें कायदे करणारी एक मंडळी आहे, ती जे जे काय करिते, व जे जे नेम ठरविते, त्यांच्या अनुसारानें राज्यकारभार च लतो. (हें उत्तर देऊन नारायणास वाटलें कीं, मीं आज अ काय सभाजयच केला आहे. मग तो जयमुंद्रेनें इकडे तिकडे सव च्या मुखांकडे पाहूं लागतो. विष्णु व जगू हे गालच्या गा हांसतात; गोपाळा तर मोठ्यानें खदखदां हांसूं लागतो.)

गोपाळ—नारायणराव, तुला ठाऊक नाहीं अशी गोष्ट आमच्या ह खोलींत नाहींच, असें आम्हांस खचीत वाटतें.

नारा०—मलाही तसेंच वाटतें, गोपाळा.

मामा—बरें, नाना, ह्या चौरंगावर जी चहादाणी विटूनें आणून ठेवि आहे, तिवें झांकण काय म्हणून जोरानें वर उडतें! आणि ती फसफस शब्द करून धूर कां बाहेर येतो! ह्या दोन गोष्टींचीं क जगूस समजाऊन दे बरें, पाहूं.

नारा०—मामा, ह्यांत काय आहे! हें सांगावयाचें तर अगदीं स आहे. ह्या गोष्टीचें कारण दुसरें काय असावयाचें आहे! ह्या कारण पाण्याची वाफ.

मामा—होय हें खरें, पण ज्या हौदांतून तें पाणी भरलें त्या हौदा पाण्यांत कांहीं वाफ नाहीं.

नारा०—पाणी कढलें म्हणजे उष्णतेच्या योगानें त्याची वाफ होते.

मामा—होय. पण हें घोकींव उत्तर. परंतु कशी, कोणत्या रीती उष्णतेच्या योगानें हौदांतील पाण्याची वाफ होते, हें उलगडून आम्हां सांग. (हें ऐकून नारायण गोंधळतो; ह्यावर त्यास उत्तर

5.   1894 (?); Major Thomas Candy; *Marathi Fifth Book*, 12th
stereotyped ed. (1894), pp. 22-23.

The photographic reproduction of the two pages from Candy's most
popular textbook for the Fifth standard shows that nearly all the graphic
elements — script, punctuation and typography — are fully standardized.
They show little change in comparison with the earlier typographically
and lithorgaphically printed books. See Chapter 7 : Specimen Passage 6
(1867) and Chapter 8 : Specimen Passage 3 (1883).

6

होय[1]. ती माझी[2] आई जिच्याविषयीं[3] आम्हां साऱ्यांना इतका[4] अभिमान - इतकें[5] प्रेम वाटत असे, मला कळूं लागल्यापासून[6] जिची[7] आज्ञा[8] मीं प्रत्यक्ष[10] तर काय[11], परंतु नुसती मनांतदेखील[12] उल्लंघिली[13] नाहीं, जिनें[14] मला आपल्या उपदेशानें आणि[15] आचरणानें चांगल्या मार्गास[16] लावून आईचें खरें कर्तव्य तें[17] बजावलें; जिनें[18] कधीं कोणाच्या तोंडून[19] यत्किंचित् वाईट म्हणून घेतलें[20] नाहीं, जी[21] कोणाला[22] कधींही नकोशी वाटली नाहीं; ती[23] आज आम्हां साऱ्यांना रडत ठेवून चालती झाली ![23]आतां ती आम्हांला पुनः कशानें लाभणार ?[24] आतां तिचा तो उपदेश ऐकण्याचा सुप्रसंग[25] आम्हांला कुठला येणार ?[26] आतां तिच्या प्रेमानें सांगितलेल्या शिकवणीच्या गोष्टी[27] कुठल्या ऐकायला सांपडणार ![28] मनुष्य गांवाला गेलें[29], तर तें परत येईल[30] ही आशा[31]; परंतु[32] एकदा या शेवटल्या गांवाला गेलें, म्हणजे[33] पुनः त्याचें दर्शन तरी होतें काय ? आम्ही सारीं त्या दिवशी[34] किती तरी[35] रडलों, किती तरी ओरडलो, किती शोक केला, पण काय उपयोग ! थोड्याच वेळांत आमचा शोक[36] आम्हांस[37] आंवरून[38] पुढल्या तयारीस लागावें लागलें. मेलें मनुष्य कितीहि आवडतें असो[39], तें कितीहि हवेसें वाटो[39], परंतु एकदां त्याच्यांतला प्राण निघून जाऊन माती जड झाली, म्हणजे[40] मग[40] क्षणभरदेखील[41] दृष्टीसमोर ठेववत नाहीं[41] मग त्याचा सर्व लोभ सोडावा लागतो[42], आणि सुटतोहि[42]. आम्ही म्हणजे[43] जगाच्या बाहेरलीं नव्हतों, तेव्हां आई वारल्याबरोबर[44] जे दुःखाचे उमाळे साऱ्यांस आले ते कमी कमी होऊन[45] जनरीतीप्रमाणें पुढील विधीस मंडळी लागली. बाबांची अवस्था मात्र फारच कठीण झालीं[46].

6. 1890-93; H.N. Apte; *Pan Lakshyat Kon Gheto!* 7th ed. (1960), pp.182-83.

The language of the passage, taken from a 'social' novel serialized in the weekly *Karamanuk,* is a landmark in the period style. It clearly distinguishes a genre style based on the models of nineteenth-century English novel. It is characterized by new techniques of sustained narrative register profusely punctuated by exclamations and questions used as narrative devices. Series of clauses, systematically distinguished by commas and semi-colons, increase the length of the sentence. Varied uses of tenses accentuate the use of verbal forms. Increasing weight is put on verbs, adjectives and adverbs. Most of these features have English roots though colloquialism balances the sentence rhythm moderately.

1. A single-verb device important for its varied functions—interjection, emphasizer, brevity, surprise etc.

2. Pronominal form like determiner according to E. structure + head noun + relativization beginning a series of subordinate *wh*-clauses.

3   A prolonged complex clausal chain beginning with 3 and ending at 23 supported only by commas and semi-colons. Relative pronouns are differently inflected for linkage. Subordinate clauses are reduced in value in comparison with the main clause on account of the poverty of syntactic devices to distinguish between the two types.

4,5. After E. noun phrase reference *such* + noun minus the E. accent for exclamatory force; the dash provides the emphasis.

6. Subordinate clause with verbal participle.

7. Second subordinate clause beginning with the correlative shifted in the middle of the clause as a branching device, relative pronoun in possessive.

7,8,9. After E. word order *whose command I . . .*

10. Sktism.

11,12. E. co-ordinating correlatives *not only . . . but also* transferred to M. word order with modifications.   13. Innovatory verbalization.

14. Third subordinate clause; relative pronoun in instrumental.

15. Doublet connected by additive.

16. Single adjective + noun pattern.

17. Colloquial padding for rhythm; also as reference device.

18. Fourth subordinate clause; relative pronoun in instrumental.

19,20. Passivization device supported by verbal compound.

21. Fifth and the last subordinate clause in nominative as the following main clause also has its subject in the nominative; the use of case as a concord device.

22. Use of reflexive verb for E. passivization.

23. Main clause too weak to balance the preceding subordinate clauses but strengthened by a long verbal compound of three participles + one personal verb + exclamatory mark.

24,26. Questions intensifying the narrative.

25. Sktism; coinage.

27. Adjective + noun pattern.

28. Exclamatory sentence with question word + verbal compound + exclamatory mark suggesting negation emphatically.

29,30,31,32. Short metaphor with three syntactic breaks followed by adversative connective; verbs in carefully distinguished tense order.

33. Traditional connective in the middle of the clause merged in E. correlative construction followed by colloquial padding.

34. Time relater bringing the diverted narrative back to the original time situation.

35. Adverbial intensifier repeated thrice, increasing verbalization.

36,37,38. Word order unidiomatic.

39. Parallelism by absolute clauses of similar verbal forms supported by commas.

40. See 33 above and 43 below.

41. After E. *not even a moment*; subject suppressed.

42. Verbal forms; 1. causative + emphatic operator; 2. single-verb clause for emphasis. Abstract Noun as the subject of the sentence.

43. See 33 and 40 above.

44. Verbal participle with postposition followed by a downgraded correlative clause.

45. For E. comparative idiom *less and less*.

46. After E. comparative intensification *very much*.

8.3 CONCLUSION

The foregoing specimen texts are sufficient evidence to suggest that a fully adult writing system capable of accommodating several distinct individual and genre substyles has come into being by 1890. The development of the standard since 1818 has been a continuous process of borrowing and change, which, in the Third phase shifts from the intra-sentential to the sentential sub-system in the texts, with a higher rate of adaptation at the cohesion relationship among sentences in the discourse. Both logical and rhetorical manipulation of the graphic norms, lexical and syntactic patterns and sentential structures have consolidated the inter-relationship between norms and norms, variants and variants, and norms and variants.

It is obvious by the end of the Third phase that Marathi word order has been the most obstinate subsystem. It retains its native flexibility inspite of undergoing some change. It has adopted English punctuation system to modify itself moderately. The use of the comma is particularly more frequent. It is used to point out discontinuity in syntactic breaks, relativization, parenthetical constructions and insertion, and formal and rhetorical parallelism. Of the other points, the end-of-the sentence punctuation marks have proved to be of crucial importance, not only for clarity and order of the internal components of the sentence, but also for intersentential relationships. The quotation marks are not particularly suited to Marathi syntax. The semi-colon is still a stranger in Marathi writing system and the colon has not found its proper place in the rhythmic system of Marathi word order; the dash often serves its function.

Borrowing at the lexical level is fully stabilized under the complex mechanism of substitution, transference and conversion by means of Sanskrit and traditional native devices. The grammatical categories like gender, person and number are applied to even English loan words; so that the interference at the lexical level is fully stabilized by morphophonemic principles of Marathi. There is an unprecedented activity of the revival of dormant and fossilized native lexical features and Sanskrit elements. Whether these processes of transposition of English lexical elements are related to the substratum genetic links between the two distantly related Indo-European languages is a subject of independent research. The Greek and Latin terminology converted to Sanskrit equivalents is of course a more obvious link between several lexical sets and form classes.

An important gain at the lexical level which greatly contributed to the period standard is the growth of new concepts, the use of inanimate objects as the subject of a sentence and abstract ideas absorbed into the

The Influence of English on Marathi

new prose from a variety of English textual sources. Features from old Marathi Pundit and Bakhar styles, colloquial and dialect features, are utilized to fill the gap created by the expanding sentence span. The status of adjectives and adverbs has increased under the pressure of English sentence structure. The adjective + noun and adverb + verb patterns are becoming a popular feature in imitation of English construction, of a similar kind. Several rhythmic elements and cohesive devices such as padding, connectors and linkers have increased to meet the prosodic demands of the new sentence. Amplifiers, emphasizers, intensifiers and downtoners are seen being increasingly employed to reduce the stereotypy caused by the haphazard structure of the new sentence.

Change at the micro-linguistic subsystems is minimal in this phase. At the grammatical level passivization and impersonal constructions with suppressed subject are adjusted with the object-type construction (*Karmani prayoga*) and Marathi is found to be particularly favouring this feature.

The minutely distinguished time sequence of English tense system has made considerable impact on Marathi discourse, but the tense distance which has disturbed cohesion in Marathi discourse in the earlier phase is gradually eliminated in this phase. The four-tier system of English tenses is found merging with the multi-functional participial verbal structures of Marathi. The growth of participials coming in a sequence before the personal verb modulating the underlying concept in more complex shades of tenses, movements and actions have increased greater control of the predicate side, strengthening the hitherto weak verb in Marathi sentence.

At the syntactic level, the uncontrollable clausal linkage has not only increased sentence length but established several new patterns in Marathi word order, such as the downgraded clause, insertion, parenthetical clause, correlative clauses and relativization. Marathi, unlike English, does not possess a device to distinguish between subordinate and main clauses, between clauses of lesser semantic value and those of prominence. Therefore, each clause demands an equal degree of attention and disturbs the movement of the sentence, and consequently of the whole discourse. Punctuation and lexical devices, therefore, have increased to bring about an artificial balance in the sentence. Syntactic cohesive devices other than mere lexical ones are beginning to develop in Marathi.

The most desirable influence of English verbalization has been fully realized in this phase. The traditional bent of Marathi toward nominalization was inadequate to express complex logical relationships and scale of delicacy which is essential to meet the needs of the new age. With the

verbal compounds the capacity of the predicate to carry this load has
increased considerably. The new types of sentences supported by punctuation marks are now able to indicate new cohesion relationships such
as parallelism, adversation, alternation, explanation, conclusion and causality. The subtler rhetorical relationship such as derision, shift, twisting,
substitution, reference, ellipsis etc. are also seen maturing.

At the sentential level, changes are seen in the growth of all the three
types : simple, compound and complex. The sentence span has thus
become broad, much to the credit of the punctuation devices, especially
the comma. The periodic sentence modelled on the English periods of
Johnson and Macaulay has virtually superseded the other types. The
result is basically an inflated sentence swollen with relative clauses,
modifiers, parenthetical clauses and correlatives with conjunctions. Even
the compound sentence has expanded into a juxtaposition of two complex sentences. The simple sentence has become rare and has expanded
beyond its kernel excessively. In general, the sentences exhibit grammatical extravagance having sacrificed the rhythmic necessity. The influence of English syntactical structures which dominate the left-handed
elements of the subject side destroy the balance of the sentence by often
making it amorphous.

Against the background of the total absence of compositional norms
in traditional Marathi prose, the paragraph appears to be the most significant gain in the period style. The new techniques of cohesion borrowed
from English norms of linkers, connectors—syntactic as well as lexical,
and different types of sentences have contributed immensely to make the
paragraph an oratorical entity.

In the various stages of the development of period style, a noticeable
gap between colloquial Marathi and the written prose has been growing.
Attempts made by some writers to explore the inherent potentialities of
the Marathi language have been rare. The transition in expressive tech-
nique from mere information to communication in the First phase, and
from communication to expressiveness in the Second phase is now
tending toward aesthtic use of linguistic features. Deviation from the
norm and the principle of selectivity are seen being used as purposeful
language variation. Linguistic borrowing has assumed contextual dimension and is absorbed conveniently at the stylistic level. Though the
use of English continues as a new *supraglossia,* the process of borrowing
causes little interference in the subsystems because interference has been
circumscribed to limited areas. The more literary motivations of rhythm
and creative urge are seen superseding the earlier motivations of need,
utility and compulsion. With the growth of individual and genre styles,

                                            The Influence of English on Marathi

borrowing has assumed a creative dimensions. The dominant literary forms in this phase are drama, fiction, biography and science. According to M. G. Ranade's report the books published during this phase contain 336 plays, 278 novels, 320 books on science and 96 biographies.[4] Adaptation of literary registers borrowed from English to Marathi genre styles, which can be a subject of independent research, reveals two tendencies : 1. Borrowing stylistic features as they are, when they have no possible equivalence in Marathi, and 2. adjusting the newly borrowed features by accommodating them under conservative conversions. Literary forms have, thus, become instruments of direct stylistic borrowing by 1890.

The different stages of language standardization discussed in 4.4 have reached their apex toward the end of this phase, and the period style found in the writings of different individuals of all communities and in different genres has now become the voice of the entire speech community, a visible sign of unity which is an important characteristic of a national style. The standard language as a medium of discourse in education, journalism and belletrist literature on the one hand, and spread of literacy in all communities and regions on the other, accompolished a period style which is elitist, puristic and Brahmanical. Writers of all castes from Dadoba Pandurang to Phule and Valangakar have accepted this standard. According to A. H. Limaye, out of 128 writers of the nineteenth century, 114 were Brahmans and only 14 from other castes; of these 114 Brahmans, 74 were Chitpavans.[5] The literary milieu was thus dominated by English-educated bilingual Chitpavan Brahmans, the remnants of the Eighteenth-century ruling class. The underlying continuity behind the apparent break in the socio-political conditions is notable. The Brahmans, on account of their deep roots in Sanskrit learning, found a style which discovered common links between the oratorical, verbose, Sanskrit rhetoric on the one hand and the highly oratorical prose modelled on the ornate substyles popular in Vicitorian England, and characterized by lack of precision and subtlety on the other. The hero's voice dominates the prose of the more influential essayists. It encourages incisive satire, lampooning and denunciation rather than judicial criticism, sentimentalism rather than realism, caste-wise fiction rather than the novels of wide human interests. The result of this new rhetorical synthesis of Sanskrit and English elements was noted by E. I. Howard, the then Director of Public Instruction and one of the officials responsible for language planning. He observed :

> "I believe that among almost all Brahmans, there is a tendency to overlay and overwhelm the native Marathee with the learned language, and that (in this connection), for one oriental Swift

who knows the power of his mother tongue, there are scores of oriental Johnsons who delight in a pedantic and stilted phraseology. *This evil must be guarded against.*"[6]

The dominant forms in the prose of this phase reveal exactly the *evil* trends feared by Howard. Prose-writing is found mainly providing for general taste and in conformity with popular communal prejudices. Nativistic motivations, diverted to non-aesthetic linguistic utilization and politicization, increased the loudness in the employment of literary register. This also accounts for the absence of plain prose, scientific and rational discourses, understatement, subtle humour, self-conscious autobiographies, wit and high comic register during this phase.

CHAPTER NINE
Conclusion

All the foregoing chapters end with a set of conclusions and no attempt is made here to recall all of them. A few of them, however, are listed here as we suggest some of the directions in which future investigations in the area could proceed.

The methodology and approach developed in this thesis can, we hope, be profitably applied to the study of problems in the related areas, especially comparative literature and comparative linguistics. The coordination of researches into linguistic acculturation, on the broad foundation of linguistic disciplines, is found to be most fruitful for the study of stylistic influence of one langage on the other. The study of the linguistic aspect of acculturation provides important evidence, as far as the making of a national prose is concerned, of the cultural need of the Indian literary tradition. Perhaps no other foreign cultural element has proliferated so much in the Indian soil as prose during the period of culture contact.

The specific point of view from which the language contact has been considered in our study reveals definite laws and formative processes. Language contact of the textual type leads to confrontation of two linguistic systems. The confrontation of the systems gives rise to a simultaneous occurrence of several literary-aesthetic phenomena which demand independent enquiries into their genesis in the linguistic acculturation. They also bear evidence of the fact that acculturation is, on the whole, a creative process. The contact begins with bilingualism of the literate type, develops into linguistic borrowing and consequently leads to interference and change in the textual system of the receiving language. Language standardization, which is the prerequisite of stylistic norm formation, is a natural result of these processes.

In a country like India, where large ethnic groups with different languages live, at least three layers of linguistic repertoire are found to be in operation :

1. A variety of spoken dialects at the lowest level.
2. A standard language at the middle level.
3. A *supraglossia* at the top. During the period of linguistic acculturation, the *supraglossia* is affected and replaced by the language of the dominant group.

The most characteristic feature of linguistic acculturation in the nineteenth-century India is that the following three processes are found running very close to each other :

1. Language standardization : a linguistic process.
2. Influence of a foreign language : a socio-cultural process.
3. The emergence of a national prose style : a stylistic process.

It is interesting to note that in England these three processes took place in different periods of history and often independent of each other : 1. Language standardization from the midfourteenth to late fifteenth century, when the Midland dialect was established as Standard English, 2. the influence of French and Italian from A.D. 1060 to about 1400, and 3. the making of a national prose style from A.D. 1600 to 1760. The speed in the standardization of Marathi prose and the rapid development of a period style are attributable to the over-all influence of a foreign language, and so also to the peculiar historical and sociological conditions. That a language which did not earlier have even standard norms of written prose should change so rapidly and cope with the new needs with a well-developed prose style speaks of the potential of the Marathi language as a system.

However, our study reveals that the development of the period style did not take place in a straight line of historical linguisitic change. The process of stylistic norm formation under the influence of English during the three phases of the language contact shows that different motivations, from need to fancy, were active behind linguistic borrowing. A kernel of radical transition is found in both structural and para-structural subsystems of text. The transition first affects the existing norms of graphic as well as sentential subsystems. Gradual adjustment of borrowed features in other subsystems appears in later stages of the influence. This is followed by selection, synthesis of alien and native features, and elimination of competing variants with their paradigmatic and syntagmatic arrangements in the textual system.

A broad survey of the Marathi texts written during the period of influence reveals that certain subsystems are more susceptible to change than

                                   The Influence of English on Marathi

others (cf. Conclusions under 6.4, 7.3 and 8.3). Linguistic conservatism is an important dimension in stylistic influence. Phonaesthetic reasons dominate both graphic and structural changes. Concrete semantic categories are easily tranferred into the receiving language, while rhythmic features such as nonsense paddings and pillow words, suprasegmental features and most culture-specific features are not accepted in the stylistic system of the receiving language. The total effect is that of enlargement of the system. During the earlier stages the subsystems are seen expanding and remoulding themselves according to the behaviour of the changing norms and their variants, the borrowed norms often working at cross-purposes. Borrowing at one subsystem affects the other subsystems. Degeneracy at certain subsystems, especially at the prosodic level, is most clearly evident. This develops a secondary subsystem of written prose within the main system. The superficial elements borrowed from the foreign language are tried all at once, creating pigeon-holes in the linguistic structure, as the receiving language is put to increasing pressure by the rapidly increasing bilingualism. A kind of pseudo-style sets in as interim stylistic devices absorb indiscriminate and random borrowings. The stylistic system converts this chaos by means of new norms. Frequent deanglicization is noticeably operative in each phase, the substituting factor being the vanishing *supraglossia*. This process of Sanskritism avoids creolization of the written system. Further research in the phenomenon, which is a peculiar result of the linguistic acculturation in India during the nineteenth century, would be a valuable contribution to the study of language engineering. The dormant role Sanskrit plays in the deep structure of Marathi in the process of influence needs a more detailed investigation. The revived autochthonous elements which become active during the period of influence also need further study on historical lines.

Of the other areas which need further investigation, only a few are statable in concrete terms at this stage of research. Even these assume a number of hypotheses that need to be verified with studies of a similar kind. Statements claiming to be universal cannot be made on the basis of a comparative study of two languages in contact. The methodology of investigating stylistic influence employed in the present study has to be tested on broader range of language communities and their literary cultures. It is also essential to verify whether stylistic influences in all the Indian languages reveal definite patterns. Since the influence of English on the national languages of India has occurred in a similar cultural environment, comparison will be easier. The resulting conclusions will be contributory to acculturation studies. In view of the noticeable negligence of British linguistics of this area, Indian linguists will have to take a lead.

The role of stimulus diffusion in the linguistic nativistic movements of the subcontinent during this period needs to be studied from a literary point of view, to see whether this phenomenon reveals culture-specific literary-aesthetic norms of style in all the Indian languages. Microscopic studies dealing with the change in particular stylistic features between two different points of time, tracing the chronology of particular norms in textual system, may be undertaken for more accurate explanation of changing literary-aesthetic norms within the tradition. For example, the late emergence of poetic style in Marathi under the influence of English may suggest, contrary to the accepted view, that prose is perhaps more sensitive to change, or at least a less conservative medium of expression than poetry.

The theory that Marathi is a case of total acculturation between Dravidian and Aryan languages needs to be examined and the results compared in order to see how far the autochthones dominate the deep structure of Marathi even in the later periods of further acculturation processes.

Evaluation of stylistic influence in relation to the receiving literature does not exist in literary studies because of the lack of delicate scale of analysis appropriate to stylistic studies. Future studies in comparative literature would need models for the analysis of stylistic influence of one language on the other. When we enter the contiguous area of literary influences in world literture, the theory of the 'universals' of literature begins to pose serious problems : Whether the representation of reality in literature is dependent upon the 'world-view' determined by the langauge of a community? If this is true, can linguistic influence transplant an alien world-view in the literary tradition of a different language community? Whether properties implicit in the borrowed signs are imposed on the newly designated things within the borrowing culture's world-view, influencing also its style in the long run? If so, to what extent? Does literate bilingualism encourage plagiaristic tendencies in the whole generation of bilingual writers? What is the aesthetics of literary influence? If style is the deviation from the norm, how to evaluate the literature of the norms which are themselves deviant?

There is ample scope to study these problems in colonial literatures. Perhaps aesthetic norms derived from Graeco-Roman tradition may not be adequate for this purpose and it may be necessary to explore Eastern poetics to evolve more satisfactory norms. The genesis of new literary-aesthetic norms and the related phenomena, during the process of change in Indian literary culture. constitute an area which demands serious critical attention.

                                    The Influence of English on Marathi

NOTES AND REFERENCES

CHAPTER ONE

1. Cf. G. B. Gramopadhye, *Marathi Bakhar Gadya* (1963), preface, pp. 1-11; R. V. Herwadkar, *Marathi Bakhar* (1975), p.3 and 199; R. S. Jog, *Marathi Vangmayabhiruchiche Vibhangamavalokan* (1959), Ch.2; S. R. Kulkarni, *Prachin Marathi Gadya* (1970), pp. 57-58, 64; A. K. Priyolkar, *Granthik Marathi Bhasha ani Konkani Boli* (1966), p. 36; D. W. Potadar, *Marathi Gadyacha Ingraji Avatar* (1976), pp. 1-10; G. B. Sardar, *Arvachin Marathi Gadyachi Purvapithika* (1971), p.1.

2. See John Beames, *A Comparative Grammar of the Modern Aryan Languages of India* (1966), p. 103; Sten Konow, *Linguistic Survey of India*, vol. VII (1967), p.9.

3. Meyer Schapiro, "Style" in *Anthropology Today*, ed. A. L. Kroeber (1953), p. 288.

4. Cf. D. K. Bedekar, Intr. in *Vishrabdha Sharada*, ed. H. V. Mote, vol. 1 (1972), pp. 13-40; Jules Bloch, *Formation of Marathi*, trans. V. G. Paranjape (1941), p. 323; Vishnushastri Chiplunkar, *Nibandhamala* (1926), pp. 5,19,95-108, 139; R. B. Gunjikar, *Sankalit Lekh*, vol. I (1942), pp.193,342; R. S. Jog (ed.) *Marathi Vangmayacha Itihas*, vol. V : 1 (1973), p. 3; R. B. Joshi, *Marathi Bhashechi Ghatana* (1923), p. 520; N. C. Kelkar, *Samagra Kelkar Vangmaya* vol. 11 (1938), pp. 516-31; S. K. Kolhatkar, *Lekhasangraha* (1932), pp. 585, 605, 616, 617-40, 665; M. M. Kunte, *Raja Shivaji* (1924), p. 3; A. K. Priyolkar, op. cit., p.41; M. G. Ranade, *The Miscellaneous Writings* (1915), pp.2-11; D. P. Tarkhadkar, *Maharashtra Bhasheche Vyakaran* (1865), pp. 3-4; B. G. Tilak, *Samagra*

Lokmanya Tilak, vol. 6 (1976), p. 927; John Wilson, "Notes. . .," in *Marathi-English Dictionary* by J. T. Molesworth (1975), p.29.

5. See V. S. Naipaul, *The Area of Darkness* (1970), p. 213.

6. See Ravinder Kumar, *Western India in The Nineteenth Century* (1968); Arthur Mayhew, *The Education of India* (1926); Ramkrishna Mukherjee, *Rise and Fall of the East India Company* (1958); L. S. S. O'Malley, *Modern India and the West* (1941); *Language and Society in India : Proceedings of a Seminar* (1969); Anil Seal, *The Emergence of Indian Nationalism* (1971).

7. Refer Ch. 3.1, pp. 99-100.

8. Refer Ch. 3. 2.1 and 3.5, pp. 100-107 and 128-32.

9. See V. K. Gokak, *English in India* (1964), p. 5; Akhileshwar Jha, "The Sex-bound Literary Tradition," *New Quest* 12 (1978), pp. 373-82; Braj B. Kachru, "English in South Asia," in *Current Trends in Linguistics,* vol. 5, ed. T. A. Sebeok (1969), pp. 627-78; S. M. Katre, *The Formation of Konkani* (1942), p. 148; M. G. Krishnamurthi, "Literary Studies in India," *New Quest : 15* (1979), pp. 165-73; R. C. Majumdar (ed.), *British Paramountcy and British Renaissance,* part II (1965), p. 45.

10. D. W. Potadar, *Marathi Gadyacha Ingraji Avatar* (1976).

11. See J. R. Firth, *Papers in Linguistics 1934-1951* (1957), p. 55; Richard Temple, *Oriental Experience* (1883), pp. 152, 225; Charles E. Trevelyan, *On the Education of the People of India* (1838), pp. 37, 38; T. B. Macaulay's Minute, quoted in *Life and Letters of Lord Macaulay,* vol. 1 by G. O. Trevelyan (1908), p. 448.

12. See Bhalchandra Nemade, "The Revolt of the Underprevileged," *Journal of Asian and African Studies,* vol. XIV : 3-4 (1980).

13. See John Beames, op. cit., pp. 1-121; S. K. Chatterji, *Languages and Literatures of Modern India* (1963); also *Indo-Aryan and Hindi* (1942), pp. 102-4, 126; P. D. Gune, *An Introduction to Comparative Philology* (1950), Ch. 1; Sten Konow, op. cit., pp. 1-28; Alfred Master, *A Grammar of Old Marathi* (1964), pp. 1-2, 33-39; S. M. Katre, op. cit., pp. 95-97.

14. We have coined the term *supraglossia* to connote the special functions of a kind of creolized variety of *lingua franca*, which has been a historical phenomenon in the linguistic culture of India.

                                            The Influence of English on Marathi

As a cultural medium it works as a literary language, a medium of intellectual intercourse in the multilingual communities of the sub-continent. The hierarchical layers : 1. The spoken dialects, 2. the literary varnacular language fairly standardized for use in different parts of India, and 3. the *supraglossia*, perform independent functions. *Supraglossia* as a language of culture is a parallel medium with a fair degree of continuity like Sanskrit and the Prakrits. The term *diglossia* defined by Charles A. Ferguson, *Word :* 15 (1959), pp. 325-40 is inadequate for this phenomenon because it refers to two variants of the native language, the higher one superposed on the lower. See also Valter Tauli, "The Theory of Language Planning," *Advances in Language Planning,* ed. Joshua A. Fishman (1974), p. 64; J. A. Fishman, "The Sociology of Language," in *Advances in the Sociology of Language,* vol. 1 (1971), pp. 235 ff.

15. See Note 1; also S. G. Tulpule, *An Old Marathi Reader* (1960).

16. Frantz Fanon, *The Wretched of The Earth* (1977), pp. 196-97.

17. Cf. D. K. Bedekar, *Towards Understanding Gandhi* (1975), Ch.3.

18. O'Malley, *Modern India and the West,* p. 764.

19. Rene' Wellek and Austin Warren, *Theory of Literature* (1966), p. 265.

20. Cf. A. L. Kroeber, *Style and civilizations* (1957), p. 149; also *Anthropology* (1967), pp. 245, 248.

21. Otto Jespersen, *Language : Its Nature, Development and Origin* (1954), p. 260.

22. Compare the early essays of Lokahitavadi, *Lokahitavadinchi Shatapatre* (1940) with his booklet *Jatibhed* (1974), in which he admitted caste hierarchy.

23. See V. K. Rajavade, *Kanishtha, Madhyam va Uchcha Shalantil Svanubhava* (1931), p. 33.

24. See M. G. Ranade, op. cit., pp. 12-54; D. P. Tarkhadkar, "Atmacharitra" in *Raobahaddur Dadoba Pandurang* (1947), p.157.

25. See details in Ch. 4.2.1, 4.2.2.

26. See Einar Haugen, "Languages in Contact," *Proceedings of the Eighth International Congress of Linguists, 1957* (1958), pp. 771-810; Harry Hoijer, "The Relation of Language to Culture," *Anthropology Today,* ed. A. L. Kroeber (1953), p. 561; A. L. Kroeber, *Anthropology* (1967), pp. 245, 248; Uriel Weinreich, *Languages in Contact* (1953), p.6.

27. See H. D. Sankalia, "India's Language c. 300 B.C.—A.D. 1960, *"Linguistics and Language Planning in India,* ed. N. G. Kalelkar (1969), pp. 12-19.

28. Edward Sapir, *Culture, Language and Personality,* ed. David G. Mandelbaum (1962), p.33.

29. J. R. Firth, *Studies in Linguistic Analysis* (1957), p.22.

30. Cf. A. R. Kelkar, "Some Notes on Language and Literature," *Indian Linguistics,* vol. 31:3 (1970), pp.1-2.

31. Andre' Martinet, *A Functional View of Language* (1962), pp. 135 and 137.

32. Ibid., p. 137.

33. See Einar Haugen, op. cit., p.773; also "Problems of Bilingualism," *Lingua,* vol. 2:1 (1949), pp. 272-90; P. S. Ray, *Language Standardization Studies in Prescriptive Linguistics* (1963); Uriel Weinreich, "Research Frontiers in Bilingual Studies, " *Proceedings of the Eighth International Congress of Linguists, 1957* (1958), pp. 786-97. Also see articles on the subject in *Readings in the Sociology of Language,* ed. Joshua A. Fishman (1972).

34. Cf. John W. M. Verhaar, "Method, Theory, and Phenomenology," *Method and Theory in Linguistics,* ed. Paul L. Garvin (1970), p.65.

35. Cf. Melville J. Herskovits, *Man and His Works* (1956), pp. 526-30.

36. Cf. Edward Sapir, *Language : An Introduction to the Study of Speech* (1949), p. 219.

37. Harry Hoijer, "Linguistic and Cultural Change," *Language,* 24 : 4 (1948), p. 342.

38. Ralph Beals, "Acculturation," in *Anthropology Today,* ed. A. L. Kroeber (1953), p. 635.

39. A. Martinet, preface to *Language in Contact* by Uriel Weinreich, pp.8-9.

40. Charles A. Ferguson, "Language Development," *Language Problems of Developing Nations,* eds. J. Fishman, Ferguson and Das Gupta (1968), p.32.

41. Lubomir Dolezel, "Toward a Structural Theory of Content in Prose Fiction," in *Literary Style : A Symposium,* ed. S. Chatman (1971), p. 95.

42. Tzvetan Todorov, *The Poetics of Prose* (1977), p.20.

                                        The Influence of English on Marathi

43. Archibald A. Hill, *Introduction to Linguistic Structures* (1958), p.406.

44. Alphonse G. Juilland, "Charles Bruneau : Review of L'Epoque Realiste," in *Essays on the Language of Literature,* eds. S. Chatman and S. R. Levin (1967), p. 378.

45. A. Martinet, *Functional View*, p. 135.

46. Wallace L. Chafe, "Internal Reconstruction in Seneca," *Language,* 35 : 3 (1959), p.483.

47. Naomi S. Baron, *Language Acquisition and Historical Change* (1977), Ch. 1.5.

48. Einar Haugen, *Bilingualism in the Americas* (1956), p.42.

49. James M. Anderson, *Structural Aspects of Language Change* (1973), p.215.

50. Harold Weinreich, "The Textual Function of the French Article," *Literary Style : A Symposium,* ed. S. Chatman (1971), p.221.

51. See Nils E. Enkvist, *Linguistic Stylistics* (1973), p.142; M. A. K. Halliday, Angus McIntosh and Peter Strevens, *The Linguistic Sciences and Language Teaching* (1970), pp. 27,97,246; M. I. Isayev, *National Language in the U.S.S.R. : Problems and Solutions* (1977), p. 306; D. D. Lee, "The Linguistic Aspect of Wintu" Acculturation, " *American Anthropologist,* vol. 45 : 3 (1943), p. 435; David Robey (ed.), *Structuralism* (1973), pp. 6-9; H. G. Widdowson, "Stylistics," *The Edinburgh Course in Applied Linguistics*, ed. J. P. B. Allen and S. Pit-Corder (1974), p.206.

52. See H. S. Babb (ed.), *Essays in Stylistic Analysis* (1972), p. 5. For different concepts of style, see Roland Barthes, *Writing Degree Zero*, intr., pp.7-12; Richard Ohmann, "Speech, Action and Style," in *Literary Style,* ed. S. Chatman (1971), p.243; Nils E. Enkvist, "On Defining Style," in *Linguistics and Style,* ed. John Spencer (1964), pp. 10-27.

53. Cf. A. R. Kelkar, "On Aesthesis," *Humanist Review* : 2 (1969), p. 226.

54. Michael Riffaterre, "Criteria for Style Analysis," *Word,* 15 (1959), p. 154.

55. Efim Etkind, "Comparative Stylisitics," *Diogenes,* 57 (Spring, 1967), pp.33-46.

56. Roman Jakobson, "Linguistics and Poetics," *Style in Language*, ed. Thomas A. Sebeok (1964), p.352.

57. See Nils E. Enkivist, *Linguistic Stylistics* (1973), Ch. 4; John Spencer and Michael J. Gregory, "An Approach to the study of Style," in *Linguistics and Style* ed. John Spencer (1964), pp. 99-102.

58. See Jeffrey Ellis, *Towards a General Comparative Linguistics* (1966), pp.33-61, 102.

59. Lubomir Dolezel, op. cit., Note 41.

60. Uriel Weinreich, *Languages in Contact*, pp.3-6.

61. Cf. Ju. M. Lotman et al., "Theses on the Semiotic Study of Cultures," in *The Tell-Tale Sign : A Survey of Semiotics,* ed. Thomas A. Sebeok (1975), p.80.

62. See Winfred P. Lehmann, *Historical Linguistics : An Introduction* (1966); Holger Pederson, *Linguistic Science in the Nineteenth Century,* trans. John M. Spargo (1931).

63. See Jeffrey Ellis, *Comparative Linguistics;* U. Weinreich, *Languages in Contact.*

64. J. Ellis, ibid.

65. Several analytical works, works on translation theory and the methods of the Russian formalists and Prague School have been utilized for the textual analysis of several Marathi works, though a small number of selected specimen passages are presented for demonstration in Chapters 6, 7 and 8 of the present study.

66. Halliday, McIntosh and Strevens, *The Linguistic Sciences,* pp. 246-49.

67. Cf. J. D. McCawley, "English as VSO Language," in *Semantic Syntax*, ed. Pieter A.M. Seuren (1974), p.94.

68. Cf. James M. Anderson, *Structural Aspects of Language Change,* p. 215.

69. See David Lodge, *Language of Fiction* (1966), p.85; Rene' Wellek, *Discriminations* (1970), p.337.

70. J. Ellis, *Copmarative Linguisitics,* p. 37.

CHAPTER TWO

1. Benedetto Croce, *Aesthetic : As Science of Expression and General Linguistic* (1962). p.136.

2. M. J. Herskovits, *Man and His Works*, p. 530.

3. There is no reference to any of the old Marathi prose classics in the writings of William Carey, S. K. Chhatre, Balshastri Jambhekar, Bhau Mahajan, Lokahitavadi, Dadoba Pandurang, Baba Padamanji, R.B. Gunjikar, Krishnashastri Chiplunkar, Phule, Vishnushastri Chiplunkar, B. G. Tilak, G. G. Agarkar, H. N. Apte and others.

4. See Major Candy's writings; Robert Drummond, *Illustrations of the Grammatical Parts of the Guzerattee, Mahratta and English Languages* (1808); Mountstuart Elphinstone's correspondence, J. T. Molesworth, Preface to *Marathi-English Dictionary*, p. XXV; E. I. Howard's correspondence; Macaulay's Minute and other works also reveal the ignorance of the existence of old Marathi prose.

5. I. M. P. Raeside lists 339 mss. of the single cycle of Mahanubhava prose in "A Bibliographical Index of Mahanubhava Works in Marathi," *Bulletin of the S.O.A.S.*, vol. XXIII, part 3 (1960), pp.464-507; S. M. Katre, *Introduction to Indian Textual Criticism* (1941),p. 28. The Marathi Department of Marathwada University alone has over 3000 mss. lying unpublished.

6. See Durga Bhagvat, "A Critical Bibliography of Folklore in Maharashtra," *Journal of the Asiatic Society of Bombay*, 39/40 (1964-65), pp. 273-320; *Marathwadyatil Lokakatha*, ed., Y. M. Pathan (1962), preface, pp. 1-29.

7. S. R. Kulkarni, *Prachin Marathi Gadya*, pp. 57-58.

8. Ibid., p. 64; S. G. Tulpule, *An Old Marathi Reader*, (1960), p.3.

9. See note 5; V. L. Bhave also mentions 6000 mss., see "Puravani", in *Maharashtra Sarasvat*, 5th ed. (1963), p.670.

10. See the style of passages C 1 to C 5 in the Annexure.

11. See Mahimbhat, *Leelacharitra*, ed. V.B. Kolte (1978), intr., pp.67-74.

12. Cf. I. M. P Raeside, "The Mahanubhava Sakala Lipee," *Bulletin of the S.O.A.S.*, vol. XXXIII, Part 2 (1970), p. 328 ff.

13. See R.V. Herwadkar, *Marathi Bakhar*, 2nd ed. (1975).

14. Ibid., p. 199; M. T. Patwardhan, *Pharsi Marathi Kosh* (1925), preface, p.4; A. K. Priyolkar, *Granthik Marathi Bhasha.*, p.40.

15. See G. B. Grampopadhye, *Peshavedaptraratil Marathi Bhasheche Svarup* (1940); Y. M. Pathan, *Marathi Bakharitil Pharsiche Svarup* (1973).

16. See Note 3; R. S. Jog, *Vihangamavalokan*, pp. 211-12; G.B. Sardar, *Purvapithika*, p.1.

17. See B. G. Jambhekar, *Jeevanavritta va Lekhasangraha*, vol. 2 (1950), pp. 154-55; and Baba Padamanji, *Arunodaya*, 3rd ed. (1963), pp. 10-11, 15, 25, 32; John Wilson, *Marathi-English Dictionary*, ed. Molesworth; and also references to old texts in Tarabai Shinde, *Streepurush Tulana*, ed. S.G. Malashe, 2nd ed. (1975).

18. See Bibliography.

19. M. M. Kunte, *Raja Shivaji*, p.2.

20. Baba Padamanji, *Arunodaya*, pp. 10,11,12,15,32,54,76.

21. See R. W. Chambers, *On the Continuity of English Prose* (1932); Ian A. Gordon, *The Movement of English Prose* (1966), pp.8-9; James Sutherland, *On English Prose* (1957), p.10.

22. Gordon, ibid, p.9.

23. See. M. K. Damle, *Shastriya Marathi Vyakaran*, ed. K. S. Arjunwadkar (1970), pp. 76, 82, 85, 310, 554, 677, 752; Krishnashastri Godbole, *Marathi Bhasheche Navin Vyakaran* (1967), Notice; V. K. Rajavade, "Marathitil Shuddhalekhanasambandhi...," in *Granthamala* (?); D. P. Tarkhadkar, *Maharashtra Bhasheche Vyakaran*, 4th ed. (1865), p. 13; also "Atmacharitra" op. cit., p.85; R. B. Joshi, *Praudhabodh Marathi Vyakaran* (1889), p.2.

24. S. M. Katre, *Formation of Konkani*, p. 97.

25. M. M. Kunte, *Raja Shivaji*, p.16.

26. See Dadoba Pandurang Tarkhadkar, *Maharashtra Bhasheche Vyakaran*, pp. 21-22; Jagannathshastri Kramawant et al., *A Dictionary of the Marathi Language* (1829), preface; Gangadhar Shastri Phadke, *Maharashtra Bhasheche Vyakaran* (1836), p.6.

27. i. *Bhausahebanchi Bakhar*, (1955); ii. Raghunath Yadav Chitre (?), *Panipatachi Bakhar* (1955); iii. *Holkaranchi Kaifiyat* (1954); iv. excerpt from "Shrimant Bhausahebanchi Kaifiyat," *Marathi Bakhar Gadya*, ed. G. B. Gramopadhye (1963).

28. For example, see *Bhausahebanchi Bakhar*, p.7.

29. Ibid., p.77.

30. See G. B. Gramopadhye, *Peshavedaptaratil Marathi*, pp. 291-320.

31. R. B. Joshi, *Marathi Vyakaran*, pp. 292-95.

2. S. K. Kolhatkar, *Lekhasangrah*, pp. 589-95.

33. Cf. S. K. Chatterji, *Indo-Aryan and Hindi*, p. 126.

34. See Note 29, and also Annex. D2.

35. John Beames, *Comparative Grammar*, p.189.

36. Cf. Claudio Guillen, *Literature as System : Essays Toward the Theory of Literary History* (1971), Ch.3.

ANNEXURES TO CHAPTER 2 :

A1 : *Sachitra Kahanya*, ed. K. A. Joshi (?), pp. 41-42.

A2 : "Laxminarayankalyan," *Granthamala* (1906), pp.6-7.

B1 : "Vaidyak," *Prachin Marathi Gadya Granth* (1938), p.14.

B2 : Niranjan Madhav, *Advaitamrit Gadyatika*, ed. S. R. Kulkarni (1968), p.76.

C1 : Mahimbhat, *Leelacharitra : Ekank*, ed. H. N. Nene (1953), p.23.

C2 : Chakradhar, "Drishantapath," in *Sutrapath* (1959), p.83.

C3 : Bai Deva Vyasa, "Pujavasar," in *Sutrapath* (1959), pp. 55-56.

C4 : Narendra and Parasharam (?), *Smritisthal*, ed. V. N. Deshpande (1960), p.7.

C5 : *Panchopakhyan*, ed. V. B. Kolte (1979), pp. 109-10.

D1 : Keshavacharya and others, *Mahikavatichi Bakhar*, ed. V. K. Rajavade (1924), p.39.

D2 : *Bhausahebanchi Bakhar*, ed. V. S. Chitale and S. N. Joshi (1955), pp. 86-87.

D3 : *Kavyetihasasangraha*, ed. G. S. Sardesai, Y. M. Kale and V. S. Vakarkar (1930), pp. 51-52.

E1 : Ekanath, *Ekanathi Bharud, 1* (1961), pp.7-8.

E2 : *Prachin Marathi Gadya*, ed. S. G. Tulpule (1961), pp. 120-21.

F1 : *Manapatra*, Ms. No. 23, Marathi Department. Marathawada University Aurangabad.

F2 : Mahimbhat (?), *Shri Govind Prabhu Charitra*, Ms. No. 327, Marathi Dept. Marathwada Univ., Aurangabad.

F3 : Bajirao I, *Sanad by Raje Shahu Chhatrapati*, Marathi Dept., Marathwada Univ., Aurangabad.

1. See Claude Levi-Strauss, *Structural Anthropology* (1963), p. 21. Also see B. Malinowsky, "The Dilemma of Contemporary Linguistics, " *Language in Culture and Society*, ed. Dell Hymes (1964), p.63; M. J. Herskovits, *Man and His Works, pp. 539 ff.* Otto Jespersen, *Language*, p. 260; A. L. Kroeber. *Anthropology*, p. 467; A. Martinet, *Elements of General Linguistics* (1964), pp. 166-67; E. Sapir, *Culture, Language and Personality*, p. 35; Ferdinand de Saussure, *Course in General Linguistics* (1960), pp. 6-7.

2. See S. M. Pinge, *Europeanancha Marathicha Abhyas. . .* (1960), pp. 1- 44.

3. See G. N. Madgaonkar, *Mumbaiche Varnan* (1961), esp. Chapters 1 and 2.

4. See Edgell Rickword, "The Social Setting (1780-1830)." *The Pelican Guide to English Literature,* vol. 5, ed. Boris Ford (1961), p.13.

5. See E. W. Said, *Orientalism* (1978); Introduction, Dickens, David Copperfield, p.3.

6. Ibid. p.22 ff.; and H. G. Rawlinson, "Indian Influence on the West," in O'Malley, *Modern India and the West* (1941).

7. All the contemporary writers record this fact. See Bibliography for the works of Balshastri Jambhekar, N. V. Joshi, Lokahitavadi, G. N. Madgaonkar, Baba Padamanji, D. P. Tarkhardkar and Moroba Kanhoba Vijaykar.

8. See Baba Padmanji's letter in *Dnyanodaya*, ed. B. P. Hivale (1942), pp. 108-9; Pherozeshah Mehta, *Some Unpublished and Later Speeches and Writings,* ed. Jeejeebhoy (1918), p.7; Jotirao Phule, *Samagra Vangmaya* (1969), pp. 43, 90, 136, 315, 486, D. P. Tarkhadkar, "Atmacharitra," p. 177.

9. See R. V. Parulekar (ed.), *Selections from the Records of the Government of Bombay* : Part I (1953), p. 91. R. Kumar, *Western India*, Ch. 2.

10. R. Kumar, ibid., p. 45.

11. See A. Mayhew, *The Education of India*, p.9 ff.

12. Quoted in D. P. Tarkhadkar's "Charitra," by A. K. Priyolkar, p. 375.

13. Quoted by K. B. Kulkarni in *Adhunik Marathi Gadyachi Utkranti* (1956), p.1.

The Influence of English on Marathi

14. Quoted in D. P. Tarkhadkar's, "Charitra," p. 374.

15. Quotation from Eric Stokes, *The English Utilitarians and India* (1959), p. 45. See also E. Trevelyan, *On the Education*, p. 193.

16. Quoted by Mayhew in *The Education of India*, p. 26.

17. Quoted by R. Mukherjee, *Rise and Fall*, p. 380.

18. Eric Stokes, *The English Utilitarians and India*, p. 51.

19. The eye-witness was Vishnubhat Godse, see his autobiography *Majha Pravas* (1966), p. 101. Also see *Dnyanodaya*, ed. B. P. Hivale, pp. 138-54; Pat Barr, *The Memsahibs* (1978), Chapters 7 and 8; S. G. Malshe, *Sattavani Uthavachi Samakalin Katrane* (1977).

20. See R. B. Gunjikar, "Apalya Bhasheche Pudhe Kay Honar?" *Vividhadnyanavistara* 21 : 9-10 (1889), pp. 207-17.

21. Some of the more important names are : Harry Arbuthnot Acworth, Major Candy, Grant Duff, Sir Bartle Frere, Thomas Graham, A. Grant, E. I. Howard, George Jervis, C. A. Kincaid, Molesworth, the Rev. Nesbit, Dr. J. Stevenson and Dr. John Wilson.

22. See N. C. Kelkar, *Samagra Kelkar Vangmaya,* vol. 7 (1938), p. 304; R. C. Majumdar (ed.) *British Paramountcy and Indian Rennaissance,* Part II (1965), Chapter 2.

23. See O'Malley (ed.), *Modern India and the West*, p. 649.

24. Ibid., p. 648.

25. See *The Teaching of English in England* (1935), p. 20.

26. See J. A. K. Thomson, *The Classical Background of English Literature* (1950), p. 223 ff.; Ian A. Gordon, *English Prose*, p.157.

27. G.H. McKnight, *The Evolution of the English Language* (1968), Ch. XVI.

28. See for example, George Jervis's *Prasiddhipatra*. Molesworth's preface to his *Dictionary,* and Candy's statement in *Dnyanodaya*, ed. Hiwale (1942), pp.186-89.

29. See the Addressess presented to Mary Carpenter and her correspondence in *Vishrabdha Sharada,* ed. H. V. Mote, vol. 1 (1972), pp. 100-07, *Dnyanodaya,* ed. Hivale, p.28.

30. See Note 11 in Chapter 1; and also see the documents relating to Mountstaurt Elphinstone in R. V. Parulekar's (ed), *Selections,* Part I (1953).

31. See B. Jambhekar, *Jeevanvritta,* pp. 2-3; G. N. Madgaonkar, *Mumbaiche Varnan,* preface, p.2; D. P. Tarkhadkar, *Puranika*

(1881), p. 4; L. M. Halabe, *Muktamala* (1959), preface to First ed., p.3.

32. Cf. Richard Temple, *Men and Events* (1882), p. 502; R. V. Parulekar (ed), *Selections,* Part I, p. 91.

33. J. Paul Sartre, Preface to F. Fanon's, *The Wretched of the Earth,* p.7.

34. See Nurullah Syed and J. P. Naik, *History of Education in India* (1943), pp. 63-64.

35. See Marathi works in Bibliography esp. by Vans Kennedy, William H. Bell, T. Candy, David Capon, William Carrey, Robert Drummond, Mrs. Farrar, George Jervis, John McLennan, Dr. J. Stevenson, John Wilson and Madam Wilson.

36. See R. V. Parulekar (ed.), *Selections,* Part I, pp 92 ff.

37. See A. R. Kelkar, "Marathi as a State Language : A case study in Language Planning," *New Quest :* 23 (1980), p. 269.

38. B. Jambhekar, *Jeevanvritta.* vol. II (1950), p. 153; N. Syed and J. P. Naik, *History of Education,* p. 137; A Seal, *Indian Nationalism,* pp.89-93.

39. A. Mayhew, *The Education of India,* p. 13.

40. E. Stokes, *English Utilitarians and India,* p. 43.

41. See Jervis's statement and other details in N. Syed and J. P. Naik, op. cit. p. 139.

42. See Note 38; and also Lord Mayo's denunciation of the Filtration theory in O'Malley's, *Modern India and the West,* pp. 652-53.

43. G. R. Potter, *Macaulay* (1959), p. 15.

44. See Correspondence in R. V. Parulekar (ed.), *Selections,* Part III (1957), p. 61.

45. See M. G. Ranade, *Miscellaneous Writings* (1915), pp.52-53; *Vividhadnyanavistara* 3:10 (1871), p. 148; 6:7 (1873), pp. 130-31 and 21 : 9-10 (1889), pp. 209-11; N. V. Joshi, *Pune Varnan* (1971), p. 78; J. Stevenson's letter quoted in K. B. Kulkarni, op. cit., Append., p. 37; D. P.Tarkhadkar, "Charitra" in *Raobahadur Dadoba Pandurang* (1947), p. 301.

46. For caste-wise distribution of students see R. V. Parulekar (ed.), *Selections,* Part II (1955), p. 262; and Part III (1957), p. 205. Also see N. Syed and J. P.Naik, *History of Education,* pp. 298-99.

47. V. Chiplunkar, *Nibandhamala,* p. 19; Jotirao Phule, *Samagra Vangmaya,* pp 3, 82, 172; G. K. Gokhale, *The Select Gokhale*

(1968), p. 329; M. N. Wankhede "Education and Social Reform in Maharashtra," in A. K. Bhagwat (ed.), *Maharashtra — A Profile* (1977), p. 324 ff.

48. N. Syed and J. P. Naik, *History of Education,* p. 315.

49. See *Elphinstone School-Paper,* vol. IV (1863); M. S. Gole, *Brahman ani Tyanchi Vidya* (1895), Chapters 3 and 11; S. Nagarajan, "The Decline of English in India : Some Historical Notes," in *English and India,* ed. M. Manuel and K. Ayyappa Paniker (1978), p. 163.

50. For example, no writer in the nineteenth century Maharashtra seems to have known the names of Emile and Charlotte Bronte, George Eliot, Thomas Hardy, Anthony Trollope, William Morris, Samuel Butler, Charles Reade and Oscar Wilde; while writers like Walter Scott, Reynolds, Meadows Taylor, Lord Lytton were more popularly read.

51. R. Temple, *Men and Events,* p. 432.

52. See M. N. Srinivas, "A note on Sanskritization and Westernization," *Caste in Modern India and Other Essays* (1970).

53. Cf. R. Kumar, *Western India,* Chapter VIII; O'Malley (ed.), *Modern India and The West,* p. 651 ff.; A. Seal, *Indian Nationalism,* pp. 92-93.

54. R. Mukherjee, *Rise and Fall,* p. 327.

55. Cf. R. W. Chambers, *Continuity of English Prose* (1932), p. 58.

56. See Bhalchandra Nemade, "Marathi Kadambari," *Anushtubh* (Sept.-Oct. 1980), pp. 44-46.

57. See T. N. Atre, *Gavagada* (1959), esp. Chapter 4.

58. R. Temple, *Men and Events,* p. 497.

59. See *Dnyanodaya,* (ed.), B. P. Hivale; and Baba Padamanji, *Arunodaya, p. 89.*

60. Cf. Jotirao Phule, *Samagra Vangmaya,* pp. 121, 135.

61. See A. K. Priyolkar, "Devanagari Lipitil Pahila Mudrit Granth," in *Dr. Kolte Gaurav Granth* (1969), p. 138.

62. See D. K. Bedekar and A. R. Kelkar "Marathi Literature, 1870-1970," in *Maharashtra—A Profile,* ed. A. K. Bhagwat (1977), pp. 228-50; N. R. Phatak's Preface to V. K. Joshi and R. K. Lele's *Vrittapatrancha Itihas,* vol. 1 (1950).

1. Cf. B. Malinowski, "The Dilemma of Contemporary Linguistics," in *Language in Culture and Society,* ed. D. Hymes (1964), p. 63.

2. Cf. Melville J. Herskovits, *Man and His Works,* p. 526.

3. See Eric Stokes, *The English Utilitarians,* Intr., p. VIII; also see Macaulay's assessment of Hindu culture in his "Minute," G. Trevelyan, *The Competition Wallah,* pp. 319-30.

4. See Erskine Perry's "Note on Education," in N. Syed and J. P. Naik, *History of Education,* p. 137; O'Malley (ed.), *Modern India and The West, p. 365.*

5. Quoted in D. P. Tarkhadkar, "Atmacharitra," ed. A. K. Priyolkar, p. 373.

6. See B. Jambhekar, *Darpansangraha,* ed. V. K. Joshi and S. M. Sahasrabuddhe (1946), p. 4; Lokahitavadi, *Shatapatre,* ed. S. R. Tikekar, esp. Essays :1, 5, 12, 31, 38, 46, 54 and 94.

7. Renate Zahar, *Frantz Fanon : Colonialism and Alienation* (1974), p. 14 ff.

8. See list of British bilingual writers under Note 21 in Ch.3, the names of Mountstuart Elphinstone, William Jones, Lord Minto, Monier Monier-Williams, Major Wilkinson and several others who encouraged native writing can be added to the list.

9. A characteristic example of this attitude is seen in Macaulay's letter quoted by G. O. Trevelyan in *Life and Letters of Lord Macaulay* (1908), p. 468, where he states : "The tropical fruits are wretched. The best of them is inferior to our apricot or gooseberry ... a plantain is very like a rotten pear." For a detailed interpretation of different attitudes of British writers toward Indian culture, see Allen Greenberger, *The British Image of India : A study in the Literature of Imperialism* (1969). The more sober view of the racial relationship is reflected in E. M. Forster's *A Passage to India* (1924, rpt. 1976).

10. Nirad C. Chaudhari, *The Continent of Circe* (1966).

11. See Martin Montgomery quoted in R. Mukherjee's *Rise and Fall,* p. 380.

12. Cf. Braj Kachru, "English in South Asia," in *CTL,* vol. 5, ed. T. A. Sebeok (1969), pp. 630-34; also articles by S. K. Chatterji, L. M. Khubchandani and P. B. Pandit in *Language and Society in India : Proceedings of Seminar* (1969).

13. See M. Herskovits, *Man and His Works,* p. 532; M. L. Samuels, *Linguistic Evolution with Special Reference to English* (1972), pp. 92 ff.; J. M. Anderson, *Structural Aspects,* pp. 2 ff.

14. Cf. Lokahitavadi, *Shatapatre,* p. 127; R. B. Gunjikar, *Sankalit Lekh* vol. 1, p. 43; V. Chiplunkar, *Nibandhmala,* pp. 67, 556-628; M. G. Ranade, *Miscellaneous Writings,* pp. 39, 52-53.

15. See R. B. Patankar, *Saundaryamimansa* (1974), Intr., p. 14; Braj Kachru, op. cit. Note 12; also J. H. Greenberg, *Essays in Linguistics* (1957), p. 74.

16. J. R. Firth, *Papers in Linguistics,* p. 55.

17. V. S. Naipaul, *An Area of Darkness,* p. 209.

18. Ibid., p. 211.

19. E. Haugen, *Bilingualism,* p. 99.

20. See Ch. 3.3.5, The Third Phase for nativisitc reactions.

21. M. Herskovits, *Man and his Works,* p. 532.

22. See Franklin C. Southworth, "Detecting Prior Creolization," in D. Hymes (ed.), *Pidginization and Creolization of Languages* (1971), pp. 255-73; also see V. Khaire, *Dravid Maharashtra* (1977) and "Itihaspurva Marathamoli" in *Marathi Sanshodhan :* 11 (1978); S. B. Joshi, *Marathi Sanskriti* (1952).

23. See Ch. 6.3 : analysis of Specimen Passage No. 1.

24. A. L. Kroeber, *Anthropology,* p. 248.

25. Ju. M. Lotman et al., "Theses on The Semiotic Study of Cultures," in *The Tell-Tale Sign,* ed. Sebeok, p. 58.

26. Roman Jacobson in *Style in Language,* p. 351

27. Efim Etkind, *Diogenes* : 57, pp. 39-40.

28. Gerald D. Berreman, "Aleut Reference Group Alienation, Mobility and Acculturation," *American Anthropologist,* 66:2 (1964), p. 245.

29. V. S. Naipaul, *An Area of Darkness,* p. 208; also see E. B. Havell, *The History of Aryan Rule in India* (1918), intr., p. X, wherein he confesses that the British had failed in raising both material and spiritual aspects of national art in India.

30. Cf. R. Barthes, *Elements of Semiology* (1969), pp. 58-88.

31. See E. Said, *Orientalism,* pp. 51 ff.

32. The syllabuses and the textbooks in the curriculums of schools and universities reveal that no such courses were taught throughout the nineteenth century. For further details see *The Teaching of English in England* (1935); *Elphinstone School-Paper* (1863); S. P. Sinha, *English in India* (1978); S. Nagarajan, "The Decline of English in India," in *English and India,* ed. Manuel and Paniker (1978).

33. See V. Chiplunkar, *Nibandhmala,* pp. 569 ff., 668 ff.

34. Statements by some of the writers indicate the new role that the prose writer displayed. For example see V. Chiplunkar's famous bravado: "I am the Sivaji of the Marathi language ...," in L. K. Chiplunkar, *Vishnushastri Chiplunkar Yanche Charitra* (1894), p. 282; also see V. K. Oak comparing S. K.Chhatre, B. G. Jambhekar, H. K. Pathare and G. N. Madgaonkar with Hooker, Dryden, Temple and Addison in *Vividhadnyanavistara,* 10:3 (1877?).

35. See Bhalchandra Nemade, *Tukaram* (1980), Chs. 2 and 3.

36. Cf. J. Das Gupta and J. Gumperz, "Language, Communication and Control in North India," in *Language Problems of Developing Nations,* eds. Fishman and others, pp. 156 ff.; K. S. N. Pillai, "Prose in Search of an Identity," *Quest* : 100 (1976), pp. 39-44.

37. Cf. V. S. Naipaul, *India : A Wounded Civilization* (1979), pp. 125 ff.

38. See S. K. Chatterji, *Indo-Aryan and Hindi,* pp. 102 ff. ; also the translations of Sanskrit works during the nineteenth century in S. G. Date's *Marathi Granth Suchi 1800-1937,* 2 vols. (1943).

39. Akhileshwar Jha, "The Sex-bound Literary Tradition," *New Quest :* 12 (1978), pp. 373-82.

40. M. S. Gole, *Brahman ani Tyanchi Vidya* (1895), Preface, p.3.

41. D. P. Tarkhadkar, *Kekavali* (1865), Intr., p.6.

42. See S. K. De, *History of Sanskrit Poetics,* vol. 2 (1960), pp. 45 ff. 77 ff.

43. C. D. Narasimhaiah, "Commonwealth Literature : Problems of Response," *The Literary Criterion,* vol. XIV, No. 3 (1979), p. 3.

   The Influence of English on Marathi

44. C. Guillen, *Literature as System,* p. 61.

45. Rene' Guenon, *East and West* (1941), p. 44 ff.

46. See G. Lukacs, *Studies in European Realism* (1972), Ch. 8.

47. J. K. Lele, Personal conversation.

48. See Alberuni, *Alberuni's India,* (1888), esp. Ch. 5.

49. For the different connotations of the term see Tom E. Kakonis and James C. Wilcox, *Forms of Rhetoric* (1969); also see Morris M. Croll, *Style, Rhetoric and Rhythm* (1966), p. 358; Aristotle, *Rhetoric and Poetics,* bk. 1, pp. 99 ff. ; Northrop Frye, *Anatomy of Criticism* (1973), pp. 245-47, 263 and 326.

50. R. F. Jones, *The Seventeenth Century* (1965), pp. 75-110; J. Sutherland, *On English Prose,* p. 67; G. Highet, *The Classical Tradition* (1967), p. 325.

51. T. S. Eliot, *Selected Prose* (1953), p. 287; J. A. K. Thomson, *The Classical Background,* p. 133; G. Highet, loc. cit., p.327.

52. R. F. Jones, loc. cit., pp. 85 ff.

53. This conviction is largely the influence of the Greek Tradition. See J. A. K. Thomson, loc. cit. Ch. 1.

54. O. Jespersen, *Growth and Structure of the English Language* (1970), p.16.

55. Cf. P. S. Ray, "The Formation of Prose," *Word* : 18 (1962), p. 324.

56. C. E. Trevelyan, *On Education,* p. 83.

57. Ibid., p. 203.

58. Ibid., p. 218.

59. O'Malley (ed.), *Modern India and the West,* p. 579; also see M. G. Ranade, *Miscellaneous Writings,* pp. 27,31; Percival Griffiths, *The British Impact on India* (1965), pp. 484-87.

60. C. E. Trevelyan, op. cit., p. 37. Emphasis added.

61. G. S. Amur, *Images and Impressions* (1979), p. 22.

62. John MacNamara in his article "Successes and failures in the Movement for the Restoration of Irish," in *Can Language Be Planned ?* eds. Joan Rubin and Bjorn H. Jernudd (1971), shows, on the basis of various census reports, how even a steady corrosion of the whole system under the influence of English took place and the Irish people had dropped Irish in

favour of English sometime between 1750 and 1850. Several languages in Post-colonial Americas have been annihilated along with the political and social structures of the native societies as a result of dominant foreign cultural elements not resisted in time. See also E. Sapir, *Culture, Language and Personality,* P. 42: E. Haugen, *Bilingualism,* pp. 102 ff.

63. Ralph Linton, "Nativistic Movements," in *American Anthropologist,* 45 : 2 (1943), p. 230.

64. E. Sapir, loc. cit., p. 35.

65. Cf. H. A. Acworth and S. T. Shaligram, preface to *Powada or Historical Ballads of the Marathas* (1891); *Elphinstone School-Paper,* IV : 12 (1883), p. 326.

66. See Hugh D. Duncan, "Art as a Social Institution," in *Modern Sociological Theory in Continuity and Change,* eds. H. Becker and A. Boskoff (1957), pp. 488-94.

67. See Ch. 7.1.

68. Cf. G. Highet, *The Classical Tradition,* p. 275.

69. See Bibliography for *Vividhadnyanavistara, Dnyanodaya* and *Nibandhmala.*

70. See 1.1.3, p. 14 and Ch. 1, Note 14.

71. Cf. V. A. Avrorin in M. I. Isayev's *National Languages in the U.S.S.R.,* pp. 310 ff.

72. J. Gumperz, "Language Problems in the Rural Development of North India," in *Study of the Role of Second Language in Asia, Africa and Latin America,* ed. Frank A. Rice (1962), p. 83.

73. See H. D. Sankalia, "India's Language c. 300 B.C.—A.D 1960," *Linguistics and Language Planning in India,* ed. N. G. Kalelkar (1969), pp.12-19. Sankalia's observation is fully supported by J. Das Gupta and J. Gumperz, op. cit., Note 36, p. 155; J. Gumperz and R. Wilson, "Convergence and Creolization," pp. 151-67; Martin Joos, "Statement and Precis : Hypotheses ... Pidgins," pp. 187-89 in *Pidginization and Creolization of Languages,* ed. D. Hymes; also Allen D. Grimshaw, "Some Social Forces and Some Social Functions of Pidgin Creole Languages," ibid., pp. 427-45; P. Garvin, "The Standard Language Problem—Concepts and Methods," in *Language in Culture and Society,* ed. D. Hymes (1964), pp. 521-26; E. Haugen, *Bilingualism in the Americas,* p. 100.

74. See Hardev Bahri, *Persian Influence on Hindi* (1960), and G. B. Gramopadhye, *Peshavedaptaratil Marathi.*

75. See A. L. Basham, *The Wonder That Was India* (1971), pp. 388-93.

76. The model of the spoken and written languages of India in relation to the *supraglossia* can be drawn as follows :

Spoken dialects like Khandeshi, Konkani etc.	:	Standard written languages like Marathi, Bengali etc.	:	Sanskrit, Prakrits, Persian, English.

77. See Glyn Lewis, *Multilingualism in the Soviet Union* (1972), and M. I. Isayev, *National Languages in the U. S. S. R.*

78. R. B. Patankar, *Saundaryamimansa,* p. 511. See also C.E. Trevelyan *On Education,* pp. 37-38; and Ramamanohar Lohiya's books in Bibliography.

79. See Note 62, and also extract from "The Fourth Report (1827) of the Bombay Native Education Society," in R. V. Parulekar (ed.), *Selections,* part II (1955), pp. 98-102.

80. Dilip Chitre, "Poetry in the Enemy's Tongue," *New Quest* : 14 (1979), p. 77.

81. See Notes 73 and 78.

82. Cf. C. A. Ferguson, "Diglossia," *Word* : 15 (1959), pp. 325-40, and "Language Development," in *Language Problems of Developing Nations,* pp. 28-32. Also see J. Byron, *Selection among Alternates in Language Standardization* (1976); P. S. Ray, *Language Standardization Studies in Prescriptive Linguistics* (1963).

83. J. Gumperz, "The Speech Community," in *International Encyclopedia of the Social Sciences,* vol. 9 (1968), p. 384.

84. R. V. Parulekar (ed.), *Selections,* Part II, pp. 108-10. Emphasis added.

85. D. Hymes (ed.), *Pidginization,* p. 187.

86. J. H. Greenberg, "Concerning Inferences from Linguistic to Non-linguistic Data," in *Language in Culture,* ed., Harry Hoijer (1955), p. 7.

87. See *Dnyanodaya,* (1st Feb. 1851), ed. B. P. Hivale (1942), p. 189.

88. D. Hymes (ed.), *Pidginization,*   p. 151.

89. See William Mackey, "The Description of Bilingualism," *The Canadian Journal of Linguistics,*   vol. 7 : 2 (Summer 1962), pp.51-85. The terms literate bilingualism/textual bilingualism are used synonymously with written bilingualism in the present study. For the detailed characteristics of the mechanism involved in spoken bilingualism, see U. Weinreich, *Languages in Contact* (1953), Ch.2, and for the survey of literature on multilingualism see V. Vildomec, *Multilingualism* (1963), Ch.1; L. S. Vygotsky, *Thought and Language* (1962), pp. 98-99.

90. U. Weinreich, "Functional Aspects of Indian Bilingualism," *Word,* 13 : 2 (1957), pp. 203-33.

91. See E. Haugen, "Languages in Contact," in *Proceedings of the Eighth International Congress of Linguists, 1957* (1958), pp. 771-810.

92. Das Gupta and Gumperz, op. cit. Note 36, p. 155.

93. A. R. Kelkar, "Marathi English : A Study in Foreign Accent," *Word* : 13 (1957), p. 268.

94. Cf. C. K. Sheshadri and J. P. B. Allen, "English as a Foreign Language...," *Working Papers on Bilingualism,* 17 (1979), pp. 66-68.

95. See for example, Specimen Passage 10 in Ch. 4, and *Vishrabdha Sharada,* vol.1, ed. H.V. Mote (1972).

96. See Note 34.

97. See S. Nagarajan, op. cit. pp. 161 ff. , and M. K. Naik, "The Achievement of Indian Prose in English," *Cygnus,* vol. 2:1 (1980), pp. 19-32.

98. J. D. O'Connor, *Better English Pronounciation* (1971), pp. 174-75.

99. Hans Vogt, "Language Contacts," *Word* : 10 (1954), p. 369; also see V. Vildomec, *Multilingualism,* pp. 119 ff.

100. Cf. J. Ellis, *Comparative Linguistics,* pp. 27-28.

101. R.V. Parulekar (ed.), *Selections,* Part II, p. 91.

102. S. Nagarajan, op. cit. p.165.

103. E. Haugen, *Bilingualism in the Americas,* p. 101; also see V. Humboldt quoted in J. H. Greenberg, op. cit. Note 86, p.3.

104. See O. Jespersen, *Language,* p. 147; R. Jakobson and M. Halle,

Fundamentals of Language (1956), pp. 59 ff. and L. S. Vygotsky, *Thought and Language*, p.110; V. Vildomec, *Multilingualism*, pp. 179-229; "Conclusions and Applications," in U. Weinreich, *Languages in Contact*, pp. 116-122. Also see review of "The use of Vernacular Languages in Education, UNESCO, 1953" by William E. Bills in *Language in Culture and Society*, ed. D. Hymes (1964).

105. S. Nagarajan, op. cit. p. 169.

106. B. Kachru, "Towards Structuring Code-mixing, An Indian Perspective," in *Indian Bilingualism*, eds. P. Gopal Sharma and S. Kumar (1977), pp. 188-209.

107. Cf. A. R. Kelkar, "Bhasha Pradushan," in *Marathi Bhashecha Arthik Sansar* (1977), pp. 64-87.

108. Cf. E. Sapir, *Language* Chs. 7 and 9; F. de Saussure, *Course in Linguistics,* part III; L. Bloomfield, *Language* (1957), Chs. 25-27; C. F. Hockett, *A Course in Modern Linguistics* (1958), Chs. 47-54.

109. Cf. U. Weinreich, *Languages in Contact*, pp. 51-52; V. Vildomec, *Multilingualism*, p.90.

110. See Bibliography : Hans Vog, U. Weinreich, A. R. Kelkar, William Mackey, E. Haugan, Joshua A. Fishman, V. Vildomec, and E. Glyn Lewis.

111. J. B. Johnson, "A Clear Case of Linguistic Acculturation," *American Anthropologist*, 45 : 3 (1943), p. 428.

112. See W. Mackey, "The Description of Bilingualism," *The Canadian Journal of Linguistics*, vol. 7 : 2 (1962), p. 68. He distinguishes *interference*, which according to him, belongs to *langue*, from *borrowing* which is a feature of *parole*.

113. A. Martinet, *Functional View*, p. 139.

114. See H. Pederson, *Linguistic Science,* p. 315; J. M. Anderson, *Structural Aspects of Language Change* (1973), pp. 192 ff. ; W. Lehmann, *Historical Linguistics,* pp. 140 ff.

115. See V. Vildomec, *Multilingualism,* pp. 111 ff.

116. U. Weinreich, *Languages in Contact,* p. 25; and H. Vogt, "Language Contacts," *Word,* 10 (1954), pp. 372-74.

117. See A. Martinet, *Functional View,* p. 138, and also *Elements of General Linguistics;* p. 165; H. Hoijer, "Linguistic and Cultural Change," *Language,* 24 : 4 (1948), p. 340; E. Sapir, *Cul-*

ture, Language and Personality, pp. 28-30; M.L. Samuels, *Linguistic Evolution*, Ch.6, J. M Andersen, *Structural Aspects*, p. 172.

118. E. Sapir, *Culture, Language and Personality*, pp. 28-29.

119. See R. Brown and A.Gillman, "The Pronouns of Power and Solidarity," in Sebeok (ed.), *Style in Language*; also U. Weinreich, "Functional Aspects...," *Word* 13 : 2 (1957), p.213.

120. Cf M. L. Samuels, *Linguistic Evolution, pp. 109 ff.*

121. Cf. J. M. Anderson, *Structural Aspects*, pp. 175 ff.

122. Cf. A. Martinet, *Elements of General Linguistics* (1964), pp. 151 ff.; L. S. Vygotsky, *Thought and Language*, pp. 98-110.

123. J. M. Anderson, loc. cit., p. 179.

124. O. Jespersen, *Language*, p. 260.

125. See E. Sapir, *Language*, pp. 205-6.

126. See C. A. Ferguson, "Background to Second Language Problems,"in *Study of the Role of Second Languages*, ed. F. A. Rice (1962),pp.1-7; "Language Development", in *Language Problems of Developing Nations*, eds. Fishman and others; U. Weinreich, *Languages in Contact*, pp. 102-3; and E. Haugen, "Problems of Bilingualism," *Lingua*, 2 : 1 (1949), pp. 272-90.

127. See J. Byron, *Selections Among Alternates*, pp. 103 ff.

128. Cf. Paul Wexler, *Purism and Language* (1974), pp. 10, 319-20.

129. See Chapter 7.1 and 7.3.

130. See M. L. Samuels, *Linguistic Evolution*, p. 109; and C. F. Hockett, *A Course in Modern Linguistics*, pp. 546, 561.

131. See Fedot Filin, *Theoretical Aspects of Linguistics* (1977), p. 50; R. Barthes, *Writing Degree Zero*, pp. 19-20.

132. P. S. Ray, "The Formation of Prose," *Word* : 18 (1962), p. 318.

133. Molesworth, *Marathi-English Dictionary*, Preface, p. XIX.

134. For comparison with the linguistic situation in the U.S.S.R. see Fedot Filin *Theoretical Aspects*; A. E. Darbyshire, *A Grammar of Style* (1971), pp. 48 ff. , 96 ff.

135. See Chapter 6.2 and 6.4.

136. O. Jerpersen, *Efficiency in Linguistic Change* (1941), p. 87.

   The Influence of English on Marathi

137. See Chapter 6.1.

138. The two-year course in Marathi was found to be too hard for the Educational Officers sent out from England, and E. I. Howard, the then Director of Public Instruction pleaded for the relaxation of the standard. The request, however, was promptly rejected by the Chief Secretary. For correspondence in this regard, see *Elphinstone School-Paper,* vol. IV, p. 75.

139. George H. McKnight, in *The Evolution of the English Language* (1968), shows how the eighteenth century British society was particularly concerned with linguistic purism and ridiculed 'barbarisms' in language use. See esp. pp. 37, 310-13.

140. See S. G. Malshe, "Avval Ingrajitil Granthanirmitichi Nandi," *S. N. D. T. Mahila Vidyapith Journal,* V (1975), pp. 45-73.

141. K. K. Chatterjee, "Indian English: Problems of identity," *Quest* : 99 (1976), p.60.

142. See Chapter 8.1 and 8.3.

143. For the table showing school masters of different castes posted in different schools at district headquarters of Maharashtra, see R. V. Parulekar (ed.) *Selections,* Part II, p. 262.

144. See Gangadharshastri Phadke, *Maharashtra Bhasheche Vyakaran* (1836), Preface, p.3; D. P. Tarkhadkar, *Atmacharitra,* ed. Priyolkar, p. 85. Also Ch. 7.1.

145. M. K. Damle, *Shastriya Marathi Vyakaran,* p. 103.

1. See Nils Enkvist, *Linguistic Stylistics*, Ch. 1; and "On Defining Style," in J. Spencer (ed.), *Linguistics and Style* (1964); S. Chatman (ed.), *Literary Style*, Intr., p. x; D. Freeman (ed.), *Linguistics and Literary Style*, Ch. 1; H. S. Babb (ed.), *Essays in Stylistic Analysis*, Intr., pp. 3-9; Crystal and Davy, *Investigating English Style*, (1969), Intr. , pp. 9-10.

2. Robert Adolph, *The Rise of Modern Prose Style*, Intr. , p.9.

3. For the criticism of Bernard Bosanquet's views in this regard see R. B. Patankar, *Saundaryamimansa*, pp. 107 ff., 385-86. The Linguists and aestheticians' dilemma regarding the 'literariness' of language, according to Patankar, is the result of bipolarity of arts. See ibid., pp. 71-72, 140, 312.

4. See S. Chatman (ed.), *Literary Style*, Editor's Intr., p. xii; see B. Croce's statement, "At a certain stage of scientific elaboration, linguistic, in so far as it is philosophy, must merge itself in Aesthetic : and this indeed it does without leaving a residue," in *Aesthetic*, p. 152.

5. A. R. Kelkar, "Language : Linguistics : The Applications," in *Language and Society in India*, vol. 8 (1969), pp.1-13.

6. R. Wellek, *Discriminations*, pp. 332-43.

7. Nils Enkvist, *Linguistic Stylistics*, Ch. 4; R. Wellek, *Discriminations*, pp. 332 ff.

8. R. Barthes, *Writing Degree Zero*, p. 26.

9. Lotman et al. , "Theses on the Semiotic Study of Cultures (As Applied on Slavic Texts), " in *The Tell-Tale Sign*, ed. Sebeok (1975), pp. 61 ff.

10. A. Martinet, *Functional View*, p. 157; also see L. S. Vygotsky, *Thought and Language*, pp. 149-50.

11. Cf. T. Todorov, "The Place of Style in the Structure of the Text," in *Literary Style*, ed. Chatman, pp. 29-37 and the following discussion, pp. 39-44; C. Guillen, *Literature as System*, pp. 228-31.

12. E. Sapir, *Culture, Language and Personality*, p.33.

13. R. Barthes, *Elements of Semiology*, Ch.3.

14. M. Riffaterre, "Criteria for Style Analysis," *Word* : 15 (1959), p. 171, and "Stylistic Context", *Word* : 16 (1960), pp. 207-18.

The Influence of English on Marathi

15. H. G. Widdowson, "Stylistics," in *The Edinburgh Course in Applied Linguistics*, vol.3, eds. Allen and Pit Corder (1974), p. 206.

16. Jan Mukarovsky, "The Esthetics of Language," in *A Prague School Reader*, ed. P. Garvin (1974), p. 44.

17. W. Lehmann, *Historical Linguistics*, p. 216.

18. W. Mackey, "The Description of Bilingualism," *The Canadian Journal of Linguistics*, vol. 7 : 2 (1962), p. 68; and "The Description of Bilingualism" in *Readings in the Sociology of Language*, ed. Fishman (1972), p. 557.

19. See Conclusions of Chapters 6, 7 and 8.

20. A. E. Darbyshire, *A Grammar of Style*, pp. 47 ff., and R. Barthes, *Writing Degree Zero*, pp. 21 ff.

21. J. Sutherland, *On English Prose*, p. 3.

22. Donald Ross, "Difference, Genres and Influences," *Style*, vol. 11 : 3 (1977), pp. 262-63.

23. Heinrich Wolfflin, "Introduction to Principles of Art History," in *Essays in Stylistic Analysis*, ed. H. S. Babb, p. 28.

24. Douglas A. Russell, *Stage Constume Design : Theory Techniqe and Style* (1973), p. 211.

25. Samuel Johnson, "Preface to Shakespeare," *Shakespeare Criticism : A Selection*, ed. D. Nichol Smith (1963), p. 87.

26. M. Schapiro, "Style," in *Anthropology Today*, ed. A.L. Kroeber (1953), p. 287.

27. Mario Castelnuovo-Tedesco, "Problems of a Song-writer," in *Reflections on Art*, ed. Sussanne K. Langer (1961), pp. 301-10.

28. O. Jespersen, *Growth and Structure*, pp. 5 and 16.

29. From "Concerning Inferences. . . ," Joseph Greenberg in *Language in Culture*, ed. H. Hoijer (1955), p. 13.

30. H. Hoijer in his article, "The Sapir-Whorf Hypothesis," sees cross-cultural communication through the essential character of language, i.e., the manifestation of a culture through its distinctness. See *Language in Culture*, ed. Hoijer (1955), pp. 92-105.

31. See Benjamin Lee Whorf, *Language, Thought and Reality*, ed. J. B. Carroll (1971).

32. R. Wellek and Warren, *Theory of Literature*, p. 265.

33. J. Mukarovsky, "Standard Language and Poetic Language," in *Linguistics and Literary Style*, ed. D. Freeman (1970), pp. 43 ff.

34. The problems peculiair to individual style *beyond* those of the period style may very well have their own existence, and individual style may give a certain impetus to the formation of period style *collectively*; however, this discussion is outside the scope of the present study.

35. Karl Kroeber, *Styles in Fictional Structure* (1971), p.5.

36. R. M. Ohmann, "Prolegomena to the Analysis of Prose Style," in *Essays in Stylistic Analysis*, ed. Babb (1972), p. 41.

37. Gerald L. Bruns, "The Originality of Texts In a Manuscript Culture," *Compartive Literature*, vol. 32 : 2 (Spring 1980), pp. 113-29.

38. Robert Escarpit, "Sociology of Literature," *International Encyclopaedia of The Social Sciences*, vol. 9, ed. David L, Sills (1968), pp. 419 ff.

39. See Chapter 8.3.

40. Josephine Miles, "The primary Language of Poetry in the 1540's and 1640's," in *Essays in Stylistic Analysis,* ed. Babb, p. 136.

41. Louis T. Milic, "Against The Typology of Styles", in *Issues in Contemporary Literary Criticism,* ed. Gregory T. Polletta (1973), p. 254.

42. Cf. Ezra Pound, *A B C of Reading* (1961), where he states that "Most arts attain their effects by using a fixed element and a variable," p. 201.

43. Juri Tynianov quoted in T. Todorov's *The Poetics of Prose* (1977), "The element enters simultaneoulsy into relation with the series of similar elements belonging to other systems or works, even to other series, and further with the other elements of the same system (it has an autofunction and a synfunction)," p. 251.

44. A. Martinet, *Functional View*, p. 140.

45. P. S. Ray, "The Formation of Prose," *Word*, 18 (1962), p. 318. This fact can be related to the statement by P. Wexler : "Variants of the same language may co-exist in one speech community only if they are stylistically or functionally differentiated," *Purism and Language* (1974), p. 317.

46. The sources of the model are : M. Herskovits, *Man and His Works,* p. 528; E. Haugen, "The Analysis of Linguistic Borrowing," *Language,* 26. (1950), p. 227; J. M. Anderson, *Structural Aspects,* Ch. 1; Werner Winter, "Basic Principles of the Comparative Method," *Method and Theory in Linguistics,* ed. P. Garvin (1970), p. 148; and Ralph Beals, "Acculturation," *Anthropology Today,* ed. Kroeber, (1953), p. 621.

47. Cf. W. Winter, ibid., p. 148.

48. For example, M. A. K. Halliday conceives 4 levels of analysis, whereas Todorov formulates a 3-level model that includes verbal, syntactic and semantic levels. Darbyshire also proposes 3 levels, but the model of D. Crystal and D. Davy is fairly useful for analysing texts in a single language, for it distinguishes between extra-linguistic phonic and graphic substance from that of the intra-linguistic phonetic and graphetic. This model is based upon the 4-level system consisting of graphetic-phonetic, graphological-phonological-orthographic, lexical-grammatical and semantic levels. Mackey's model, however, has the maximum number of levels, i.e., five : Phonological-graphic, grammatical, lexical, semantic and stylistic.

49. Juri Tynianov quoted by T. Todorov, op. cit. Note 43, pp. 250-51.

50. E. Haugen, *The Ecology of Language,* sel. & intr. by A. S. Dil (1972), p. 165.

51. Cf. Virginia Tufte, *Grammar as Style* (1971), p.8.

1. Bapurao Naik's *Typography of Devanagari,* 2 vols. (1971), traces the history of Devanagari typography, occasionally referring to the writing system; also see A. K. Priyolkar, *Printing Press in India* (1958).

2. See G. McKnight, *The Evolution of the English Language,* p. 423; Mindele Treip, *Milton's Punctuation and Changing English Usage 1582-1676* (1970), Preface, p.X.; Park Honan, "Eighteenth and Nineteenth Century English Punctuation Theory, "*English Studies,* vol. 41 : 1-6 (1960), pp. 92-102; Percy Simpson, *Shakespearean Punctuation* (1911), Intr., pp. 8 ff. Also cf. Evelyn M. Simpson, "A Note on Donne's Punctuation," *The Review of English Studies,* vol. IV (1928), p. 300; Walter J. Ong, "Historical Backgrounds of Elizabethan and Jacobian Punctuation Theory," *PMLA,* LIX (1944), 349-60; T. Julian Brown, "Punctuation", *Encyclopaedia Britiannica* (1977).

3. T. Candy, *Viramchinhanchi Paribhasha* (1850; rpt. 1963); D. P. Tarkhadkar, *Maharashtra Bhasheche Vyakaran,* pp. 325 ff.; R. B. Gunjikar, *Sankalit Leth :* 1, pp. 193-94; R. B. Joshi, *Marathi Bhashechi Ghatana,* p. 527; V. K. Rajavade, "Marathitil Shuddhalekhana-sambandhi . . . ," *Granthmala,* pp. 1-19; *Vividhadnyanavistara* 3 : 2 (1870), p. 29 and 9 : 6-10.

4. Molesworth, *Marathi-English Dictionary,* Preface, p. XXI.

5. B. Jambhekar, "Report of the Board of Education for 1842," in *Jeevanavritta,* p. 154.

5. Compare the graphic components of the photocopied Specimen Passages No. 2 in this Chapter with No.1 and No. 6 in Chapter 7. Also see Bibliography for the books published in Marathi during 1818-1850.

7. S. K. Kolhatkar, *Lekhasangraha,* pp. 595 ff.

CHAPTER SEVEN

1. D. P. Tarkhadkar, "*Atmacharitra*," ed. A. K. Priyolkar, p. 157.

2. Quoted in K. B. Kulkarni, *Adhunik Marathi Gadyachi Utkranti.* (1956), p. 53. Emphasis added.

3. See Note 3 in Chapter 6, and *Dnyanodaya*, ed. Hivale (Feb. 1, 1851), pp. 186-89. For the assessment of Candy's work by V. K. Oak and others, see K. B. Kulkarni, loc. cit., pp. 55, 193, 204, 217, 348 ff.; *Vividhadnyanavistara* 22 : 1-2 (1890), p. 24.

4. Quoted in K. B. Kulkarni, loc. cit., p.22.

1. See Chapter 4.3.2; see prefaces and introductions in V. J. Kirtane, *Jayapal* (1876); D. P. Tarkhadkar, *Kekavali* (1865); Jotirao Phule, "Gulamgiri," in *Samagra Vangmaya*; M. S. Gole, *Brahman ani Tyanchi Vidya.*

2. See *Vividhadnyanavistara* 3 : 10 (1871), p. 148; R. B. Gunjikar, *Sankalit Lekh*, pp. 30-54.

3. M. G. Ranade, *Miscellaneous Writings*, pp. 13-14, 21.

4. M. G. Ranade, ibid. p.33.

5. A. H. Limaye, *Marathi Prakashananche Svarup* (1972), p. 257.

6. Quoted in K. B. Kulkarni, *Adhunik Marathi Gadyachi Utkranti*, p. 66. Emphasis added.

A SELECT BIBLIOGRAPHY

MARATHI

Bloch, Jules. *Formation of Marathi.* Trans. V.G. Paranjape. Pune : V. G. Paranjape, 1941.

Carey, William. *Dictionary : Mahratta Language.* Serampore : ?, 1810.

Chapekar, N. G. "Marathi Bhashcchi Payamalli". *Maharashtra Sahitya Patrika,* 17 : 3 (1944).

Chauhan, Devising. "Marathi va Pharshi : Uttarardh". *Maharashtra Sahitya Patrika,* 41 : 163 (1967), pp. 16-22.

Chiplunkar, Vishnushastri. Nibandhamala. 3rd ed. 1874 to 1883; rpt.Pune : Chitrashala, 1926.

Damle, Moro Keshav. *Shastriya Marathi Vyakaran.* Ed. Krishna Keshav Shrinivas Arjunwadkar. 4th ed., 1911; rpt Pune : Deshmukh ani Co.,1970.

————— *Shuddhalekhan Sudharana athava Sarkari Bandava.* Kolhapur : V. G. Vijapurkar, 1905.

Date, S. G. *Marathi Granth Suchi 1800-1937.* 2 Vols. Pune : S. G. Date, 1943.

Date, S. G. ,Kale, D.V. and Barve, S. N. *Marathi Niyatakalikanchi Suchi.* Vol. I and 2 : 1-4. Bombay : Mumbai Marathi Granth Sangrahalaya, 1969-1977.

Dnyanodaya. *Dnyanodaya : Dnyanodayachi Pahili Shambhar Varshe* (1842-1941), Vol.I. Ed. B. P. Hivale. Bombay : Dnyanodaya Board of Management, 1942.

Godbole, Krishna hastri. *Marathi Bhasheche Navin Vyakaran.* rpt. Bombay : Krishnashastri Godbole, 1867.

Godse, Vishnubhat.   *Majha Pravas*, 4th ed. Ed. D. W. Potadar. Pune : Venus, 1966.

Gramopadhye, G. B.   *Bhasha Vichar ani Marathi Bhasha*. Pune: Venus Prakashan, 1964.

————.   *Marathi Bakhar Gadya*. 2nd ed. Pune : Venus Prakashan, 1963.

————.   *Peshavedaptaratil Marathi Bhasheche Svarup*. Pune : Nerlekar (?), 1940.

————.   *Ramchandra Bhikaji Gunjikar Yanche Sankalit Lekh*, Vol. 1. Bombay : R. K. Tatnis, 1942.

Howard, Edward I.   "Bhashantar." 1859; rpt. in *Marathi Sanshodhan-4*, Bombay : Marathi Sanshodhan Mandal, 1971.

————.   *Prasiddhipatra*. Bombay :Bombay Native School Book and School Society, 1825.

Joshi, Narayan Vishnu.   *Pune Shaharache Varnan*. 2nd ed., 1868; rpt. Ed. G. D. Khanolkar. Bombay :   Sahitya Sahakar Sangh, 1971(?).

Joshi, R. B.   *Marathi Bhashechi Ghatana*, 2nd ed. Pune : M. R. Joshi, 1923.

————.   "Marathit Parabhashetun Shabda Ghene." *Vividhadnyanavistara*,   36 : 6 (1905), pp. 252-56.

————.   *Praudhabodh Marathi Vyakaran*. 6th ed., 1889; rpt. Pune : M. R. Joshi, 1923.

Joshi S. B.   *Marhati Sanskriti*. Pune : S. J. Bhagavat, 1952.

Joshi, V. M.   "Marathit Apratyaksha Nivedanpaddhati." *Vividhadnyanavistara*,   56 : 10 (1925), pp. 294-411 (?).

Kennedy, Vans.   *Dictionary of the Maratha Language*, Parts 1 and 2. Bombay : ?, 1824.

Kolhatkar, S. K.   *Kolhatkarancha Lekhasangraha*. Ed. V. S. Khandekar, et al. Bombay : G. D. Khanolkar, 1932.

Kolte, V. B.   "Adhyakshiya Bhashan." *Maharashtra Sahitya Patrika*, 39 : 155 (1965).

————.   *Mahanubhava Sanshodhan*.   Malkapur : Arun Prakashan, 1962.

————.   *Prachin Marathi Sahitya Sanshodhan*. Pune : Shri Lekhan Vachan Bhandar, 1968.

Kramawant Jaggannathashastri et al.   *A Dictionary of the Marathi Language*. Bombay : ?, 1829.

————.   *Maharashtra Bhasheche Vyakaran*. 1822 (?); rpt. Bombay : Marathi Sanshodhan Mandal, 1954.

                                        The Influence of English on Marathi

Kulkarni, Krishnaji Bhikaji. *Adhunik Marathi Gadyachi Utkranti.* Bombay: K. B. Kulkarni, 1956.

Kulkarni, Krishnaji Pandurang. *Marathi Bhasha: Udgam va Yikas*, 2nd ed. Pune: Kamalabai Bhide, 1950.

Kulkarni. Shridhar Rangnath. *Prachin Marathi Gadya: Prerana ani Parampara.* Bombay: Sindhu Publications, 1970.

Limaye, Ananta Hari. *Marathi Prakashananche Svarup: Prerana va Parampara. Pahile Shatak 1805 - 1900.* Pune: Prasad. 1972.

————. *Lokahitavadinchi Shatapatre.* Ed. S. R. Tikekar. Aundh : Usha Prakashan, 1940.

Madagaonkar, G. N. *Mumbaicbe Varnan.* 2nd ed. 1863; rpt. Ed. N. R. Phatak. Bombay: Mumbai Marathi Granth Sangrahalaya, 1961.

Malshe, S. G. *Gatashatak Shodhitana.* Pune: Pratima, 1989. "Mahatma Phuie: Shaili ani Bhashavishesh." S. N. D. T. Mahila Yidyapith Journal II (1969), 1- 36.

Mangarulkar, Aravind. *Marathichya Yyakaranacha Punarvichar.* Pune: Pune Vidyapith, 1964.

Mate, Ganesh Babaji Nyayaratna, 2nd ed., 1867

Molesworth. James Thomas. *Marathi-Englisb Dictionary.* 3rd ed. 1831; rpt. Pune: Shubhada-Saraswat, 1975.

Nemade, Bhalchandra. *Sahityachi Bhasha.* Aurangabad: Saket, 1986. Teekasvayamvara. Aurangabad: Saket, 1990.

Padamanjee, Baba. *Arunodaya.* 3rd ed .• 1884; rpt. Bombay: Bombay Tract and Book Society, 1963.

Patwardhan. Madhavrao (Trimbak). *Bhashashuddhivivek.* Pune: L. N. Chapekar, 1938.

————. *Pharsi Marathi Kosh.* Pune: Bharat Itihas Sanshodhan Mandai. 1925.

Phadke, Gangadhar Shastri. *Maharashtra Bhasheche Vyakaran.* Bombay: Education Society. 1836.

Phule, Jotirao. *Mahatma Phule Samagra Vangmaya.* Ed. Dhananjaya Keer and S. G. Malshe. Bombay: Maharashtra Rajya Sahitya ani Sanskriti Mandal, 1969.

Pinge, Shriniwas Madhusudan. *Europeanancha Marathicha Abhyas va Seva.* Aurangabad: S. M. Pinge, 1960.

Potadar, Datto Waman *Marathi Gadyacha Ingraji Avatar.* 3rd ed. Pune: Venus Prakashan, 1976.

Priyolkar, A. K. "Devanagari Lipitil Pahila Mudrit Granth" in Dr.

Kolte Gaurav Granth. Ed. Madhukar Ashtikar. Amaravati : Gaurav Granth Prakashan Samiti, 1969.

——————. "Molesworthachya Koshachi Mula Yojana." *Maharashtra Sahitya Patrika,* 39 : 155, (1965), pp. 30-45.

Rajavade, V. K. *Kanishtha, Madhyam va Uchcha Shalantil Svanubhava ... .* Satara : V. S. Vaidya, 1931.

——————. *"Marathi Shuddha Lekhana Sambandhi ...."* *Granthamala (?).*

Sane, K. N. et al. "Marathi Bhashechi Lekhanapaddhati." *Marathi Shalapatrak,* Vol. 9 : Nos. 6-10, June 1898 — Oct. 1898.

Sardar, Gangadhar Balkrishna. *Arvachin Marathi Gadyachi Purvapithika,* 3rd ed. Pune : Modern Book Depot, 1971.

Savarkar, V. D. *Bhasha Shuddhi.* Bombay : G. M. Joshi, 1958.

Tarkhodkar, Dadoba Pandurang. *Maharashtra Bhasheche Vyakaran.* 4th ed., 1836; rpt. Bombay : Tarkhadkar (?), 1865.

——————. "Marathi Bhasheche Vyakaran : Prastavana," rpt. in *Marathi Sanshodhan - 6.* Bombay : Marathi Sanshodhan Mandal, 1972.

——————. *Mothya Maharashtra Vyakaranachya Satavya Avrittichi Puranika.* Bombay : Tarkhadkar (?), 1881.

——————. "Atmacharitra" in *Raobahaddur Dadoba Pandurang.* Ed. A. K. Priyolkar. Bombay: K. B. Dhavale, 1947.

Tarkhadkar, D. R. *Bhashantarapathamala* : 1, 28th ed. Bombay : Nirnayasagar Press, 1945. 2, 39th ed., 1964. 3, 40th ed., 1965.

Tilak, B. G. *Samagra Lokamanya Tilak,* Vols. 3 , 5 and 6. Pune : Kesari Prakashan, 1976.

Tulpule, S. G. (ed.). *Yadavakalin Marathi Bhasha,* 2nd ed. Pune : Venus, 1973.

Vaidya, C. V. "Marathi Bhasha ani Tichyavar Itar Bhashancha Parinam. " *Vividhadnyanavistara,* 37 : 8 (1906), pp. 308-315.

Vividhadnyanavistara. Several anonymous articles, see esp. Vols. 3 (1870-71), 6 : 7 and 10 (1873), 10 : 3 (1876 ?), 21 : 6,9 and 10 (1889), 22 : 1 (1890), 36 (1905), 37 (1906) and 56 : 10 (1925).

Anon.   *The Teaching of English in England being the Report of the Departmental Committee ...* London : His Majesty's Stationery office, 1935.

————.   "Theoretical Aspects of Linguistics." *Social Sciences Today.* Moscow : USSR Academy of Sciences, 1977.

————.   *Working Papers on Bilingualism,* Nos. 15-19. Toronto : The Ontario Institute for Studies in Education, 1978.

Adolph, Robert.   *The Rise of Modern Prose Style.* Cambridge, Mass. : The M.I.T. Press, 1968.

Allen, J. P. B. and Corder, S. Pit.   *The Edinburgh Course in Applied Linguistics,* Vol 3. London : Oxford Univ. Press, 1974.

Allen, J. P. B. and Van Buren, Paul (eds.).   *Chomsky : Selected Readings.* London : Oxford Univ. Press, 1971.

Anderson, James M.   *Structural Aspects of Language Change.* New York : Longman, 1973.

Babb, Howard S. (ed.).   *Essays in Stylistic Analysis.* New York : Harcourt Brace Jovanovich, 1972.

Bach, Emmon and Harms, Robert T. (eds.).   *Universals in Linguistic Theory.* New York : Holt, Rinehart and Winston, 1968.

Bahri, Hardev.   *Persian Influence on Hindi.* Allahabad : Bharati Press Publications, 1960.

Ballhatchet, Kenneth.   *Social Policy and Social Change in Western India* 1817-1830. London : Oxford Univ. Press. 1957.

Baron, Naomi S.   *Language Acquisition and Historical Change.* Amsterdam : North-Holland Publishing Co., 1977.

Barthes, Roland.   *Barthes : Selected Writings.* Ed. Susan Sontag. London: Fontana, 1983.

————.   *Elements of Semiology,* trans. Annette Lavers and Colin Smith. London : Jonathan Cape, 1969.

————.   *Writing Degree Zero,* trans. Annette Lavers and Colin Smith. London : Jonathan Cape, 1970.

Beals, Ralph.   "Acculturation" in *Anthropology Today : An Encyclopedic Inventory.* Chicago : The Univ. of Chicago Press, 1953. pp. 621-635.

Beames, John.   *A Comparative Grammar of the Modern Aryan Languages of India.* 3 Vols. Delhi : Munshiram Manoharlal, 1966.

Berreman, Gerald D.   "Aleut Reference Group Alienation, Mobility and Acculturation". *American Anthropologist.* 66 : 2 (1964), pp. 231-250.

Bhagwat, A. K. (ed.). *Maharashtra — A Profile.* Kolhapur : V. S. Khandekar Amrit Mahotsav Satkar Samiti, 1977.

Brosnahan, L. F.   *The Sounds of Language : An Enquiry into the Role of Genetic Factors in the Development of Sound systems.* West port, Conn.: Greenwood Press, 1982.

Brower, Reuben A. (eds.).   *On Translation.* Cambridge : Harvard Univ. Press, 1959.

Brown, Huntington.   *Prose Style : Five Primary Types.* Minneapolis : The Univ. of Minnesota Press, 1966.

Brown, T. Julien.   "Punctuation." *Encyclopaedia Britannica.* 1977.

Bruns, Gerald L.   "The Originality of Texts In a Manuscript Culture" in *Compardtive Literature,* Vol. 32 : 2, (Spring 1980), pp. 113-129.

Bryant, Margaret M.   *Modern English and Its Heritage.* New York : The Macmillan and Co., 1962.

Byron, Janet.   *Selection among Alternates in Language Standardization : The Case of Albanian.* The Hague: Mouton, 1976.

Casagrande, Joseph B. "Comanche Linguistic Acculturation : I." *International Journal of American Linguistics.* 20 : 2 (1954), pp.140-151.

————.   "Comanche Linguistic Acculturation : 2." *International Journal of American Linguistics.* 20 : 3 (1954), pp. 217-237.

Catford, J. C.   *A Linguistic Theory of Translation : An Essay in Applied Linguistics.* London : Oxford Univ. Press, 1965.

Chafe, Wallace L.   "Internal Reconstruction in Seneca." *Language.* 35 : 3 (1959), pp. 477-495.

————.   *Meaning and the Structure of Language.* Chicago: The Univ. of Chicago Press, 1970.

Chambers, R. W.   *On the Continuity of English Prose from Alfred to More and his School.* London : Humphrey Milford, 1932.

Chatman, Seymour and Levin, Samuel R. (eds.). *Essays on the Language of Literature.* Boston : Houghton Mifflin Co., 1967.

Chatman, Seymour (ed.). *Literary Style : A Symposium.* London : Oxford Univ. Press, 1971.

Chatterji, Suniti Kumar. *Indo-Aryan and Hindi : Eight Lectures.* Ahmedabad : Gujarat Vernacular Society, 1942.

——————. *Languages and Literatures of Modern India.* Calcutta : Bengal Publishers, 1963.

——————. "The Study of Modern Indian Languages." *Indian Linguistics.* 7, 1939 (rpt. 1965), pp. 357-371.

Chomsky, Noam. *Language and Mind.* New York : Harcourt Brace Jovanovich, 1972.

Communications Research Centre, Univ. College, London. *Aspects of Translation.* Ed. A. H. Smith. London : Secker and Warburg, 1958.

Congress of Linguists, London 1952. *Proceedings of the Seventh International ...* London : C.I.P.L., 1956.

Congress of Linguists, 1957. *Proceedings of the Eighth International ...* 1957. Oslo : Oslo Univ. Press, 1958.

Croce, Benedetto. *Aesthetic : As science of expression and general linguistic,* trans. Ainslie, Douglas. London : Vision Press, 1962.

Croll, Morris W. *Style, Rhetoric and Rhythm.* Princeton : Princeton Univ. Press, 1966.

Crystal, David and Davy, Derek. *Investigating English Style.* London : Longmans, Green and Co., 1969.

Cunningham, J. V. (ed.). *The Problem of Style.* Greenwich, Conn. : Fowcett, 1966.

Darbyshire, A. E. *A Grammar of Style.* London : Andre Deutsch, 1971.

Das Gupta, Jyotirindra and Gumperz, John. J. "Language, Communication and Control in North India." in *Language Problems of Developing Nations.* Ed. Joshua A. Fishman et al. New York John Wiley and Sons, 1968.

Davidson, William and Alcock, Joseph Crosby. *English Grammar and Analysis.* London: Allman and Son, 1902.

de George, *The Structuralists : From Marx to Levi-Strauss.*

Richard T. and
de George
Fernande M. (eds.).   New York : Anchor Books,1972.

Dharkar, C. D. (ed.).   *Lord Macaulay's Legislative Minutes*. London :
                             Oxford Univ. Press, 1946.

Dolezel, Lubomir and   *Statistics and Style*. New York : American
Bailey, Richard W.   Elsevier Publishing, 1969.

Dozier, Edward P.   "Two Examples of Linguistic Acculturation : The
                             Yaqui of Sonora and Arizona and the Tewa of
                             New Mexico." *Language*, 32 : 1 (1956), pp. 146-
                             157.

Duncan, Hugh D.   "Art as a social Institution" in *Modern Sociologi-
                             cal Theory in Continuity and Change*. Ed.
                             Howard Becker and Alvin Boskoff. New York :
                             Holt, Rinehart and Winston, 1957, pp. 488-494.

Editorial Board,   *Theoretical Aspects of Linguistics*. Moscow :
Social Sciences   U.S.S.R Academy of Sciences, 1976.
Today.

Ellis, Jeffrey.   *Towards a General Comparative Linguistics*. The
                             Hague : Mouton, 1966.

Elphinstone School.   *Elphinstone School-Paper*, Vol IV : 2 to 6
                             and 11 (1863).

Emeneau, M. B.   "India as a Linguistic Area." *Language*, 32 : 1
                             (1956), pp. 3-16.

Enkvist, Nils Erik.   *Languistic Stylistics*. The Hague : Mouton, 1973.

————————.   "On Defining Style : An Essay in Applied Lin-
                             guistics" in *Linguistics and Style*. Ed. John
                             Spencer. London : Oxford Univ. Press, 1964.

Escarpit, Robert.   "Sociology of Literature." *International Ency-
                             clopedia of the Social Sciences*, Vol. 9, Ed. David
                             L. Sills. the Macmillan Co. and The Free Press,
                             1968, pp. 417-425.

Etkind, Efim.   "Comparative Stylistics : A Guide to the Art of
                             Translation." *Diogenes*, 57 (Spring, 1967), pp.
                             33-46.

Fanon, Frantz.   *The Wretched of the Earth*. Trans. Constance
                             Farrington. Harmondsworth : Penguin Books,
                             1977.

Ferguson, Charles A.   "Diglossia." *Word*, 15(1959), pp.325-340.

————————.   *Language structure and language Use*. Sel. intr.
                             Anwar S. Dil. Standford : Stanford Univ. Press,
                             1971.

Filin, Fedot.   *Theoretical Aspects of Linguistics.*   Moscow :
                       U.S.S.R. Academy of Sciences, 1977.

Finch, C. A.   *An Approach to Technical Translation.* Oxford :
                       Pergamon Press, 1969.

Firth, J. R.   *Papers in Linguistcs 1934-1951.*
                       London : Oxford Univ. Press, 1957.

————————. (intr.).   *Studies in Linguistic Analysis.* Oxford : Basil
                       Blackwell, 1957.

Fishman, Joshua   *Advances in Language Planning.* The
A. (ed.).   Hauge : Mouton, 1974.

——————————.   *Advances in the Sociology of Language 1.* The
                       Hague : Mouton, 1971.

——————————.   *Language in Socio-cultural Change.* Sel. and intr.
                       Anwar S. Dil. Stanford : Stanford Univ. Press,
                       1972.

Fishman, Joshua A.,   *Language Problems of Developing Nations. New*
Ferguson, Charles A., York : John Wiley and Sons, 1968.
Das Gupta, Jyotirindra
  (eds.).

Fishman, Joshua   *Readings in the Sociology of Language.*
A. (ed.).   The Hague : Mouton, 1972.

Freeman, Donald   *Linguistics and Literary Style.* New York:
C. (ed.).   Holt, Rinehart and Winston, 1970.

Fries, Charles C.   *"Have* as a Function Word." *Language Learning,*
                       1 : 3 (1948), pp. 4-8.

Garvin, Paul L. (ed.). *Method And Theory in Linguistics.* The Hague :
                       Mouton, 1970.

——————————.   *A Prague School Reader on Esthetics,*
(ed. and trans.).   *Literary Structure and Style.* Washington: Geor-
                       getown Univ. Press, 1964.

Gelb, I. J.   *A Study of Writing : The Foundations of Gram-*
                       matology. Chicago, Ill. : The Univ. of Chicago
                       Press, 1952.

George, K. M.   *Western Influence on Malayalam Language and*
                       Literature. New Delhi : Sahitya Akademi, 1972.

Gleason, H. A., Jr.   *Linguistics and English Grammar.* New York :
                       Holt, Rinehart and 'Viston, 1965.

Griffiths, Sir Percival. *The British Impact on India. ?* : Frank Cass and
                       Co., 1965.

Gordon, Ian A.   *The Movement of English Prose.* London : Long-
                       mans Green and Co., 1966.

Gray, Louis H.   *Foundations of Language.* New York: The Macmillan Co., 1958.

Greenberg, Joseph H. *Essays in Linguistics.* Chicago: The Univ. of Chicago Press, 1957.

————— .   *Language. Culture and Communication.* Sel. intr. Anwar S. Dil. Stanford: Stanford Univ. Press, 1971.

————— . (ed.).   *Universals of Language. Cambridge,* Mass.: The M.LT. Press. 1963.

Greenberger, Allen J. *The British Image of India*: A Study in the Literature of Imperialism (1880-1960). London: Oxford Univ. Press, 1969.

Greer, Rita.   *An Introduction to Art and Craft.* London: Pitman Publishing, 1974.

Guenon, Rene'.   *East and West.* Trans. William Massey. London: Luzac and Co., 1941.

Guillen, Claudio.   *Literature as System: Essays Toward the Theory of Literary History.* Princeton: Princeton Univ. Press, 1971.

Gumperz, John J.   *Language in Social Groups.* Sel. intr. Anwar S. Dil. Stanford, Ca1.: Stanford Univ. Press, 1971.

————— .   "Linguistic and Social Interaction in Two Communities." *American Anthropologist.* 66: 2 (1964), pp. 37-53.

————— .   "The Speech Community." *International Encyclopedia of the Social Sciences.* Vol. 9. The Macmillan Co. and The Free Press, 1968.

Hall, Gordon.   'A *Help in acquiring a knowldge of English,*... 1818 (?).

Halliday, M. A. K.   *Language as Social Semiotic: The Social Interpretation of Language and Meaning.* London: Edward Arnold, 1978.

Halliday, M. A. K., McIntosh, Angus and Strevens, Peter. The Linguistic Sciences and Language Teaching. London: The ELBS and Longman Group, 1970.

Haugen, Einar.   "The Analysis of Linguistic Borrowing." Language. 26 (1950), pp. 210-231.

————— .   *Bilingualism in the Americas: A bibliography and Research Guide.* Alabama: American Dialect Society, 1956.

————— .   *The Ecology of Language.* Sel. intr. Anwar S. Dil. Stanford, Cal.: Stanford Univ. Press, 1972.

————— .   *The Norwegian Language in America:* A Study

in Bilingual Behaviour, 2 Vols. Philadelphia, Penn. : Univ. of Pennsylvania Press, 1953.

——————. "Problems of Bilingualism." *Lingua,* 2 (1949), pp. 272-290.

Hardan, G. *Language as Choice and Chance.* Groningen : P. Noordhoff N. V., 1956.

——————. *Quantitative Linguistics.* London : Butterworths, 1964.

Herskovits, Melville J. *Man and His Works.* New York : Alfred A. Knopf, 1956.

Highet, Gilbert. *The Classical Tradition : Greek and Roman Influences on Western Literature.* London : Oxford Univ. Press, 1967.

Hill, Archibald A. *Introduction to Linguistic Structures.* New York : Harcourt, Brace and Co., 1958.

Hockett, Charles F. *A Course in Modern Linguistics.* New York : The Macmillan Co., 1958.

——————. "The Problem of Universals in Language" in *Universals of Language.* Ed. Joseph. H. Greenberg. Cambridge, Mass.: The M.I.T. Press, 1963.

Hoijer, Harry (ed.). *Language in Culture :* Conference on the Interrelations of Language and other Aspects of Culture. Chicago : The Univ. of Chicago Press, 1955.

——————. "Linguistic and Cultural Change." *Language,* 24 : 4 (1948), pp. 335-345.

Honan, Park. "Eighteenth and Nineteenth Century English Punctuation Theory." *English Studies,* 41 : 1-6 (1960), pp. 92-102.

Hymes, Dell (ed.). *Language in Culture and Society : A Reader in Linguistics and Anthropology.* New York : Harper and Row, 1964.

——————. *Pidginization and Creolization of Languages :* Proceedings of a Conference held at the Univ. of the West Indies, Mana, Jamaica, April 1968. London : Cambridge Univ. Press, 1971.

Isayev, M. I. *National Languages in the U.S.S.R. : Problems and Solutions.* Moscow: Progress Publishers, 1977

Jakobson, Roman and Halle, Morris. *Fundamentals of Language.* The Hague : Mouton, 1956.

Jensen, Hans.	*Sign, Symbol and Script : An Account of Man's Efforts to Write,* trans. George Unwin. London : George Allen and Unwin, 1970.

Jespersen, Otto.	*Analytic Syntax.* London : George Allen and Unwin, 1937.

———.	*Efficiency in Linguistic Change.* Kopenhagen : Ejnar Munksgaard, 1941.

———.	*Essentials of English Grammar.* London : George Allen and Unwin, 1933.

———.	*Growth and Structure of the English Language.* ? : Oxford Univ. Press, 1970.

———.	*Language : Its Nature, Development and Origin.* London : George Allen and Unwin, 1954.

———.	*Mankind, Nation and Individual : From a Linguistic Point of View.* London : George Allen and Unwin, 1946.

———.	*A Modern English Grammar on Historical Principles,* parts 1 and 2 (1928), parts 3-7 (1954). London : George Allen and Unwin.

Johnson, Jean Bassett.	"A Clear Case of Linguistic Acculturation." *American Anthropologist,* 45:3 (1943), pp. 427-434.

Jones, Richard Foster.	*The Seventeenth Century : Studies in the History of English Thought and Literature from Bacon to Pope.* London : Oxford Univ. Press, 1965.

———	*The Triumph of the English Language: A Survey of Opinions Concerning the Vernacular from the Introduction of Printing to the Restoration.* Stanford, Cal.: Stanford Univ. Press, 1966.

Kachru, Braj B.	"English in South Asia" in *Current Trends in Linguistics.* Vol. 5, Ed. Thomas A. Sebeok. The Hague : Mouton, 1969.

Kale, G. R.	*Lessons in English Translation.* Bombay : Macmillan and Co., 1949.

Kalelkar, N. G.	*Marathi.* New Delhi : Indian Council for Cultural Relations, 1965.

——— (ed.).	*Linguistics and Language Planning in India.* Poona : Deccan College, 1969.

Kane, P. V.	*History of Sanskrit Poetics.* Delhi : Motilal Banarsidass, 1971.

Katre, S. M.	*The Formation of Konkani.* Bombay : Karnatak Publishing House, 1942.

—————————. *Introduction to Indian Textual Criticism.* Bombay : Karnatak Publishing House, 1941.

Kelkar, Ashok R. "Marathi English : A Study in Foreign Accent." *Word,* 13 (1957), pp. 268-282.

Kintgen, Eugene R. "Reader Response and Stylistics." *Style,* Vol. 11:1 (Winter 1977), pp. 1-18.

Kinsella, Valerie. *Language Teaching and Linguistics : Surveys.* Cambridge : Cambridge Univ. press, 1978.

Klima, Edward S. "Negation in English" in *The Structure of Language : Readings in the Philosophy of Language.* Ed. Jerry A Foder and Jerrold J. Katz. Englewood Cliffs, N. J. : Prentice-Hall, 1964.

Koch, Walter Alfred. "On the Principles of Stylistics." *Lingua,* 12 : 4 (1949 ?), pp. 411-422.

Konow, Sten. "A Marathi Idiom." *Indian Linguistics,* rpt. ed., Vol. IV, part III:4 (1966), pp. 345-352.

—————————. *Linguistic Survey of India,* vol. VII. 2nd ed., 1927; rpt. Delhi : Motilal Banarsidass, 1967.

Kottler, Barnet and Light, Martin (eds.). *The World of Words.* Boston : Houghton Mifflin Co., 1967.

Kroeber, A. L. *Anthropology.* Calcutta : Oxford and IBH Publishing, 1967.

Kroeber, A. L. *Anthropology Today : An Encyclopedic Inventory.* Chicago : The Univ. of Chicago Press, 1953.

—————————. *Style and Civilizations.* Ithaca, N. Y. : Conneff Univ. Press, 1957.

Kroeber, Karl. *Styles in Fictional Structure.* Princeton, N. J. : Princeton Univ. Press, 1971.

Kumar, Ravinder. *Western India in the Nineteenth Century : A Study in the Social History of Maharashtra.* London : Routledge and Kegan Paul, 1968.

Lass, Roger (ed.). *Approaches to English Historical Linguistics : An Anthology.* New York : Holt, Rinehart and Winston, 1969.

Lee, D. D. "The Linguistic Aspect of Wintu.' Acculturation." *American Anthropologist,* 45:3 (1943), pp. 435-440.

Lehmann, Winfred P. *Historical linguistics : An Introduction.* Calcutta : Oxford and IBH Publishing, 1966.

Levi-Strauss, Claude. *Structural Anthropology.* Trans. Claire Jacobson

Lewis, E. Glyn.

and Brooke Grundfest Schoepf. Harmondsworth : Penguin Books, 1963.

Multilingualism in the Soviet Union : Aspects of Language Policy and Its Implementation. The Hague : Mouton, 1972.

Lieberson, Stanley.

Language Diversity and Language Contact. Ed. intr. Anwar S. Dil. Stanford : Stanford Univ. Press, 1981.

Linton, Adelin and Wagley, Charles.

Ralph Linton. New York : Columbia Univ. Press, 1971.

Linton, Ralph.

"Nativistic Movements." *American Anthropologist,* 45:2 (1943), pp. 230-240.

Lodge, David.

Language of Fiction. London : Routledge And Kegan Paul, 1966.

Lotman, Ju. M., Uspenskij, B. A., Ivanov, V. V., Toporov, V. N. and Pjatigorskij, A. M.

"Theses on the Semiotic study of Cultures (As Applied to Slavic Texts)" in *The Tell-Tale Sign : A Survey of Semiotics.* Ed. Thomas A. Sebeok. Lisse/Netherlands : The Peter de Ridder Press, 1975.

Love, Glen, A. and Payne, Michael.

Contemporary Essays on Style. Glenview, Ill. : Scott, Foresman and Co., 1969.

Macaulay, Lord.

The Complete Works of Lord Macaulay, vol. VIII : 2. London : Longman Green and Co., 1914.

Mackey, William.

"The Description of Bilingualism." *The Canadian Journal of Linguistics,* Vol. 7 : 2 (Summer 1962), pp. 51-85.

Mackey, William Francis and Ornstein, Jacob (eds.).

Sociolinguistic Studies in Language Contact : Methods and Cases. The Hague: Mouton, 1967.

Martin, Harold C.

Style in Prose Fiction : English Institute Essays 1958. New York : Columbia Univ. Press, 1959.

Martinet, Andre.

Elements of General Linguistics. Trans. Elisabeth Palmer. London : Faber and Faber, 1964.

————.

A Functional View of Language. Oxford : The Clarendon Press, 1962.

Master, Alfred.

A Grammar of Old Marathi. Oxford: Oxford Univ. Press, 1964.

Mayhew, Arthur.

The Education of India : A Study of British Educational Policy in India, 1835-1920 .... London : Faber and Gwyer, 1926.

                                    The Influence of English on Marathi

McKnight, George, H. *The Evolution of the English Language from Chaucer to the Twentieth Century.* New York : Dover Publications, 1968.

Miles, Josephine. *Style and Proportion : The Language of Prose and Poetry.* Boston : Little, Brown and Co., 1967.

Milic, Louis Tanko. *A Quantitative Approach to the Style of Jonathan Swift.* The Hague : Mouton, 1967.

Morris, Charles. *Signs, Language and Behaviour.* New York : Prentice-Hall, 1946.

Morris, Edward P. "A Science of Style." *Transactions and Proceedings of the American Philological Association,* Vol. XLVI. Boston : Ginn and Co., 1915, pp. 103-118.

Mukherjee, Ramkrishna. *The Rise and Fall of the East India Company : A Sociological Appraisal.* Berlin : VEB Deutscher Verlag Der Wissenschaften, 1958.

Murry, J. Middleton. *The Problem of Style.* Oxford : Humphrey Milford, 1922.

Naik, Bapurao S. *Typography of Devanagari,* 2 vols. Bombay : Govt. of Maharashtra, 1971.

Navalkar, G. R. *The Student's Marathi Grammor.* Bombay : Education Society's Press ?, 1894.

Nemade, Bhalchandra. "Against Writing in English : An Indian Point of View." *New Quest,* 49 (Jan.-Feb. 1985).

————. "A Case Study of Bilingual Poetry" in *Indian Readings in Commonwealth Literature.* Ed. G. S. Amur et al. New Delhi : Sterling, 1985.

————. "The concept of Nativism in Literature." *New Quest,* 45 (May-June 1984).

————. "Literary Aspects of Anglo-Marathi Confrontation." *Jadavpur Journal of Comparative Literature,* 25 (1987).

————. "Marathi Novel 1950-1975." Trans. G. N. Devy. *Setu* II : 1 (1986).

————. "Modern Indian Fiction : A Clear Case of Acculturation." *Osmania Journal of English Studies,* 13 (1983).

————. "The Revolt of the Underprivileged : Style in the Expression of the Warkari Movement in Maharashtra." *Journal of Asian and African*

              Studies, Vol. XIV: 3-4 (1980).

————. "A Theoretical Framework of Influence Study in Indo-Anglian Context" in *Comparative Literature: Theory and Practice.* Ed. Amiya Dey and S. K. Das. New Delhi: Indian Institute of Advanced Study, Shimla and Allied Publishers, 1988.

————. "Towards a Definition of Modernity in Modern Marathi Literature." *Mahfil,* 6 (1970).

————. *Tukaram.* New Delhi: Sahitya Akademi, 1980.

Nida, Eugene A. *Language Structure and Translation.* Sel. intr. Anwar S. Dil. Stanford, Cal.: Stanford Univ. Press, 1975.

Ohmann, Richard M *Shaw: The Style and the Man.* Middletown, Conn.: Wesleyan Univ. Press, 1962.

O' Malley L. S. S (ed.). *Modern India and the West: A Study of the Interaction of their Civilizations.* London: Oxford Univ. Press, 1941.

Ong, Walter J. "Historical Backgrounds of Elizabethan and Jacobean Punctuation Theory." *PMLA* Vol. LIX (1944), pp. 349-360.

Parret, Herman. *Discussing Language: Dialogues with Wallace L. Chafe. Noam Chomsky and Others.* The Hague: Mouton, 1974.

Parulekar, R. V. (ed). *Selections from the Records of the Government of Bombay:* Education. Parts I to III. Bombay: Asia Publishing House, 1953, 55, 57.

Pederson, Holger *Linguistic Science in the Nineteenth Century.* Trans. John W. Spargo. Cambridge, Mass.: Harvard Univ. Press, 1931.

Pillai, K. S. Narayana. "Prose in Search of An Identity." *Quest,* 100 (1976), pp 39-44.

Potter, G. R. 'Macaulay', London: Longmans, Green & Co., 1959.

Prakash, Karat. *Language and Nationality Politics in India.* Bombay: Orient Longman, 1973.

Priyolkar, A. K. *Printing Press in India.* Bombay: Marathi Samshodhan Mandal, 1958.

Pulgram, Ernst. "Proto-Indo-European Reality and Reconstruction." *Language.* Vol. 35 No. III (1959), pp. 421- 426.

Quirk, Randolph et al. *A Grammar of Contemporary English.* New York: Seminar Press, 1972.

Ranade, M. G. *The Miscellaneous Writings of* .... Poona : Ramabai Ranade, 1915.

Ray, Punya Sloka. "The Formation of Prose." *Word,* 18 (1962), pp. 313-325.

——— *Language Standardization Studies in Prescriptive Linguistics.* The Hague : Mouton, 1963.

Rice, Rank A. (ed.). *Study of the Role of Second Languages in Asia, Africa and Latin America.* Washington D.C. : Centre for Applied Linguistics of the Modern Language Association of America, 1962.

Riffaterre, Michael. "Criteria for Style Analysis." *Word,* 15 (1959), pp. 154-174.

———. "Stylistic Context." *Word,* 16 (1960), pp. 207-218.

Roberts, Murat H. "The Science of Idiom : A Method of Inquiry into the Cognitive Design of Language.' *P.M.L.A.,* Vol. LIX, 1944, pp. 291-306.

Robey, David (ed.). *Structuralism : An Introduction.* Oxford : Clarendon Press, 1973.

Ross, Donald Jr. "Differences, Genres, and Influences." *Style,* Vol. 11 : 3 (Summer 1977), pp. 262-273.

Rubin, Joan and Jernudd, Bjorn H. *Can Language Be Planned?* Honolulu : The Univ. Press of Hawai, 1971.

Said, Edward W. *Orientalism.* London : Routledge and Kegan Paul, 1978.

Samuels, M. L. *Linguistic Evolution with Special Reference to English.* Cambridge : Cambridge Univ. Press, 1972.

Sapir, Edward. *Culture, Language and Personality.* Ed. David G. Mandelbaum. Berkeley : Univ. of California Press, 1962.

———. *Language : An Introduction to the Study of Speech.* New York : Harcourt, Brace and Co., 1949.

Saussure, Ferdinand. *Course in General Linguistics.* Trans. de. Wade Baskin. London : Peter Owen, 1960.

Savory Theodore. *The Art of Translation.* London : Jonathan Cape, 1957.

Sawyer, Janet B. "Aloofness From Spanish Influence in Texas English." *Word,* 15 (1959), pp.270-281.

Sayce, R. A. "Literature and Language." *Essays in Criticism.*

Vol. 7 : No. 2, 1957, pp. 119-133.

Sayyid, Abdul-Latif. *The Influence of English Literature on Urdu Literature,* London : Forster Groom, 1924.

Schapiro, Meyer. "Style" in *Anthropology Today.* Ed. A. L. Kroeber. Chicago : The Univ. of Chicago Press, 1953.

Schorer, Mark, Miles, Josephine and McKenzie, Gordon (eds.). *Criticism : The Foundations of Modern Literary Judgement.* New York : Harcourt, Brace and Co., 1948.

Seal, Anil. *The Emergence of Indian Nationalism : Competition and Collaboration in the Later Nineteenth Century.* Cambridge : Cambridge Univ. Press, 1971.

Sebeok, Thomas A. (ed.). *Style in Language.* Cambridge, Mass. : The M. I. T. Press, 1964.

Sen, Priyaranjan. *Western Influence in Bengali Literature.* Calcutta : Univ. of Calcutta, 1932.

Sen, Sukumar. "A Comparative Grammar of Middle Indo-Aryan." *Indian Linguistics.,* Vol. 12, 1952-53, rpt. 1965, pp. 211-354.

————. "Historical Syntax of Middle Indo-Aryan." *Indian Linguistics.* Vol. 13, 1953, rpt. 1965, pp. 355-473.

Sharma, P. Gopal and Kumar, Suresh (eds.). *Indian Bilingualism.* Agra : Kendriya Hindi Sansthan, 1977.

Smith, Carlota S. "Sentences in Discourse : an Analysis of a Discourse by Bertrand Russell." *Journal of Linguistics.* Vol. 7, No. 2, 1971, pp. 213-235.

Southworth, Franklin C. "The Marathi Verbal Sequences and their Co-occurrences." *Language,* Vol. 37 No. 2, 1961, pp. 201-208.

Spencer, John (ed.). "An Approach to the study of style " in *Linguistics and Style.* Ed. John spencer. London : Oxford Univ. Press, 1964.

Spicer, Edward H. "Linguistic Aspects of Yaqui Acculturation." *American Anthropologist,* 45 : 3, part 1, 1943, pp. 410-426.

Spitzer, Leo. *Linguistics and Literary History : Essays in Stylistics.* New York : Russell and Russell, 1962.

Srinivas, M. N. "A Note on Sanskritization and Westernization" in *Caste in Modern India and Other Essays*. 1962. rpt. Bombay : Asia Publishing House, 1970.

Stokes, Eric. *The English Utilitarians and India*. Oxford : Oxford Univ. Press, 1959.

Sturtevant, E. H. *Linguistic Change : An Introduction to the Historical Study of Language*. Chicago : Phoenix Books, The Univ. of Chicago Press, 1968.

Sutherland, James. *On English Prose*. Canada ? : Univ. of Toronto Press, 1957.

Syed, Nurullah and Naik, J. P. *History of Education in India during the British Period*. Bombay : Macmillan and Co., 1943.

Temple, Sir Richard. *Men and Events of My Time in India*. London : John Murray, 1882.

——————. *Oriental Experience*. London : John Murray, 1883.

Thomson, J. A. K. *The Classical Background of English Literature*. London : George Allen and Unwin, 1950.

——————. *Classical Influences in English Prose*. London : George Allen and Unwin, 1956.

Todorov, Tzvetan. *The Poetics of Prose*. Trans. Richard Howard. Oxford : Basil Blackwell, 1977.

Trager, George L. "Spanish and English Loanwords in Taos." *International Journal of American Linguistics*, No. 4, Oct. 1944, pp.144-158.

Traugott, Elizabeth Closs. *A History of English Syntax : A Transformational Approach to the History of English Sentence Structure*. New York : Holt, Rinehart and Winston, 1972.

Trevelyan, Charles E. *On the Education of the People of India*. London : Longman, Orme, Brown, Green and Longmans, 1838.

Trevelyan, Sir George. *The Competition Wallah*. London : *Macmillan* and Co., 1895.

Trevelyan, Sir G. O. *Life and Letters of Lord Macaulay*, Vol. 1. London : Thomas Nelson and Sons, 1908.

Tufte, Virginia. *Grammar as Style*. New York : Holt, Rinehart and Winston, 1971.

Tulpule, S. G. (ed.). *An Old Marathi Reader . Pune : Venus, 1960.*

Ullmann, Stephen. *Language and Style*. Oxford : Basil Blackwell, 1964.

UNESCO.   *The Use of Vernacular Languages in Education.* Monographs on Fundamental Education No. 8. Paris : UNESCO, 1953.

Vildomec, Veroboj.   *Multilingualism.* Leyden : A. W. Sythoff, 1963.

Vogt, Hans.   "Language Contacts." *Word,* 10 (1954), pp. 365-374.

Vossler, Karl.   *The Spirit of Language in Civilization.* Trans. Oscar Oeser. London : Kegan Paul, Trench, Trubner and Co., 1932.

Vygotsky, L. S.   *Thought and Language.* Ed. trans. Eugenia Hanfmann and Gertude Vakar. New York : The M. I. T. Press and John Wiley and Sons, 1962.

Weinreich, Uriel.   "Functional Aspects of Indian Bilingualism." *Word,* 13 : 2 (1957), pp. 203-233.

——————.   *Languages in Contact : Findings and Problems.* New York : The Linguistic Circle of New York, 1953.

——————.   "Research frontiers in bilingualism studies" in *Proceedings of the Eighth International Congress of Linguists... 1957.* Oslo : Oslo Univ. Press, 1958, pp. 786-797.

Wellek, René.   *Concepts of Criticism.* Ed. Stephen G. Nichols Jr. New Haven : Yale Univ. Press, 1963.

——————.   *Discriminations : Further Concepts of Criticism.* Delhi : Vikas Publications, 1970.

——————.   *A History of Modern Criticism : 1750-1950,* in four volumes. Vol.1 : The Later Eighteenth Century, Vol. 3 : The Age of Transition. London : Jonathan Cape, 1955.

Wellek, René and Warren, Austin.   *Theory of Literature.* Harmondsworth : Penguin Books, 1966.

Wexler, Paul N.   *Purism and Language : A Study in Modern Ukrainian and Belorussian Nationalism (1840-1967).* Bloomington : Indiana Univ., 1974.

Whorf, Benjamin Lee.   *Language, Thought and Reality.* Ed. John B. Carroll. Cambridge, Mass. : The M. I. T. Press, 1971.

Widdowson, H. G.   *Stylistics and the Teaching of Literature.* London : Longman, 1975.

The Influence of English on Marathi

| Williams, C. B. | *Style and Vocabulary : Numerical Studies.* London : Griffin, 1970. |
| Wimsatt, W. K., Jr. | *The Prose Style of Samuel Johnson.* New Haven : Yale Univ. Press, 1963. |

HINDI

| Mishra, Vishvanath. | *Hindi Bhasha aur Sahitya par Angrezi Prabhav (1870-1920).* Dehradun : Sahitya Sadan, 1963. |

INDEX

This index does not refer to the pages in *Notes and References* (189-218) and *Bibliography* (219-239). The reader may refer to these sections for detailed information.

The Influence of English on Marathi

The Influence of English on Marathi